JOHN EYBERG aka JUANITO HAYBURG aka BIKERJOHN
www.juanitohayburg.com

CRAZY MEXICAN GRILL, 3019 YARBROUGH, EL PASO TX: START, (14:00) 11JUN2011
FINISH, on or before 25JUL2011

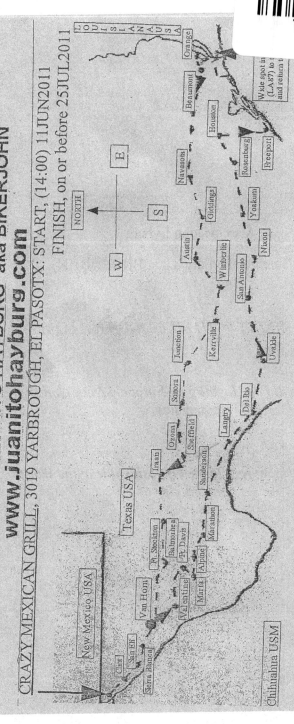

Map hand-drawn 21MAY2011 from GRAN ATLAS AGUILAR; FREDY ERAZO ESTRADA, MEDELLÍN, COLÓMBIA

¡With a daughter in Austin and a son in Houston,

this is the year for pedaling!

Also by John Eyberg

(a.k.a. Juanito Hayburg a.k.a. BIKERJOHN)

BICYCLE SAFETY WITH BIKERJOHN (out of print)

La Ruta de Familia de Hayburg en Europe y Asia: Con Esposa
(available)

La Familia Hayburg: On the Opposite Side of the World
(available)

DRY'D, FRY'D, AND SKY'D BY HEADWINDS AND HEAT:

My Trans-Texas Bicycle Odyssey

John Eyberg

(a.k.a. Juanito Hayburg a.k.a. BIKERJOHN)

iUniverse, Inc.
Bloomington

Dry'd, Fry'd, and Sky'd by Headwinds and Heat:
My Trans-Texas Bicycle Odyssey

iUniverse books may be ordered through booksellers or by contacting:

iUniverse
1663 Liberty Drive
Bloomington, IN 47403
www.iuniverse.com
1-800-Authors (1-800-288-4677)

ISBN: 978-1-4759-5380-0 (sc)
ISBN: 978-1-4759-5381-7 (e)
ISBN: 978-1-4759-5382-4 (dj)

Printed in the United States of America

iUniverse rev. date: 11/19/2012

This book is dedicated to all road users, whether motorized or not, on foot, one wheel or more, single axle or multi-axle.

Ever since organisms, specifically we humans, have moved from location to another on terrestrial Earth, the routes have evolved from casual to well trod footpaths to formally established public thoroughfares. The "public" aspect regularly conflicts with the "private" aspect, and eminent domain is the final arbitrator—of great note are the abandoned railroads; does that well-graded roadbed revert back to the landowner whose property it trespasses, or does it become a rail-trail, still to be used by the public?

Indeed, because the public routes can be and are used by all of us, we have an obligation to maintain such roads in the best condition possible while accommodating many users, aka multi-modal.

There are a few circumstances in which road users do need to be segregated, which is why there are cut-curb sidewalks in urban and suburban settings for pedestrians, lane lines, signage, and instructions. These rules of the road are universal since nearly seven billion of us (A.D. 2012) will use the transportation system from birth to death. The rules are essential to maintain effective and efficient use. Demonstrating the ability to follow the rules also shows that road users have maturity and intelligence, otherwise they would be nothing but a dangerous hazard on the boulevards.

As a regular road user, whether bicycling or in a motorized vehicle, I strongly believe that the paved path enhances civilization. Superior transportation systems, roads in particular, which aid and abet personal movement, means a more developed society. One caveat, though: no matter how safe, how improved, how 'perfect' the route, it's effectiveness all comes down to the single most important factor: the individual road user. Should she or he choose to abuse the privilege of using the road by not following the rules, she or he creates the most *unsafe* road and should not be allowed to use it until demonstrating the ability to keep themselves and other road users safe. Our multi-modal transportation schemes reflect us, our democratic obligation to each other, the world economy, and our future.

I believe Mr. George R. Chatburn effectively summarizes this on the first page of his book, Highways and Highway Transportation:

"The highways of a nation, whether they be of the land or sea, or both, are most vital elements in its progress and could almost as well as transportation be considered the measuring rod of civilization."

¡Bicycle Safety is NO accident!

CONTENTS

Abbreviations I commonly used

a/c	air conditioning
ACC	Austin Community College
A-D	Austro-Daimler
aka/AKA/a.k.a	also known as
ATLM	Audio-Tactile Lane Marker
ATM	Automated Teller Machine
AVGAS	aviation gasoline
B&N	Barnes & Noble Bookstore
BC	British Columbia, Canada
BNSF	Burlington Northern Santa Fe (railroad company)
BBQ	bar-b-que
CBP	Customs and Border Protection
CR	county road
CV	aircraft carrier, conventionally powered (fossil fuel)
CVN	aircraft carrier, nuclear reactor powered
DART	Dallas Area Rapid Transit
DHL	initials of company founders: Adrian **D**alsey, Larry **H**illblom, Robert **L**ynn
DHS	Department of Homeland Security
DHT	Danny Herman Trucking
DIY	do-it-yourself
DFW	Dallas-Fort Worth
DOT	Department of Transportation
EPCC	El Paso Community College
FedEX	Federal Express

FM	Farm-to-Market
FR	Farm Road
GH&SA	Galveston, Houston and San Antonio (railroad company)
HEB	large grocery/dry goods store chain in Texas, **H**oward **E**dward **B**utt, first president
HPV	Human Powered Vehicle
IA	Iowa
ID	identity card (typically my driver's license, although I may also carry a passport)
KS	Kansas
KFC	Kentucky Fried Chicken
kph	kilometers per hour
kms	kilometers
KOA	Kampgrounds of America
LA	Louisiana
MPO	Metropolitan Planning Organization
MO	Missouri
mph	miles per hour
MRE	meal-ready-to-eat
MS	multiple sclerosis
MVT	Mesilla Valley Transportation
NM	New Mexico
NRHP	National Register of Historic Places
NWT	Northwest Territories, Canada
NSW	New South Wales, Australia

OTC	Overland Trail Campground, Fort DavisTX-USA
OTR	over the road
PO	Post Office
POE	Port of Entry
PTSD	Post-Traumatic Stress Disorder
RFN	Robert F. Nixon
RR	Ranch Road
SP	Southern Pacific (currently bankrupt railroad company)
SPF	Sun Protection Factor
TX	Texas
TxDOT	Texas Department of Transportation
UBS	United Blood Services
UCMJ	Uniform Code of Military Justice
UPS	United Parcel Service
US	United States
USA	United States of America
USM	United States of Mexico
USNS	United States Naval Ship
USPS	United States Postal Service
UV	ultraviolet
WA	Washington state
YISD	Ysleta Independent School District, El PasoTX-USA

PREFACE

I wrote this book because of the great fortune I have known throughout my life, though certain moments might not have felt exactly that way. I have, as far as I can remember, always traveled to some extent. When growing up, my now deceased father was a chemical engineer with Boeing, thus we were located at either WichitaKS or SeattleWA, with memorable travel between the two.

My high school years took place in RollaMO, where I had the opportunity to develop deep and lasting friendships, where we spent much on my Grandparents' large ranch, being river rats on the transecting Meramec River and other Ozark streams—almost always in the absence of adults. Looking back, it miraculous that any of us survived! My beloved Grandmother recommended that I join the Navy after graduation from RHS to "see the World". Unexpressed, though, was her, and my parents, unexpressed fear that I might end up in Vietnam. However, my orders sent me out to the 4th Fleet, boarding my first ship, the USNS Marias (T-AO57), in Karachi, Pakistan.

While I had bicycled a fair amount locally while a youngster, but it was when the Marias was anchored out in *di Napoli, Italia,* that I made my first adult purchase: A 10-speed *Gitane* (This was a French product being sold in Italy—EU being practiced long before the well-known formal association.) upright bicycle. While moving it from AFSOUTH to the shore, several *Neapolitans* willingly helped me assemble it, another precursor of the co-operation essential to the much later amalgamation of European nations.

Since my first push-bike acquisition in 1975, I have pedaled over 100,000 miles/160,000 kilometers, both commuting and touring, solo or in the company of a few others, notably with one of my younger brothers, Nils. I often pedaled in adverse conditions, always confident of my ability to make basic repairs and 'make do' wherever stopped for the night. Previous to my Trans-Texas Bicycle Odyssey, my previous lengthy solo tour was the Southern perimeter of Missouri, began 05JUL1983, before beginning my Senior year as an undergraduate at the University of Missouri-Columbia.

During the intervening twenty-eight years, many bicycles (two have endured spectacularly: my Specialized Stumpjumper lasted12 years, and my current ride, Advanced Transportation Products Doublevision tandem recumbent, soon-to-surpass 12 years), I remain happily married, father of two wonderful children, excellent employment as a teacher with the outstanding Ysleta Independent School District. Those are the primary factors which combined to reduced my long-distance biketouring to long weekends—and helped my mass to gain a pound for each year. Full of trepidation, I ambitiously embarked on a long anticipated biketour across Texas, from home in El Paso, Eastward, generally staying South of I-10, crossing the Sabine River to a turn-around point, then returning West, generally staying North of I-10.

Most important to me when writing this book is my long-held belief that, while few people will actually ever partake in such a strenuous physical activity, there is an audience that would enjoy vicarious participation, possibly even be inspired to strike out on their own in a less-demanding manner, and learn the true worth of others with whom we share the Earth, Texas in particular. From an educational standpoint, I feel "You don't know until you go!", and am especially keen use my experiences to help young people make their own transition into adulthood. My zeal for being with most other humans and amazing digital capacity of today has given me a phenomenal ability to access virtually everybody, as well as being accessible. I urge you to friend me on Facebook and follow me on Twitter.

Reluctantly, this book is also an acknowledgement that the perspective I present is the result of having lived—another way of saying, with a nod toward my mortality, that the end is much closer than the start.

INTRODUCTION

I have grown as a writer over the past several decades, starting out with blatant plagiarism while a high school student for the amusement of a few close friends who certainly wouldn't turn me into the authorities. My next period a strong growth came when aboard my first ship, when I acquired a rather rickety portable typewriter. It was perfect for me and complemented my military duty in visual communications as a Signalman. I spent many, *many,* long nights of gazing at the surrounding sea for lights, whether from another ship, shore, or some other sources. That meant using white lights at night in the immediate proximity were forbidden—viewing such can cause temporary blindness to the dilated eye. I recall that most of the time, the only ship present was the one keeping me out of the water. While in high school, I passed a typing course, part of which dealt with not looking at the keys while pounding away. Aboard the Marias, my typing paper were roll-ends from the crypto teletype machines, worthless to anyone—unless retrieved from the trash—and those remains becoming an endless supply for me.

All of those elements came together, making me a true multi-tasker where I could type away to my hearts content *and* (sit) the watch.

Tragically, those roll-ends had a built-in self-destruction device: they were highly acidic, and by the time I was able to get around to looking at those memoirs, some fifteen years after becoming civilian, they had disintegrated into nothing.

Regardless, the immense beneficial relief of writing had taken hold of me, and I continued to take notes, especially while bicycling. I have over twenty years of nearly illegible scribbles, source material for reference. I often expanded my writing from those notes, organizing it into longer and longer summaries. It was almost a decade after my first ship-board typing that I launched into a formal attempt at making a living from writing with my first book, an elementary school pamphlet titled "BICYCLE SAFETY WITH BIKERJOHN". That was extremely unproductive though I did bicycle extensively while researching. Undeterred, I continued writing annual summaries of sorts, once again authoring a second and third book a decade later concerning travels with my family.

Which brings me to my latest tome, five years later, this accounting of my biketour most of the way across Texas in both directions. Of course I feel growth; I've experimented with different formats with each successive book, and am certain this is my finest. It is a bit unconventional, I'll admit. Instead of "logical" chapters, I've chosen to write this travelogue from night to night, hence every place I overnighted become both the ending and beginning. At the opening, a map shows where I speculated my route would take me. At the closing, a map show the actual route I ended up using, along with the final statistics. Also in the closing pages, I acknowledge those many people and sources that assisted me in every way, from verifying my numbers to saving my life. Most importantly the incidents, events, and people described within are very real and actually occurred at the time and date as described. I have altered only *one* name due to my concern about her/his fragility.

This book is, of course, quite different from my first elementary school pamphlet in construction. In the 1970s and early '80s, the digital revolution was pre-natal and manual pen-and-paper was *de rigueur* when notetaking for later transcription. Nowadays, my notetaking is primarily on Twitter—with barely a few handwritten remarks on paper—and heavy emphasis is placed on internet access along with the electronic writing. However, those rote typing skills I learned almost forty years ago in high school on the *qwerty* keyboard still holds the highest place of practical use despite the rapid speed and near-instantaneous transmission capabilities today.

Even though walking can be a pain, I can still pedal, and most importantly, read and write.

Some things never change.

May you enjoy reading this journal of my pedaling across Texas!

ACKNOWLEDGMENTS

Without question, I would not have been able to accomplish any of this terrific adventure without assistance. The actual manuscript writing would only be full of typos without the spell check feature on my computer, along with Google(Maps),Wikipedia, my Facebook friends and Twitter followers, including my dated website, www. juanitohayburg.com. For helping me to verify facts and provide supporting data, I relied upon the Texas Historical Commission (especially the physical plaques) (www.thc.state.tx.us), the Texas State Historical Association (www.tshasonline.org), Texas Highways, Federal Highway Administration, American Association of State Highway Officials, and many chamber of commerces. All contributed significantly. These wonderful institutions made it possible for me continue pedaling: Alterations by Mina, Texas Boot & Shoe-Pebble Hills, Al& Elizabeth's Postal Annex on Yarbrough & Montwood, McCrae Car Care, Frame Fixer Enterprises, The Bagel Shop, Signifier Signs,Tony Lewis Collision & Paint, El Paso MPO, Whataburger, Subway, Tandems Ltd., Crazy Cat Cyclery, El Paso Bicycle Center, BIKEPARTSUSA, S.C. Johnson & Company, Bridgehunter.com, Hostel Shoppe, UPS, FedEX, Tripadvisor, Virtual Tourist, and Parkland High School, Ysleta I.S.D. It goes without saying that my encounters with numerous kind strangers, now friendly collaborators, the U.S. Border Patrol—especially Agents Lily & Jay—Sutton County Sheriff Bill Webster (ret.), and most importantly, my wife, Ellen. I thank all of you. *Keep on pedaling safely!*

Dry'd, Fry'd, and Sky'd by Headwinds and Heat:

My Trans-Texas Bicycle Odyssey

"You're going to bicycle across Texas from El Paso to Louisiana in one of the hottest and driest Summers on record? Are you *CRAZY?*" was the e-mail from my good friend, KJ.

My reply seemed logical and simple: "Probably, but with our daughter in Austin, our son in Houston, and only three specific commitments to my district, I have a block of time that will allow me to pedal to *and* from the Sabine River. I've been wanting to do this for decades!"

Maybe KJ was right, I could be crazy. After all, I had not had this extensive a biketour since 1983, 28 years ago—and 28 pounds/13 kgs lighter. Besides gaining so much weight during the intervening years, did I gain more intelligence as well?

Yes. I was definitely smarter now. After all, acknowledging my possible lack of sanity should be an indicator—though not necessarily my lucidity. Perhaps it was my megalomania? Anyway, I was happily married to Ellen, and we have two grown children, both of whom are successful. My career as a teacher at fantastic Parkland High School in the exceptionally fine Ysleta Independent School District was in it's 22 year and I was performing at near-best in my assignment as a Vocational Adjustment Co-ordinator/Transition Specialist/ Work-Study teacher. I was participating as much as possible with the El Paso Metropolitan Planning Organization (MPO) regarding our region's cycling routes. With my son's help, I had established a website (www.juanitohayburg.com) as well as Facebook, Twitter, and Linked-In accounts. And I was still pedaling, sometimes joking that

1

my first marriage was to my bicycle—that relationship was longer, albeit much less stronger!

Since my 1983 circum-Missouri bicycle odyssey, taken during my last undergraduate Summer at the University of Missouri-Columbia, I have pedaled on numerous shorter excursions which included Big Bend National ParkTX; Medellín-to-Miro's-mountain-home, Colombia; El Paso-Las Cruces; El Paso-Alamogordo; El Paso-Artesia; Boy Scouts of America Cycling Merit Badge counselor for my son's troop, 192; and daily riding when in-town, with special emphasis on biking to-and-from Parkland High School most school days during the 2010-11year.

The PHS pedal is a 14 miles/23kms one way trip which usually takes me 1.5 hours, including a death-defying 3 miles/5kms of hostile Global Reach, the Northern extension of Yarbrough Drive, but more importantly, the connector between Montana Boulevard and Walter Jones/Spur 601/Liberty Expressway/Sergent Sims/Old Ironsides entrance to Ft. Bliss East/Biggs Field. The hostility only occurs during certain times of day, specifically the morning and evening rush hours, Monday through Friday, and, thankfully, only by a infinitely small ignorant percentage of the knowledgeable motorists. Of course, all it takes is one of those massive (motor) vehicles to barely tap my vehicle and I'd be down, wrecked on the road, possibly seriously injured or even dead.

I invited thousands of people to my (14:00) send-off from The Crazy Mexican Grill, 3019 N. Yarbrough, on Saturday, 11JUN2011. One invitee, Susan, actually showed up. I was delighted to see she had brought Liz, my former department chair. My wife brought another guest, Ruth. Not exactly the crowd I had anticipated, but the weather might have stopped a few—it was a dry 101°F (38°C) with no clouds in sight.

Only the foolhardy, or supremely confident, would be attempting my feat.

I like to think of myself in the latter category.

Within a half-mile, I turned East onto Montwood and stopped in the shade of a Mesquite tree at the Bank of the West, double-checking all of my straps and packs. Ahead of me, a neat red Focus pulled off the road and the driver, another good friend, Mike, strode toward me.

"I would've made it to your start," he told me, "but your timing was not exactly the best."

We had an animated discussion for several minutes before we were both off and away, each on our own mission. I had forty-three days and a wakeup to complete mine.

I had barely gone uphill and passed Lomaland Drive when I heard the disheartening *hissssss* of a front tire going flat. I couldn't believe it! A hole was being punctured in my fundamental belief in my Trouble Free Touring. The tube hadn't been in for more than a week!

I was in front of the Milan spa, and knew that to be the cause of my flat.

I *still* haven't resolved my ill will toward Milano, Italy, after having to overnight there with my family on a 2004 trip. It was bad karma! How long will I suffer? Obviously, I have to return to break the Milano Curse.

Then a golden beemer whipped around me and pulled into the church parking lot, and saw my closest friend from work.

"I wasn't exactly sure where the Crazy Mexican Grill was," Gil greeted me, "but I remembered you telling me your route out of town."

Elated that he had shown up, I began pushing my Doublevision tandem recumbent off the street.

"Get over into the shade to repair that," came his gentle directions, "it's too hot in the Sun. What can I do to help?"

"You've already given me good help by directing me to the shade, Gil, but there's nothing more you can do," I assured him. "If I can't repair this by myself, then I shouldn't be pedaling anywhere!"

I quickly stripped out the faulty tube, checked the rim and tire for anything that might have caused the flat, then installed a new, slimed BikeNashbar 20-inch tube. Pumping it up partially to achieve the correct seating, I deflated it, then reinstalled the wheel, and pumped it to its full 110psi/ 7.6bar. Solid! Literally, it was hard as the cement sidewalk we stood upon.

"On second thought, Gil, there is something you can do. Can you take this busted tube, and I'll get it from you next month?" I asked.

He was glad to do so, and admired my preparation for the heat, specifically carrying fresh water.

"I have almost three gallons (11 liters) of fresh water; two water bladders apiece are in those blue denim holster-like bags hanging from each side of my seat were created for me at Alterations by Mina," I told him. "In fact, she has done a lot of work for me—see the seat bag, and that folded orange material is a tarp-tent, a very special job by her."

"Do you think she could do some delicate work on my flight jacket?" he asked.

"I don't know why not, but you'd have to talk with her first," I responded. "If you rush, you can catch her before closing time at sixteen hundred. Just go back down Montwood, turn right on Yarbrough for a mile to the light at Pebble Hills, and look in the Karen Plaza strip, behind the Seven-Eleven. Anyway, I'm ready to go. Thanks for taking that tube, Gil. See you next month!"

Yes, it was hot. Really hot. I felt the Sun beating down, but I also felt protected, having coated all of my exposed skin with NO-AD SPF60 Sunblock at home. I took another swig out of my Tour de Tolerance Water Bottle, one of the items that is included for all participants in the annual October fundraiser bike ride. I felt good, ready to get gone.

This mid-day departure might not be the best thing, but since I had stayed up all night to help with Project Celebration (a safe party-environment for the new graduates that goes all night until 5am), I needed *some* rest before beginning my own 2000 mile/3219 kilometer bicycle tour. And I had to get pedaling on that as soon as possible; every day counted.

Continuing my cycling, I listened for any more *hissssssing* and consciously avoided any debris that might cause another flat. I was feeling very good until I turned off Pellicano onto Berryville when it became unbelievably hard to turn the crank. I crossed Eastlake drive and coasted into the Western shade of a purpose built structure, the Valero mini-mart gas station, stopping beside a water machine.

The derailleur cable had snapped. If it's not one thing, it's another. Maybe these were signs that perhaps I *should* wait until tomorrow morning for a much cooler departure? No, and within two hours, I had replaced the cable. Unfortunately, I unknowingly had fed the wire through the incorrectly positioned housing, not discovering the error until I had put the final tighten on the cable bolt. I sure didn't want to spend another two hours repairing *that*. Resigning myself to the fact that the cable will likely break again, I only hoped it wouldn't happen soon.

"Trouble Free Touring" indeed!

While the shade had made my work immeasurably easier, I was still guzzling liquids, primarily water and Gatorade. A Red Bull route driver approached me and commented that the product he carried was just as effective. I agreed, having often sought it out while pedaling in the Ciclovia or Tour de Tolerance or anytime I was particularly exhausted. So who was I to turn down a free can of it, albeit warm? It was different yet familiar; something akin to a decades-ago Lik-M-Aid candy, which would effervesce in my mouth.

Measuring the zenith of the Sun with my hand, I saw possibly an hour of ride time. I was desperate to get underway, get farther than Horizon City. I had been jokingly telling people that I might not get farther than Clint, the next town along the way. Now it was looking as though I might have unintentionally set myself up for not even progressing that far.

With the ball of light descending behind me, I pedaled steadily East on Darrington Drive, thinking about campsites. I could layover by the landfill, but that thought was erased when I passed it speeding downhill in the setting Sun—the Beta 1 cyclocomputer mounted on my underseat handlebar indicated I was at 29mph/46kph. My new Magura HS33 hydraulic brakes ensured a smooth stop at the crossover of I-10, before proceeding South, down into the floodplain of the Rio Grande.

It had been a long time since I had been out this way, and the next stop sign at North Loop (Farm-to-Market 76) was absent, having been replaced by traffic lights. Making the lawful right turn, I wondered what else had changed over the years since last coming out here?

I remembered a short-cut into Clint, and made a quick left turn on Celum, a narrow, winding, well-paved road. This had not changed; it was more like a lovely, tree-bordered driveway that crossed a water-filled aqueduct and a single railroad track before curving away. It continued, bordered by homes, Texas A&M extension, and Clint city offices before passing the water tower and intersection with Alameda Avenue.

My most prominent memory at that moment was of Flick's Pizza, in the middle of a business strip on Alameda, close to Clint High School, and compelled by a desperate hollowness in my stomach. Turning right, I slowly pedaled, anxious to not miss my evening meal site. But it was not there. Having passed the business district, I made a U-turn and began slowly moving East, this time beside them, stopping in front of an empty space. Seeing a couple exiting the Lencho's Meat market, I called out,

"¿Donde está Flicks?"

"¡No mas!" was the response.

I couldn't believe it; the much-anticipated hot anchovy pizza drowned with tumblers of ice-cold water that had powered me here disappeared along with the last rays of Sunlight.

Oh, well, San Elizario is just a little bit further, and now I envisioned myself at the Horseshoe Adobe restaurant, enjoying delicious *fajitas* or *burritos*, and surely polishing off a basket of *tortilla* chips as well. Maybe I could find a campsite beside the *Presidio*, or Billy the Kid's jail? I pedaled the wide, smooth, debris-free shoulder of what was now Texas 20, waving at families enjoying the twilight in their more dispersed farms. It was not too long before I had to stop, turn on my own bike lights in the stark darkness of this remote Texas corner.

I pedaled with a concerned sort of delight. My target was a street light, which must surely be San Eli, but I wasn't getting any closer. I thought back three-and-a-half decades, when, aboard ship, I had been told that on a quiet sea, the red glow of a cigarette butt is visible for five miles. If that was true, then a white light on a calm warm night like tonight, might be visible for ten miles?

Good thing I love bicycling, and was particularly keen for this cross-state trip. It seemed a good long while before I came abreast that one light, but it was among the many that lined the streets of the busy community of Fabens.

Fabens!

Somehow I had neglected to observe that my route through Clint and Eastward movement on Alameda was not the way to San Elizario. Did I miss this because of my exuberance, or exhaustion? But, heck, Fabens was farther along my intended route anyway, and I really had gone a long distance despite my late start and repairs. I waited for a green light, and continued moving East, looking for potential camp sites.

After seeing a possibility, I turned North on 4th Street, crossed the tracks, passed public schools, turned West on Camp Street and pedaled back to the main drag through town where I knew I could find the needed food. I continued North, passing a small eatery, and came to a grocery store. I met two guards outside, who informed me that it had just closed and wouldn't re-open 'till mid-morning, after church. On the North side of the parking lot was a Subway, also closed, so I wheeled across the street toward McDonalds and KFC when I remembered passing a small eatery. I decided to support as much non-chain business as possible, and this would be my first opportunity to put that pledge into action.

My Doublevision tandem recumbent took up the the remaining room on the G Avenue edge of Rojeros Snacks when I parked it. An object of attention from the locals sitting at the tables under the porch or on the wall, I was unafraid of theft—I had labored all afternoon to get the heavily-loaded bicycle to that point and knew it would intimidate any who might even begin to move it. I saw customers happily eating ice creams, burgers, and other delicious looking foods (Did I mention that anything edible at that moment looked delicious?) and approached the window. I was motioned into a small dining area, and they unlocked the door for me—re-locking it before I sat down.

A few hairs stood up on the back of my neck, although I could still see my bicycle and the keys were left in the lock. Confident enough that my bike wouldn't be tampered with, I spread myself out at one of the tables and considered choice from a much larger menu—this was much more than just an ice cream stand.

I saw an unfamiliar choice, *chilindrinas*, which intrigued me. Always ready for adventure, I had to have it, and ordered the local delicacy, undeterred by quizzical looks and questions from behind the counter. It arrived very fresh, consisting of chopped cabbage, onions, and tomatoes piled on top of a waffle. What a delight this dish was, and soon occupied a place in my stomach that declared I was "full". But not quite; I followed it with an vanilla ice cream chaser, one that apparently came with this unusual meal.

Other customers saw me sitting inside, and made an attempt to enter but were thwarted by the locked door. If I can't help, then what use am I? I got up, unlocked the door, and a family of three came in to sit at the other table. The woman came from behind the counter and scowled at me while she re-locked the door. Looking around, the service window had been closed and I realized that they were actually closed for the day. I had lucked out, even if it meant some inconvenience for the cook.

I was soon retracing my route South on Fabens Road and came to the street lights at Camp Street, noting an exceedingly nice Auto Zone store on the corner. Crossing the railroad tracks, I went to the possible campsite seen earlier and became dismayed with it. I returned to the Auto Zone store, thinking that if it was so nice in the front, the backside might be very acceptable, too? I circled the closed business a few times before deciding, that, yes, I could lay down in the shadow in back. Looking above, a bright swath of stars told me no rain tonight, and knew how much less intrusive I would be without having to put up the tent-tarp. Pulling out my sleeping bag and Z-rest, I settled down between the building and my bike.

I was amazingly comfortable, and called my wife. The connection was excellent, but our conversation brief. Due to my proximity to the border, T-Mobile couldn't compete with the Mexican tower that had picked up my signal, thus making the cell call an *international* discussion, with incredibly steep rates. This was a rather expensive mistake which I resolved to never make again.

The daytime heat had given way to a surprisingly cool night, and recently blacktopped lot was now releasing the heat which had been absorbed all day. My enjoyment came to a quick end, when that most annoying sound of a mosquito buzzing in my ear made me slap at it.

My sore ear proved, once again, that either I'm not very fast or there are a multitude of these insects, each one ready to take the place of the next, or both.

I was ready, though. I had brought a Texsport no-see-um mesh fly, and an OFF Deep Woods pump-spray. I had already decided against using a tent, so the decision was easy, and I lightly coated all of my exposed skin with this highly effective repellent. I settled back down for a good night's sleep.

Almost.

The first of several Burlington Northern Santa Fe (BNSF) trains slowly rolled through, horn blasting, incredibly close. I could hear the crossbucks bell sounding loud and clear, the mechanical motion of crossing gates in need of WD-40 going down (and up), virtually see the red lights flashing, and feel seismic vibrations as the trains rumbled along. Thinking about this for a moment, my other possible campsite wouldn't be an improvement for it was close to the other main road, Texas 20, probably about the same disruptive distance. Even though it was dark out, a light flashed in my brain as I realized that either road, Alameda or North Loop, were actually routes that (motor) traffic could maintain East-West movement when a passing train prohibited North-South passage. Satisfied that I had figured out the roadway-train issue, I closed my eyes for much needed rest.

Not exactly.

A raindrop landed upon my eyelid, followed by several more all around my head. I jerked my body up, and began to off load the tent-tarp from my bike. Then the glow from an almost full-moon stopped me. There were no clouds! How, why, are there raindrops? Now fully upright, I looked closer at the load. On top was my Outdoor Products 2-liter hydration backpack, and the drinking tube extended downward, where a steady drip-drip-drip of water emanated from the bite valve.

Relieved that no tent was needed, it was obviously a siphon, and I easily remedied the spilling water by elevating the drinking tube above the pack. Having resolved that issue, I laid back down.

Unfortunately, the solution was not that easy because, while the drips had slowed, they were still falling. I lay there for a bit more, contemplating this while infrequent drops would land on me. Rising

9

once more, I was certain to fix it this time. A bungee cord held the pack securely, but it also provided the force to continue pushing the water out, into the tube, through the bite valve, and onto my weary face. I folded the tube several times on itself, effectively cutting off anyway more fluid could pass, and tucked it back under a bungee cord to secure it. Now, time for shut-eye.

I must have fallen into a deep sleep, because I next startled awake to find that a motorist had stopped on Camp Street, the bright headlights and hard stare waking me. Tense, I remained stationary but readied myself to be chased off. Actually, I had fully expected that the authorities would be visiting with me at some point during my brief overnight stay—many, many times before (OK, a long time ago, before marriage, but the memory is still with me) when the authorities would interrupt my sleep and often redirect me to another sleep site, sometimes far away. My relief was immense when the motorist—I couldn't discern if it was law enforcement or possibly the store owner or whoever—departed without asking me to do the same. I fell back into deep slumber.

OVERNIGHT ONE: FABENS

The wake-up squawk of a rooster sounded through the neighborhood. I slowly opened my eyes to a pre-dawn morning, grateful for a few hours of uninterrupted rest. However, I knew I had to vamoose—I don't think anybody much cared that I had squatted here overnight, but I sure didn't want to overstay my welcome! Besides, I've got a long way to go—only forty-two days left.

I began my morning ritual of rising and stretching, a deliberate act for over four decades. I can remember attending Rolla Junior High School in the late '60s, often starting my day in a similar manner. Instead of bicycling, I would jog a 'Green Acre Mile', which was actually much longer. My current routine is based upon the Royal Canadian Air Force work-out from a paperback I had purchased in Naples, Italy, 1975, and was then my sole source of physical fitness aboard ship. Over the decades, I'd adapted it to accommodate my aging body; I'd long ago ceased using a stopwatch for each of the targeted exercises, as well as those which antagonize my left knee (repaired several years ago) such as rope jumping, running, and even excessive walking.

Bicycling is all I can do—good thing I love it so.

Packing was easy, since I had removed so little off my bike. I was glad to not have pulled out my tent, but had I not brought it, rain would undoubtedly have soaked me. My final act was applying a layer of Equate SPF50 Sunblock to all exposed skin: nose, neck, ears, arms, and legs. I gave an extra amount to my my upper thighs which, from the sitting position on a recumbent, are extremely exposed. A few years ago, I suffered an interestingly patterned burn on my head through thinning hair because of the large vents in my Skid-lid, and now wear a BikeNashbar skullcap for excellent protection. I moved my bike off its industrial-strength kickstand and pedaled toward last night's feast.

I didn't go far before finding Ribas Bakery. Actually, I didn't find it the first time despite its prime location on the corner of Fabens Road and I Avenue. Cycling past it, I could smell the sweet fumes and had to turn around. Looking closer at the fading white-painted walls, I saw that it was open, a surprise to me because it was early Sunday morning. Everybody has a different religion; whether in a church, on two wheels, creating succulent breads—and I was glad for the plurality.

Parking prominently on the corner, I entered the business, expecting to buy numerous morsels to power my continued pedaling. Once inside, I was met with a bewildering array of treats, any of which could have satisfied my palate. I needed help in selecting a few, and asked a young girl who was there with her mother. She pointed out some *pan dulce*, and I purchased two of them (one for the child, the other for me), along with chocolate milk and a few other treats. She, and mom, were pleased to have helped me, especially since there was a reward.

I hope she learned to always try to help others, regardless of a physical reward or not, that the real reward is intrinsic. However, the biscuit was a nice way to thank her for helping me.

I was ready to roll on, returning to Alameda/Texas 20 and assumed my position on that clean shoulder. Two other cyclists were following me at about the same rate as myself, neither getting larger nor smaller in my rearview mirror.

I hadn't gone far before I came into the small community of Tornillo, perhaps more well known as one of the winding accesses to a single-lane bridge into Mexico at Caseta, one that I have motored many times. Quite recently, though, is the construction of a new well-developed port of entry, to be more directly routed through Tornillo itself. The Department of Homeland Security(DHS), along with Customs and Border Protection(CBP), sets the parameters for the new port-of-entry(POE), and once the multi-lane bridge is built, the old narrow crossing will be destroyed. Interested, I turned toward Mexico on Henderson Road, but, with no quick and easy access, I returned to Alameda on Shaffer Road.

The other two cyclists were now in front of me. It was not long before I caught up to them, exchanging friendly greetings as I passed them. They were enjoying a pleasant Sunday morning pedal, although not going nearly as far as myself—they had none of the accouterments packed around their bikes as I did.

Curiosity about the agriculture got the better of me when I saw a farmer tending to his crops, and stopped to query him.

"*Hola,*" I called out to him, "*soy Juanito. Preguntas, por favor.*"

"I understand English," he replied. "What are your questions?"

How humiliating. Perhaps my Spanish needs a bit of speech therapy?

"I know cotton is incredibly hard on the soil, do you apply much fertilizer, or what?"

"Some of the bigger farmers might because of lost Nitrogen, but I don't, rotating crops every few years instead."

"Really? What do you put in? Chiles?"

"That's New Mexico. A year or two of soybeans'll recharge the soil."

"Oh. Thanks! *¡Graciás!*" I waved to him and remounted my Doublevision, continuing East.

It wasn't too long before I saw the road bending North, away from a pull-out straight ahead, which was really a well-shaded cut-off. The old road had gone this way, but new construction and a desire to preserve the Cottonwood trees made this a wonderful rest area—too bad it was mid-morning because this would be an ideal campsite as well.

Also taking advantage of the shade was the woman biker I had passed earlier. Enjoying a chance to dismount, we both met in the shade and shared tales of how we happened to be stopped at this lovely spot. Her friend had turned off for Hidden Lakes, and one of our common motives was to lose weight. However she was returning to her home in Fabens while I was continuing on.

"*Louisiana?!*" she gasped upon learning my destination. "You'll lose too much water, and its dangerous out there—the forecast is nothing but triple digit temperatures!"

"Well," I assured her, "I'm only going to cross the Sabine, then head back. If I have enough time, I might go farther, but the thirtieth of June is my turn-around date, wherever I am."

"Do be careful," she requested, then, sizing up my bicycle, added, "I admit, it does look as if you're well prepared. I'll follow your progress on Facebook and Twitter."

Back to pedaling, I left El Paso County and entered Hudspeth County. The road became markedly different: the wide, relatively debris-free shoulder became non-existent. Fortunately, there was very little motor traffic to compete for lane use, although I'm certain that will change radically upon completion of the new POE.

My chocolate and sweets were now used up, and I could feel the fat burning off when entered the tiny community of Fort Hancock. I had read some time ago about a wonderful eatery here, but could find nothing open. Dismayed, I had a decision to make: continue pedaling East on 20, to McNary, where I would commence on the shoulder of Interstate 10, or turn North on Spur 148, where I could also take to the shoulder.

Regardless, I needed nutrition *before* attempting I-10. I looked toward McNary, and despite the promise of a water tower, I saw few trees in the distance and no buildings. Not that I could see that far anyway. Looking to my left, I saw many buildings, which had greater promise but it meant going uphill. My gut ruled; with a groan, I began pedaling. As I slowly moved up, my hopes seemed to be raised and dashed multiple times as what looked like a cafe or restaurant or some kind of eatery turned out to be a mirage, closed, or a lookalike. At the tracks, I could see gas station signs and knew that I was bound to consume whatever was available.

Then, much to my astonishment, almost hidden away, was Angies Restaurant.

Saved!

I luxuriated inside the air conditioned building, my sweat-soaked clothes chilling me to an almost frosty level of comfort. I noticed a prominent display from the March/April 1991 issue of National

Geographic Traveler that proclaimed this restaurant is home to having "...chicken fried steak beats any..." . Regrettably, Angie told me that I had arrived a bit early to verify the claim, but I could certainly have all home made food. I chose chocolate milk (two of 'em) and a tasty *chorrizo* breakfast, slowly eating to savor both the food and the climate. No need to get rush back out into the increasingly hotter day!

Besides, I had the opportunity to scuttlebutt with a soldier, V'on, who appeared ready to jump out of his own skin. He readily told me that he suffered PTSD, having been at the Iraqi front. He also said that he wasn't going to take any more of the trash his company commander was giving him, and had been speaking with him at length on his cell phone about reporting in, until the battery went out.

I was sharing my own military experiences with him, but he quickly discounted me because, you see, I have no combat experience (other than fighting with the first class, but that's a personality conflict, not armed conflict). One thing had not changed: a member of the military is government property, subject to the UCMJ, and cannot flat out refuse an order unless ready to deal with the consequences.

V'on eventually departed—something I needed, and wanted, to do myself. A half-hour later, I went outside and the heat walloped me. At least I had a tailwind. Around the corner, I saw that V'on hadn't actually left; he was now at a pay phone and was continuing to argue with a Ft. Bliss authority. I carefully mounted my Doublevision, waved to V'on, and yelled, "Don't get shot at Sunrise!"

"Don't worry about me, man. I got it all worked. . ." he yelled back.

I pedaled down the ramp onto the shoulder of I-10, with Angie's, V'on, and Ft. Hancock quickly fading out of view in my mirror. The shoulder was remarkably clean, considering the potential for excessive debris due to the significant amount of motor traffic blowing past me at six, seven, eight, times my speed, which was averaging between 5-10mph/8-16kph. I was already used to fast-moving cars and trucks, but the big rigs often had a good draft that jerked me along instantly, but left me just as quickly. I was beset by a slower tailwind which then came at me like a headwind.

I was surprise at how quickly I needed to recharge myself, sucking my water bottle to empty every half-hour. I thought how good it was that I had Mina make the blue denim water buffaloes for me, which were slung over my seat posts, port and starboard. I could stop and easily refill my water bottle by holding it below the buffalo, water would quickly siphon into it through the hose after unscrewing the bite valve.

Though pleased at this efficiency, I was becoming unhappy with two aspects: the drinking water was rapidly approaching ambient temperature, and feeling enervated.

The former I addressed by soaking the denim with water from another bladder, which, in that arid zone, actually cooled off the contents as the denim dried. Evaporative cooling is the common feature of all low-humidity, high temperature climes, thus the 'swamp' coolers prevail in building construction. In the early decades of automobile travel out West, water was often carried in a fabric canteen, which used the same principle to provide a cool drink for passengers or the vehicle itself. Unfortunately, the downside to having a cool drink is that I was using drinking water from one bladder which increased the risk of running out of water.

My answer to the latter was a partial solution to the former. My exhaustion was now due to the extreme atmospheric heat around me, sapping my energy from below and above. Once I had left the comfort of Angie's, the only way I could get cool was to escape the Sun. That meant shade, and there was very, very little of it available anywhere along that stretch of I-10. In fact, the only shade was below the rare underpass.

I skipped the first underpass, instead choosing to ride up the ramp to a truckstop. I was bitterly disappointed when, upon closer inspection, found that it was closed. Even the entrance was barricaded, denying me the chance for an overhang. I made no such mistake at the next underpass, and stopped wholly within the shadow of the bridge. I recharged my water bottle half-warm, half-cool, took a few snacks, and retired to a rather awkward resting position. My legs were angled up a cement support column while my torso was crunched out on the 45° cement apron-abutment.

This created a new challenge: gravity constantly tugged me downward, but my answer to that was to ignore it. All that counted was that I was out of the burning Sun, and, despite the difficulty, I was not alarming motorists, which is noteworthy.

Several years ago, while returning from Las Cruces on an abbreviated biketour, I experienced extreme difficulty pedaling over Anthony Gap/NM404. I knew I wasn't in the best of shape, but this was ridiculous. It wasn't until mile marker 9 that the reason became obvious: I had a flat tire! Exhausted, I chose not to repair it, and instead called my family. I invited them out for an evening meal to, say, at Edge of Texas, which, conveniently enough, just happened to be relatively close to where I lay on the broad shoulder of 404 beside my tandem.

"Oh, by the way," I added as if it was an afterthought, "could you bring the 4Runner and go a little ways up Anthony Gap to pick me and the Doublevision up first?"

I knew I'd have to tolerate snickers and rude comments later, but what amazed me were the number of New Mexico motorists who stopped beside me. Safety was not a concern as I have extreme visibility all about the tandem, but their concern was about my health. The last New Mexican to stop was none other than a state trooper, who had been alerted by a passerby that a possible injured cyclist was on the road. It might have been a cool day, but I was immensely warmed by the citizens of the Land of Enchantment.

I had learned that while removing my Doublevision completely off the roadway might be difficult or even impossible, in no way could I remain in a supine or prone position beside it. Being nearly folded over under the overpass was a small price to pay for not disrupting the flow of traffic and I was able to get sufficient rest.

Further East, I was able to exit I-10, cutting over to a 2-way frontage road though I still had to endure this furnace. Having motored I-10 many times previously, I knew my opportunities, such as they were, for shade were much greater along this side road.

Indeed, my body was soon telling me to seek shade, whereupon I found a somewhat sparse bushy site suitable to lay in. Parking my bike, I stepped over a barrier and nestled myself among the cacti for much needed rest, ignoring the pinpricks. Anything to lessen those bright rays of Sun!

Momentarily recuperated, I returned to my chro-moly steed and began turning the crank slowly. A van slowly approached me, and the driver gave me the universal sign asking me if I was "OK?" I immediately replied with "OK!" and he sped away. I was gratified to know that someone out here was aware of me, even if it meant they were greatly inconvenienced by having to turn around to check upon my status. If I'd still been resting, that motorist would've stopped to inquire about my condition.

Must be a New Mexican.

Then I thought about the irony of using the "OK" sign because it is universal for (scuba) diving and the only water around was the scant amount in my buffaloes.

At the crest of this hill, I saw several decrepit buildings, and didn't care if food or water was available; I only wanted shade. As I got closer, I could see that it might have been quite an active scene at one point in time—like the ghost truckstop I passed a few hours ago—but now it appeared to be abandoned with numerous postings against trespassing. I figured that since I was not attempting to enter the building itself, only laying in the shade of the overhead, I wouldn't get shot or arrested or whatever happens to true villains in remote areas. It was wonderful to be able to lay down completely flat without having to worry about rolling into a ditch or more treacherous situation.

Within an hour and feeling better, I once again resumed pedaling. I hadn't gone far before pushing into a bona fide rest area, where it felt good to neither be trespassing nor too close to the motorway. The only violation might be using the accessible picnic table, where I backed my tandem into the shade up a cut-curb. More satisfying was the meal-ready-to-eat (MRE) Erik had given me came in extremely handy; I ate a filling wheat snack bread, complemented by the warm water.

I thought back a month, when Erik suggested that I take the MREs, followed by scoffing at the idea that the biking plan wouldn't go exactly according to my prediction. Then I thought of previous bike journeys and I'd <u>always</u> taken emergency food because the plans rarely (??!!) seemed to work out exactly as envisioned.

Newly re-invigorated from the rations, I pedaled off.

Going around a bend, I was dismayed to not see the Border Patrol check station, then a double whammy when I didn't see it around the next bend. Glee filled my heart because there was no triple whammy, and I pedaled strongly after merging into the inspection lane. I didn't have 18 wheels, but in my own unique way, I felt as the Doublevision, longer than many of the cars in the other lane, qualified as a "truck".

Neither did the Border Patrol, who were agog at seeing me.

A passenger in a car adjacent to me yelled out, "Where're you from an' goin' to?"

"El Paso! Louisiana! Or the thirtieth of June! Whichever comes first!" I yelled back.

"More power to you, man!" he yelled as the vehicle sped East.

"So, where do you recommend I eat in Sierra Blanca, Sir?" I asked the astonished agent.

"Oh, well, yeah, go to '*La Familia*' " he told me, "take exit one zero seven, you can't miss it."

Then he added, "Be careful; going East on this road gets worse."

"Thanks!" I gratefully replied and began vigorously pedaling once more. I had been stimulated by the short conversation at the Border Patrol station, and soon left I-10 at exit 107. At the stop sign I looked about, unable to find the restaurant I couldn't miss. I pedaled uphill, but the town was diminishing so I reversed course and saw it, plain as day. Hmmmm, I must be really hungry as I pulled in front of the entrance, put the tandem on its kickstand, and entered.

Smells emanating from behind the swinging doors revved up my appetite, making the menu almost pointless.

"I'll have whatever's in the kitchen," I told the waitress hungrily.

"That's very good, Sir," she replied, "but you might want to look at the menu anyway, just to be sure."

She was right. Not only did I order an entrée steak platter, I also needed an appetizer of fried okra, and a chocolate milk, too. Interestingly, I found this meal/restaurant combination to be as equally pleasurable as Angie's many hours ago, and they kindly refilled my buffaloes with ice and water. I quickly forgot the earlier difficulties of finding shade and cold drinking water. Wanting to share my good fortune, I attempted to call my wife, but was surprised that T-Mobile service was non-existent.

Feeling well fed and strong, I went outside to see the flags on my bike streaming parallel to the ground. Palming my hand between the horizon and Sun told me one to two hours of daylight remained. When motoring this route, I always refuel at the Love's in Van Horn, which is exit 140, or 33 miles from where I stood. I knew the I-10 shoulder—it is smooth, fast cement with a distinctive white lane line and has deep ATLMs segregating it from the motor traffic lanes, and, so far, a limited amount of debris on it.

There was a preponderance of supporting evidence: tailwind, distance, fast shoulder, ample daylight, excellent battery powered lights for the inevitable darkness, fresh water. My call, and I chose to keep pedaling. Onto Van Horn!

I knew about the frontage road on the North side of I-10, and headed toward it, crossing under the interstate. I stopped at a remodeled historical marker, this one noting that this was the site of the joining of the second trans-continental railroad, 15DEC1881. A new visitors' center had been built across the road, in obvious anticipation of growth. Pedaling East on the frontage road, there was more updated construction, including restaurants, an RV park (thinking I might stay there, I hesitated for a split-second) but the urge to get along was coursing through my body.

After dipping underneath the railroad tracks, the road became slower, and I took advantage of a unregulated interstate crossing. This can be, of course, quite challenging. Knowing that I was going from a dead stop to crossing two high-speed lanes of motor vehicles moving at 80mph (129kph), I patiently waited at the edge for a huge gap in Westbound traffic. The opportunity came suddenly and I pushed off.

But the rear wheel slipped on the gravel.

My bike began to lurch over, the massive load starting to obey gravity.

I pushed hard on the right pedal and was barely able to pull out of the fall, gliding to the median, safely out of harm's way as speeding motor vehicles whooshed by. I carefully stopped on the blacktop surface, in an area that was clean and free of any debris which might throw me off.

Again, I waited patiently for a huge gap in the Eastbound traffic, and was able to cross to the shoulder without incident. I breathed a sigh of relief, and commenced pedaling East to Van Horn.

I hadn't gone too far before seeing a tractor-trailer parked on the shoulder in front of me. Scrutinizing the road behind me, I fortuitously had another gap in the traffic and was able to pass the unit on the left. Stopping in front of the Peterbuilt rig, I walked back to find out how I may be of assistance.

The skinny driver grinned at the idea that I, a bicyclist, might be able to help an 18-wheeler.

"*Mira, Señor,*" I told him, "I stop for most every motor vehicle stranded on the road, no matter how many axles. Chances are I *can't* help, but every now and then I can. It's a funny thing, but I never know until I actually do stop. I'm just glad you're OK and help is on it's way. *¡Adiós, amigo!*"

As I pedaled away, I gave a wave and two pipes on my whistle. He replied with a friendly blast from the air horns.

As the Sun approached the horizon, I was furiously pedaling in a high gear, enjoying the tailwind and employing a countdown that kept me focused. Upon seeing a mile marker sign, I began a countdown in Spanish. "*Ciento novecientos, ciento ochocientos, ciento setecientos, ciento quiñientos...*" This was not so much to reinforce my Spanish, but it was my canary in the coal mine. As long as I could make an accurate countdown, usually aloud, I was OK. However, should I be unable to do that, it was time for me to stop because my brain was beginning to fail.

I came up with this mnemonic solution a few years ago, while on a short 3-day biketour over Thanksgiving, from El Paso to Las Cruces (overnighting there at colleague Dan's home), over San Agustin Pass toward White Sands, Holloman AFB, and Alamagordo (expected overnight), then back to El Paso. Half of my second day was spent in the lowest gear, pushing up the pass, and the coast downhill only lasted a few miles. I enthusiastically pedaled the rest of the short day and well into nightfall, counting down at each mile marker. With a short seven miles to go before *ALAMOGORDO! GOLDEN CORRAL! ALAMOGORDO! GOLDEN CORRAL!*, my ability to count backwards was faltering. I might have had a large lunch at Thai Delight 45 miles/72kms back in Organ, but pedaling for many hours had used that energy and my body was now robbing other vital areas for power. And what greater power than the brain? So I knew it was time for me to stop, finding a very decent, well off the road flat space for my bike and body close to the entrance of Hollowman. It was a perfect campsite, *and* I had discovered that the countdown was an excellent predictor of when to stop.

I stopped at exit 129, Allamore, for a couple of reasons. The Sun had descended and it was now sufficiently dark enough to turn on my own battery powered lights. These lights mounted on my Doublevision are both numerous, flashing and steady, and I am a dazzling brightness in the city. However, out here, 11 miles away from Van Horn in the middle of a dark desert where the only other lights seen were from the talc mine and passing cars, my lights seemed puny and insignificant, wholly consumed by the absolute darkness.

Strange that it was so dark, after the near-full moon last night! Exhilarated that I was about an hour away from my destination, I now saw the reason for the darkness. Looking above me, I saw no stars. To the East, though, distant lightning flashed over what I knew to be the Davis Mountains. Remounting my Doublevision, I looked forward to camping somewhere in Van Horn, ready to give my tarp-tent it's first use—and hoping to not do so *before* then.

Now pedaling uphill, I was grateful that so many motor vehicles were Eastbound. The headlamps regularly illuminated the shoulder, and I was able to avoid most large debris. Debris is one of my greatest concerns pedaling anywhere, day or night. It can be anything, large to small, biodegradable or not, from paper to plastic to gravel (like what had nearly dumped me an hour ago) to glass to far worse substances that can penetrate the tire and pierce the tube. It usually tends to collect on the right, out of motor traffic lanes, close to the curb on urban/suburban streets, and is especially prone to occupy any space that is marked as a "BIKE LANE". My personal experience has been with goat-head stickers and strands from steel-belted tire scrap, both of which have caused me great problems. Whenever I have a flat tire, I analyze the cause and attempt to fix it for the short term and a long term remedy. I visually inspect the entire wheel: rim, tire, and tube, as well as running my finger or thumb along the surfaces—my skin will tear upon an unseen intrusion. Once repaired, I proclaim "no more flats for the rest of the century" but have found that sometimes it is significantly shorter than 100 years before my next flat.

I knew this topography had an inclined grade, but was it really so uphill and difficult to pedal? Undoubtedly, it was immeasurably more challenging because the strong tailwind had become a forceful headwind, doubly so when a few spitting raindrops struck my helmet like a spitwad hitting the blackboard shot by a mischievous student.

I no longer cared about counting backwards or forward in Spanish or English or even in cursive, and I began to consider camping. Then I heard one of the most compelling reasons to keep moving, a very loud, low grumble which seemed to be just off to my right. Talk about adrenalin kicking in!

I pedaled harder and finally felt relief when gravity began pulling me downhill as I passed the sign announcing Culberson County and Central Time Zone. Passing the closed weigh station, I came into visual contact with the bright lights of Van Horn. At last!

Taking the first exit, the lights were bright but I passed numerous empty or closed businesses. My personal comfort increased dramatically upon entry, but now I needed to find a campsite and food, with emphasis on the latter. It was a pleasant downhill ride, but I wasn't satisfied. I turned South on US 90 and passed under I-10.

Bingo! My answer was the Pilot Station/Wendy's Restaurant. It was perfect! I parked my bike on the sidewalk beside the windows of Wendy's, took my all-important camera bag (which contained my wallet and cell) and went inside. I was ravenous for liquid more than water or Gatorade and former YISD sub-leader Keys' words came back, "Eyberg, you need protein after exercise, especially after all that intense bicycling." I looked among the refrigerated offerings, which ran the gamut from flavored waters to exercise drinks to juices to...why, that's it! *Muscle Milk.*

As with virtually all foods, I read the ingredients list and was pleased to find that there was really nothing harmful within it. I was amused that it specifically stated there was no actual "milk" in it, and that was just a reference to similarity between this and the real thing. However, I enthusiastically grasped a bottle of Vanilla flavored and paid cash for it.

The receptionist wasn't surprised to see a bicyclist: "I'm from St. Paul, seen lot's of your kind there, an' your choosin' the right time to cycle, much cooler now than daytime."

After hearing that I'd pedaled over a hundred miles today, she added another note: "Dear, be sure you keep your water intake up; do try to avoid the mid-day Sun. Lot's of experienced bikers like you think they can beat it an' end up in the hospital. You're hearin' me, aren't you?"

I assured her that I wasn't taking my condition or the climate or anything else for granted.

Going to a table beside the window where I could see my Doublevision, I swallowed the entire drink in one long gulp. I needed more, and went to order a large Frosty. No quick slurping now, I tweeted abbreviated happenings of the day, including an archived message from Sierra Blanca.

I called my son in Houston to give the good news about my distance.

"Congratulations on your century," he said. "I hope you have more."

"So do I, but all the right elements made it possible," I replied. "If they do, I expect I'll see you within two weeks, but I'll call you before then."

"Be sure to avoid the Fourth of July weekend," he warned me, "my fianceè and I are going to D.C. then."

"No worries, mate," I told him in my best Aussie accent. "I'll be gittin' right home by then! Say, when you go home next week, please bring a pair of new gloves from my shop, eh?"

Then I called Ellen, as promised, cheerfully telling her "Yes, I made great mileage today!" leaving out the details of pedaling in darkness and the turn of weather. I promised to call her tomorrow night, "...unless I'm in a dead zone, which is probable since Far West Texas has so many of them, like when I tried to call you from Sierra Blanca..."

Realizing how late it was, I returned to the convenience store, and charged three more of the Muscle Milks: chocolate, banana, and vanilla. Back outside, I observed my surroundings. This is a truck stop, with lots of rigs parked for down time. Surely I could find someplace close where I could park for the night? After all, I had made purchases here, too, just like the truckers.

I turned my lights on and pedaled around this fine establishment, but was dismayed to see no really secure place I could lay out. Going across Van Horn Street, I went behind a closed building and considered a site close to piles of truck tires.

All of a sudden, an intensely bright pair of lights flashed onto me.

Maybe I won't stay here.

Then the headlights of the truck continued to go past me as the trucker parallel parked beside another rig a safe distance away.

That's it, then, I will stay here. I checked the sky and saw stars; no need to set up my tarp-tent tonight. Like last night, I got out my Z-rest and sleeping bag, quickly drank the Muscle Milks, brushed and flossed, then sprayed down with OFF before going into deep sleep.

OVERNIGHT TWO: VAN HORN

I woke to the sound of truckers starting their tractors in predawn darkness, getting ready for the day's run because their only way to make money is by the number of miles added to the odometer. I, too, had a long distance to cover and reset my cyclocomputer from "106.3" to "0.0". Finding a coat hanger, I rebent it to form a bracket to display my VIRTUAL TOURIST flag and ductaped it aloft on the pole. Maybe it'll identify me better and possibly be a benefit down the road? After repacking my gear, I purposely did not return to Wendy's/Pilot, instead wheeling next door to the Exxon where I met the clerk.

Pam became my source for critical information: Where is a grocery store selling water? Where is the best place for breakfast? How far to Valentine?

"Pueblo Market, on Broadway beside Motel Six. Pappas Pantry, right across the street, is the best cafe around, and Valentine is some forty miles." she said. Then came unexpected information: "It's already seventy-five degrees, hon, an' it'll be over a hundred today—again. Watch out for that Sun when you're biking," giving me a sincere smile.

Thanking her, I shook her hand and remembered passing that store last night, almost as soon as I got off the interstate. I didn't remember it being so far away, and it was a challenge to pedal back there because now I was going uphill. I was exhausted by the time I arrived at Pueblo's, I immediately bought a Heath candy bar and ate it, saving the wrapper for my bill at checkout. It might be a small store, but I was surprised that I could not find gallon containers of water, drinking or distilled.

Much to my embarrassment, I had to ask. Much to my surprise, there were no gallon jugs anyway, only a 24-pack of half-liter bottles. I was shocked to learn there was no recycling, so I filled a trash barrel with the empties after recharging my water buffaloes.

Pedaling back down the street, I rebuked myself for not stopping at that Dollar General, which surely would have water in gallon...! Oh, well, I want to support as much non-chain business as possible.

Passing Exxon, I piped my whistle and waved at Pam even though too far away to know if she saw me or not. I was glad to find a decently shaded spot for the Doublevision at Pappas Pantry, and took a seat looking through the window at it.

Whenever and wherever I've traveled, VISA has always been accepted and Pappas was no exception. I was powerful hungry; I shoveled pancakes, eggs, bacon, toast, oatmeal, and coffee down my gullet. Two nuns sitting closeby might have been shocked at my glutinous behavior, but didn't reveal it, instead giving me information concerning my route for the day.

"Yes, it's thirty-five miles to Valentine, then a mile later you turn off for Fort Davis," said the younger. "Isn't that right?" she asked the other nun.

"Very much so, but it might be a bit farther to the Fort Davis road, maybe two miles," answered the older nun. "In any case, Sir, do be careful out there. Your greatest enemy is the Sun. We'll pray for your safety."

I thanked them, then confidently assured them that with my vast experience—I had pedaled *over* a hundred miles yesterday in triple digit temperatures—would cover any difficulties I might encounter. They nodded, smiled politely, and departed.

What did they know? In fact, what did anybody know unless they were bicycling like me?

I covered my cup when the waitress came by again. My eyeballs were already floating, and more coffee in me might cause an accident. Thank goodness the bathroom was close. It seems that the enormous amount of food I'd eaten was already processed.

After paying the bill, I was disappointed to find that I had already used up a chunk of prime riding time. The Sun was almost five palms up, about (10:30). Get gone John!

Full of vigor, I went to my left, and pedaled South.

US90 is an excellent bicycling road, perhaps a notch below I-10, with a broad shoulder but no ATLMs. That was OK because there was nowhere near the amount of motor vehicles on this two-lane asphalt as on the interstate.

It was already hot, just as hot and getting hotter as I'd already been warned about. I was prepared, with bottles and waterbuffaloes full of cold water, almost 3 gallons/11 liters worth. However, I was not ready for the next challenge, despised not only by me, but bicyclists worldwide: headwinds.

I had to gear down, into my lowest range, the granny gear, so slow that a person can walk faster than a bike pedaled in the smallest chainring. That wind was a steady, unrelenting force of what was at least 50mph/80kph and I was barely able to creep along. But creep I did, and feeling all of that nourishing breakfast draining out of me with every breath.

As the day wore on, I began to feel the promised heat. I couldn't stop in the shade of the trestle where the tracks crossed overhead because the shoulder was absent right there, so I searched for other shade. I was able to recuperate a bit in a slim sheltered rest area, but I had to keep moving. Then I figured another solution: box culverts.

In the rare rainstorms, there are numerous places along the roadway where water can accumulate on one side, possibly making it impassable due to high water or simply washing the road out. To allow for passage of that water and ensuring continual use of this vital highway, a large, square cement box, open on opposite ends, is built underneath it, in sizes according to need.

Invaluable during the wet, it proved to be equally invaluable during the hot. I would park my Doublevision on the shoulder close to where I would stumble my way down, into the darkened space. Almost immediately, I would feel the relief of 15-20°F/7-10°C degrees less. Often, I would snack, drink (warm) water, and sleep. Following a half-hour break, I would return topside, refreshed, and continue grinding against the wind, until my next stop.

I had spent all day in this life-saving drill: I would count down the mile markers, and added counting down the box culverts. I quickly learned that these were always marked by a vertical, rectangular yellow sign the size of shoebox lid posted 4 feet/1.2 meters high directly on top of the midpoint.

By the time the Sun was a palm above the horizon, I came to Valentine, or, rather, to the Prada shop of artistic note. Other than being a recognized piece, I took a couple of pix before entering town proper.

This a truly small community which might not even be considered a village. I had high hopes for possibly a restaurant, cafe, some kind of an eatery, even a gas station, but was sadly disappointed. Remnants of former businesses existed, albeit tumbling down. Much to my surprise, I saw rather modern-looking schoolhouse and thought surely there must be a store or something around it. I almost biked toward it when I saw three youngsters cavorting in an above-ground swim pool.

One lad motioned for me to come their way. Upon meeting them, they were, as I suspected, quite interested in my Doublevision. I gave them my personal cards and the story of how I came to be there passing through their quaint burg. They were attentive, and before they slipped back into that oasis, I learned that nothing existed here which could induce a traveler to stay. So sad, but at least the children were immensely happy, and that is a positive note.

I parked my bike on the shoulder of the road, opened my large satchel to obtain the already opened MRE, and sat on the broken down stoop of the shuttered HiWay Cafe. I was famished, and impatiently waited for the water-activated heater to warm the meal. It made no difference what I was going to eat because, when I finally tore the plastic bag open, I couldn't get it into my mouth fast enough. I forced myself to slow down, try to enjoy it, make it last longer. I had to slow down—it was incredibly full of carbs, protein, vitamins, minerals, lots of calories of nothing but energy that my body began to resist too rapid an intake. Enjoying the peacefulness and relative lack of wind, I took care of my teeth, because wherever I stopped, and it would likely be soon, all I wanted to do was sleep.

Then, I was shocked when a man driving a pick-up truck stopped and asked if I needed water. I was dumbstruck, and probably took a full minute before I could respond.

"Well, thanks, but, no, I still have a half-gallon of water left," I explained.

"Where ever you're going from here, pardner," he told me, "that's not enough. Your forty miles that way to Van Horn, and thirty miles the other to Marfa. Ain't a thing between neither. Are you sure you don't want more water?"

"Actually," I said thoughtfully, "I probably have another half-gallon of water in another pack, so I think I'll be OK if I leave early tomorrow morning."

"Have it your way," he replied, shaking his head as if I was going to make tomorrow evening's news as another dehydrated death on US 90, "but stay outta' the mid-day Sun. An' the winds a cooker, too. Best of luck to you."

I was touched. Valentine might not have a store, gas station, or any amenities to help passerbys, but it has residents who know the area, the climate, and are ready to help.

I'd hardly turned more than ten revolutions of the crank when I was absolutely astonished by what I saw: a multi-colored stone building, the Kay Johnson Public Library. I had to do a double-take because it looked as if it had been transplanted from Lake SpringMO. A small structure of quarried colored native stones, each carefully placed and cemented, forming what I thought was probably the single most outstanding building, certainly in Valentine if not all of West Texas, although El Paso has several structures full of character, too. I hope the lions guarding the entryway prevent the ruin that had afflicted other buildings in Valentine.

I turned back to pedaling South. I now had more energy, but was battling a renewed headwind as soon as I pedaled out of town. In fact, I barely made it around a broad corner when an even greater wind buffeted me. I saw the sign for a box culvert and pushed as hard as I could.

Arriving there as the Sun was setting, I found reasonably cacti-free high ground between 90 and the fence, parking my Doublevision on it parallel to the wind, and set up for the night beside it. It was a bit tricky. I had to move slowly, putting rocks upon my Z-rest pad to keep it from blowing away, then pulling my sleeping bag between me and the pad while keeping every strapped down.

I reflected.

Whatever have I gotten myself into? Was this the end of my Trans-Texas Bicycle Odyssey? Forget Ft. Davis, which I knew was surrounded by seemingly impenetrable to bicycle mountains. I needed to go to either Marfa or back to Van Horn. Talk about being stuck being a rock and a hard place.

Marfa was closer, but headwinds will make it more difficult to pedal; Van Horn was farther, but these winds would literally blow me there within an hour. And if I go back there, then where? I passionately hated the thought of backtracking. I simply didn't know what I was going to do.

Besides being in a no-win situation, I felt there is no way my cell would reach anybody. But, what the heck, I tried calling Ellen anyway. This was my next huge shock of the day: the call went through! My joy was dashed upon glum acceptance that I was going to have to return as far as Valentine to seek fresh, clean, drinking water. Without it, I cannot go anywhere.

Laying there, a flashlight beam played over my bike and me laying beside it. Looking toward it, I heard a male voice, "Are you alright?"

I put on my hard-soled Shimano biking sandals, pulled a few personal cards out of my saddlebag, and walked toward the light.

I had a feeling the Border Patrol might show up during the night, and gave them a business card apiece, along with an explanation of this most unusual situation.

"Well, just as long as you are fine," came a female voice. "Is there anything we can help you with, food, water...."

I almost fainted when I heard it: "Water? Yes, water! I can certainly use some water."

"Bring your container over here," she said, opening up the back of their beefy patrol car.

The five gallon thermos quickly filled my water bottle, some of the cold liquid spilling onto my hand, which I lapped up. Inspired, I asked if I might be able to fill my other containers. My heart soared when they said "Yes" and "Of course".

I took the four bladders out of the buffaloes, and filled each to full from their thermos. I was overjoyed, delirious at their rescue, and of course I had know their names. Agents Lily and Jay had just saved my life as well as my Trans-Texas tour. I won't have to turn back now.

I couldn't believe my good fortune.

I called Ellen to share this incredible luck bit of luck.

"I'll be lucky to get back to sleep now," she said with irritation, "I do have to go to work tomorrow, you know. But I'm pleased for you, and you ought to post it on twitter before you use up any more battery talking to me." I felt better in every way possible, fully abetted by the delicious cold water. I may have scrubbed Ft. Davis, but now I *knew* I'd be in Marfa tomorrow by lunchtime. My Trans-Texas Bicycle Odyssey continues! I fell into deep slumber after tweeting:

Lily&Jay (usborderpatrol) just saved my life: they gave me ample water. Commendations are small compared to my gratitude. Thank you very much!

OVERNIGHT THREE: US90 BERM

I woke early, in pre-dawn gray, quite well rested. Even though the wind hadn't abated overnight, I was jubilant. I had received a new lease on life from Agents Lily and Jay last night! I quickly put together an MRE, dug a cat-hole as no cafe or gas station with a bathroom was anywhere close, and packed up.

Within a half-hour, the Sun was about to peep over the Eastern mountains and I pushed my Doublevision onto the road, After swinging my right leg over the front wheel, I began pedaling South. Ugh! Headwinds! And they feel stronger than yesterday. Double ugh!! My body responded to those winds with a shudder, a visceral groan of resignation to a repeat of yesterday. My brain forced acquiescence; I numbly pushed the crank around and around and around and around...

Within a mile, the sign for route 505 came into view. This was the cut-off to Ft. Davis I had originally planned, then deleted amid yesterday's fatiguing headwinds. It might have taken me a second, probably less, to reconsider my actions before I reinstated Ft. Davis. Anything is better than this head wind, and my body agreed, perking up as I turned at the Western terminus of 505.

I stopped, looked, and listened before slowly (I was doing *everything* slowly.) crossing the railroad tracks, wary for any loud, rumbling train. My actions seemed absurd; I could see at least a half-mile in either direction, and this fine grade had lights along with crossbucks, yet I was fearful.

I've read too much about fatalities resulting from collisions with trains. I had even experienced a near-miss in which the spare wheel on the 4Runner, re-mounted to the front, was nudged by a slow-moving train.

Yes, I was fearful, and justly so. Any train is a dominant force of land-based transportation, and all other vehicles must yield to it because of the immense distance the locomotive powered unit requires to come to a complete stop. That is just the simple physics of mass—and common sense. I don't remember reading this on the Miller Analogies Test, but it would be appropriate: a train is to a motor vehicle as a motor vehicle is to a bicycle. Perhaps it is too easy, but so clearly self-evident.

Additionally, I know from personal experience, having been rear ended by a motor vehicle 25 months ago. Fortunately, that was very low speed collision and I suffered no injury although my tandem required a significant rebuild. Other bicyclists (Specifically, Mr. Heinz Duerkop, who, two months after my incident, was murdered while pedaling on North George Dieter after being rear-ended by still at-large motorist.) are not so lucky, and have been seriously maimed or killed while the irresponsible motorist leaves the crime scene.

I'm not making excuses for us two-wheelers, but it has been my direct observation that the vast majority of problems we have are because of our own actions. Too many people on bikes refuse to follow the rules of the road, as stated in the operator's handbook. The single worst case is lack of visibility, during the day and especially at night. Another extremely hazardous situation is during group rides. Mob mentality takes over, resulting in gross abuse of the privilege of using the public roads. That is one reason I prefer solo riding, like right now.

Safely across the tracks, I wholly rejoiced at no more headwind. Then came the best surprise in this young day: I stopped in front of a road sign indicating that Ft. Davis was only 34 miles/54km away. My body rejoiced too, as extra energy surged through my legs, and I shifted from the bottom range into the middle range.

A heavy duty Jefferson County Sheriff truck stopped alongside me and the passenger window smoothly rolled down. Inside, a swarthy man clad in uniform asked, "Are you all right?"

I gave him my personal card, declaring, "Yes, I am indeed fine. You're probably mystified to see a bicyclist out here during such windy and hot weather..."

"Naw," he replied, "see'm all the time goin' to an' from Fort Davis. This is a popular road. But it is windy an' hot, be careful."

I was touched by his concern, and a bit surprised that he didn't carry extra water. I didn't really need any, it's just that everybody (official or not) who's stopped for me thus far has always offered it to me. And I for sure don't want to be dependent upon their kindness to get me through—no doubt that is exactly when I'd end up in the tough situation like last night!

Route 505 is a 9 mile/16km connector between US90 and State Highway 166, of decent pedaling that was mostly a series of low hills, not particularly gaining or losing elevation. I found it especially pleasurable because that vicious headwind was no more, replaced with a strong sidewind that sometimes blew me across the narrow two-lanes of asphalt. It was quite safe because other than the Sheriff, I saw no other vehicles, with or without motors.

At the Eastern terminus of 505, I could take the Scenic Loop to Kent, on I-10, or to Ft. Davis. I was more exhilarated than ever because it was now only 25 miles/40 km distant! I hesitated upon seeing that the first significant uphill on a diminished road that had lost the yellow centerline. Taking a breather, I took several pix of vultures feasting on a dead wild hog, then shifted back into the low range to slowly ascend.

It wasn't as long as I expected though rather steep, and was able to catch my breath again in the shade of a road cut. This became a pattern the rest of the morning: gear down for a slow ascent, shade break, whiz downhill, gear down for another slow ascent to a higher point, shade break, and so forth.

I was a bit woozy after several of these, and while at the bottom of one, I cross another cattle guard and saw two wild hogs, quite alive, under a spindly Palo Verde tree. They were in the only poor shade available, which *I* wanted. Colleague Eddie had warned me about the ferociousness of these critters, so I stayed at a safe distance and encouraged the beasts to move on. Asking them gently to move on didn't seem to be an appropriate method, so I piped my whistle long and hard, leaving me faint. They moseyed on, likely more amused by this strange creature on two wheels sounding like an inedible, noisy oversized bird. After eating another MRE, I fell fast asleep on the spot.

I woke rested, and the flags on my Doublevision showed that the wind hadn't diminished, but had changed direction—it was now a headwind. Regardless, I felt pretty good about having avoided it all morning and knew I surely didn't have that far to go before Ft. Davis, maybe 15 or 20 miles/16-32kms? I think my cyclocomputer might have been giving me readings in kilometers, which seemed closer to miles, but, heck, ...time to just go.

It was a slow uphill and against the wind, but there were several pullouts with stout rock walls where I was able to rest, albeit no shade. Then I was surprised to see a TxDOT road construction crew, putting down a layer of small rocks. The road was already slow enough, but to have to try to pedal over that, too? It wasn't easy, and at one point, I had to step off the roadway to rest under the only tree within visibility—a crackling dry Cedar. Eventually, I did reach a 5,849foot/1782meter pass, the road dramatically changed from coarse chip-seal to a smooth paved surface and the headwind became a tailwind. Thanks goodness!

I cruised downhill, into a late 1800s uninhabited community of many two-story, tin-roofed buildings that have since been added. It was identified by a historical marker as "Bloys camp meeting" and has had annual revival there ever since in August. Early on, it was one of the original Cowboy camp meeting sites where the lone ranchers and families could gather to receive religious instruction for a weekend at least once a year under leader William Benjamin Bloys. When he died in 1917, the event and area was renamed in his honor. I could see a coming together here, especially if the participants arrived on this side where a superior road would make traveling so much easier.

The tailwind now pushed me downhill on an exceptionally fine, smooth, well marked road to the Point of Rocks Roadside Park. A small car came up and parked nearby, where undoubtedly my Doublevision attracted the attention of the driver. He was John, with his wife Sandy, and were on their way to Big Bend country. What an engaging conversation we had—solved the world's problems, we did. A wet spot in the parking lot from a spring ensured why this stop was so critically important to expansion—Westward or any direction.

A plaque adhered to one of the massive boulders memorialized "Ed Waldy, John M. Dean, August Frensell; And all other stage drivers who traveled this route; Fearless heroes of frontier days; By their courage the West was made"

I remarked that the value of fresh, clean drinking water is invaluable in the desert, not only back then but today too, and told them about the lifesaving actions of Border Patrol agents Lily & Jay 14 hours ago. Then I was surprised by the generosity of Sandy and John when they offered me water, Gatorade, a banana, and an apple to help me on my way. I did not refuse. Following more small talk, they motored off as I began to pedal out of the parking lot when another motorist pulled in. Stopping beside me, the distraught man asked me about McDonald Observatory.

"Yes, you can get there from here in both directions," I told him, "because this road is a scenic loop. However, if you continue uphill, it'll take you at least another hour, maybe two, on a long, slow, winding road that is being renovated by TexDOT. I'd strongly recommend going through Fort Davis."

He thanked me and drove away in the direction I had suggested. Back on 166, I thoroughly enjoyed the tailwind and downhill, but became concerned about the price to be paid for such superior riding.

You see, it has been my experience that whenever I begin to delight in the circumstances like this good road, downhill with tailwind, there will inevitably be rotten road, uphill with headwind.

After intersecting state highway 17, turning North, then entering Ft. Davis within an hour, I began to believe that maybe, just maybe, I had paid the price already. The route between 90 and the pass into Bloys Camp meeting was difficult, but from there, it was a blissful cruise nearly all downhill until I reached my destination: Overland Trail Campground.

What was there to not like? The OTC is located in downtown Ft. Davis, has showers, laundromat, cabins, sites for tents, RVs, everything. Best of all, I arrived by late afternoon—not completely exhausted. The owner is tall, lanky Dave, a retired VietVet from Canada who maintains this impeccable area. Being South of the border hadn't yet completely destroyed the signature origins of his speech. After collecting my $14 fee, he gave me very specific directions about where I could camp, which electrical outlet was available for me to recharge my cell phone/digital camera on, and tips about where to eat. He also assured me that I didn't have to lock my bike up: "...nobody will mess with it here."

I smiled, raided his fridge (My mistake—this is *not* a hostel!), thanked him, and went outside, following his precise instructions. Mostly, but he corrected me a short time later. I could have showered and made myself real presentable, but chose to only put on my "dress" shirt (UBS flag T-shirt, captioned "The freedom to give from the heart", which I don't wear while pedaling, reserving it for occasions like this.) and extra deodorant. Ignoring his disclaimer, I locked the Doublevision anyway and made way for the Drug Store.

I was already familiar with this establishment, having been here many times before on family excursions and Scout campouts. Centrally located within the 1925 Dumas building, 113 State Street, it had the classic soda fountain, stools, long bar, and was period throughout. I knew exactly what I wanted at the bar: a traditional vanilla milk shake. That was the beginning of a much larger order, whereupon I retired to a booth to contemplate the menu.

Not that there was much contemplation on my part; I already knew steak was my choice, along with all the fixings. My appetizer was a side of green beans tasting exactly the way they ought to, which was good. So was the salad. And the well-done T-bone steak was perfect, and even its bone which I gnawed on to get every meaty morsel was delicious. And the only way to finish this outstanding meal was with pie *à la modé*—vanilla, of course. I stayed away from the coffee, knowing that it was much too late in the day for me to be ingesting caffeine. (Last July, I had taken a short 5-day, 200 mile/320km biketour through Oro GrandeNM, AlamogordoNM, CloudcroftNM, HopeNM, to ArtesiaNM. The day before departure, I made the mistake of drinking coffee throughout a school workshop and was penalized by staying awake most of the night. That necessitated a delayed start, which caused roadside camping between US54 and the fence, earning a visit from FOUR Border Patrol squad cars...!) After paying my bill, I sauntered down the street toward OTC.

I was satiated, my tummy bulging from the scrumptious meal when I passed by a distinctive store, Nel's Coffee Shop and Bookfeller. I was staring through the window when a man emerged to tell me the obvious: "it's closed, but she'll open up by seven tomorrow morning." I thanked him, took several more steps and entered the OTC compound.

I was not alarmed by the family who had erected a tent in the camping area and were admiring my bicycle. The one person most interested was a young boy, Caleb, who had never seen such a different-looking bicycle. With great pride, I went into elaborate detail telling him about my 27-speed Doublevision tandem recumbent. I had him sit in the pilot's chair, his feet not quite able to touch the pedals; he was suitably impressed. I would have given him a ride on it, but the co-pilot's chair was still packed with gear. While speaking with the parents, Jesse and Brian, I learned that they are from Round Rock, and currently touring a lot of Texas, giving their son a first-rate education. I complimented them as that was exactly what I had done for my children; "In fact, what you are doing is the best way for him to learn and bond with you, too. He might not remember anything else, but your role modeling will stay with him all his life. Congratulations!"

Brian told me, "Thank you. Don't take this the wrong way, talking with you is great and all, but we have an appointment at a Star Party tonight..."

"Oh, no, no, no," I replied, "you need to get a move on. I did the same years ago. He'll love it!"

They unplugged their own cells and motored away.

I plugged my own cell and digital camera batteries into those outlets, took care of my teeth, put out my pad and bag, then relaxed beside the Doublevision in the setting Sun. With an altitude of 5,000 feet/1524 meters and no wind, I had difficulty believing that at this time yesterday, a short 43 miles/69kms away, I was exhausted, miserable, dehydrated, and absolutely forlorn about the possibility of having to terminate my Trans-Texas Bicycle Odyssey.

I smiled at the memory, thinking about the critical essence of fresh, clean drinking water, mostly favorable winds, good nutrition (MREs might not *look* like a typical meal, but they just as good as one, if not better), and, if I can say this without getting too full of myself, having the right attitude.

What a difference twenty-four hours makes.

Overnight Four: Fort Davis

Awake before the Sun, I lay there considering the day ahead, planning to get as far as Marathon or maybe even Sanderson because I'd be going East on US90, which meant an agreeable sidewind, like yesterday. My only real problem would be pedaling to Marfa, which is South and into that discouraging headwind. In any event, I need to start doubling or tripling my distances.

Rising, I met Dave as he watered his garden.

"Another night of no rain," he commented with disappointment.

Attempting to lighten the moment, I said, "That's why I'm not using a tent, maybe sleeping out in the open will entice it..."

"That's thoughtful of you, John," he replied dead serious, "but there's been no rain for too long. The only reason any of these plants survive around here is because I water."

"So is the water table really getting low?" I asked without any hint of levity.

"At the moment it's holding. But you don't see any of the good stuff running in the streets," he told me. "Because our water is so good, we have to keep our eye for thieves who might come around with a water truck. We cannot afford to have people taking thousands of gallons at a time, eh."

"Well, I'm not a thief, but if its as good as you say, do you think I might be able to fill up my water buffaloes with it?" I asked, then added when he was slow in answering, "Only two, no more than three gallons."

"Oh, yes, that'll be fine," he confirmed.

Returning with all four, I asked, "Dave, I've got some left in one bladder. Where would you like me to put it?"

"My new seedlings can always use more, just there," he said pointing to an elevated plot.

I unscrewed the wide-mouth lid and dumped the water, causing rich black soil to bubble up and flow away.

"Geeez, man! Don't do that!" he fairly screamed at me. "That's way too much all at once! You have to water them gently! Here put the rest over here, in the basin bottom, where you won't hurt them."

I did exactly as told.

I refilled each bladder with this good drinking water and slunk back to the Doublevision. I needed to get away as soon as possible, but had to refuel my body first.

Within an hour, after coffee at Nel's and a full breakfast at the Drug Store, I pushed out to State Street and got underway to Marfa. Like Valentine yesterday evening, there was little wind in town. I anticipated that would radically change as soon as I got out onto the open road.

Pedaling South on routes 118/17, passing the stately courthouse, festooned with Flag Day bunting contrasting with the vividly green lawn. I steered to the right (going left would put my on 118, to Alpine) on 17 to Marfa. It was the reverse of how I was pushed by a tailwind into this wonderful community yesterday. Ready to work against a headwind, I got my first shock of the day: *no wind*!

Neither a tailwind, nor sidewind, and, most importantly, no headwind. This was great but I didn't want to get lulled into a false sense of security—the day was still young. It was an easy, steady gradual ascent up Mano Prieto ridge, followed by a gradual decline before a long, steady descent for miles. I had a quick conversation with a few field hands, primarily just to distribute my cards and urge them to follow me on Twitter. It is possible their fencing job was easier because fire had reduced the broad fields to little more than brown expanses awaiting rejuvenating rainfall.

As the morning grew long, the wind did arise, but it was now blowing directly out of the West. Hallelujah! I was going to be in Marfa for lunch, easy.

I was wheeling along in my lowest gear cresting the hill and admiring the Marfa water tank, a not-so-disguised cellular tower, off to my left when my Doublevision abruptly came to a halt. Mystified, I put it up on the kickstand with no idea at all about what could have possibly malfunctioned, but knowing that since I am a pretty good wrench, I'd fix it. My second shock of the day stupefied me. The Deore 9-speed Shadow derailleur normally hangs below the rear wheel cluster on the right and parallel to it, with the chain threaded through. Unbelievably, the derailleur was now *perpendicular*, jammed between spokes and tied with yellow construction twine. I was stunned; this was a brand new derailleur just two weeks ago.

I cut surprisingly long lengths of the cord away, unraveling it from between cogs. I was astounded to find the line had somehow knotted itself to one spoke, which was now completely detached from the wheel. Good thing I had requested Susan and Jack Goertz, owners of Tandems Limited, the shop where I purchased my Doublevision, to build 48-spoke, 4-cross wheels for it. I twisted the derailleur back close to its original position, but I knew it was inoperable. At least it was out of the wheel and I'd be able to coast downhill into Marfa. So close, yet so far away.

I stopped mid-street, and pulled the Doublevision onto the sidewalk in the shade of a water tower. While considering my predicament, hunger began to cloud my thinking. Feeling very trustworthy, I felt that nobody would tamper with my bike while seeking out lunch. My gut instinct was soon verified.

"That's'a hunk of machine you got there," said a guy pedaling by on an upright.

"It's great when it works, which is not right now," I told him, then identifying myself and proudly mentioning my hometown of El Paso while giving him my card. Then I asked about a restaurant and the closest bike shop.

"I'm Al, an' th' nearest is in Alpine. Bikeman John's the owner," he replied. While looking at my card, he asked, "You're not related to him...no, no, you're from El Paso. Strange how much your names are alike. Anyway, your bike is safe there, nobody'll mess with it. It's a bit late, an' if you don't mind a mobile truck, I think Food Shark is still open. Right over there, by th' tracks. You can't miss it."

Al was right.

Parked underneath an immense pavilion beside the tracks was a red food truck. A shelf below the order window held a large thermos and other condiments. I slowly read the menu board and Adam, behind the screen, took my order for a tomato-basil-sprout toasted sandwich, along with a bottomless iced tea cup. It was exactly what my famished body needed!

I was also pleased because of my timing. A line had started to form behind me, apparently the rush before Food Shark closed for the day.

To make it even more pleasant, a track crew in a special railroad coach rumbled by, drawing everybody's interest, especially the children. It was a nice lunch break, but I had work to do.

I returned to my broken bike and commenced repairing it enough to continue pedaling. I only had 25 miles/40kms to go and with a tailwind—*if* it still blew out of the West like earlier. I borrowed two bricks from city utilities by the tower, which became stands to elevate the rear wheel. After dropping it, I removed yet more of the twine, digging it out from around the axle. Then I unscrewed the derailleur from the dropout and slipped the chain out of the broken cage. I next broke the chain, glad to have spent a little extra money for a Nashbar chain tool that greatly facilitated the task. I quickly made my very expensive, 27-speed Doublevision tandem recumbent into a very expensive, single-speed Doublevision tandem recumbent.

I slowly pedaled through town on the same route I had walked an hour before. The Food Shark was gone as was the crowd, and with it so had my hopes of more iced tea. My stomach was telling me that I probably should have doubled my lunch order.

Then I saw a Stripes station—more food, and I'd be able to charge it. I pulled my bike into the shaded walk, went inside and purchased, what else, three cans of muscle milk. I explained myself and bicycle to cashier Vanessa and a few onlookers, giving each my card along with the suggestion that they follow me on Facebook and Twitter. With their good wishes and waves, I began pedaling East on US90/67.

I'd gone two blocks when the chain began slipping, skipping, and finally locking-up, refusing to move. I was distinctly fatigued as my stomach sunk; what now? I coasted across the road into the welcome overhang shade of a to-be-renovated building across from ABC Hardware. I stared at my jury-rigged one speed, saw that the outer plate on one link had twisted off a pin and unable to move beyond the front derailleur. I removed the offending link, plus two more, from the chain, returning to my East-bound journey with lightness of heart and strong tailwind pushing me uphill.

All conditions were go.

A new sign clearly designated this wonderful road as "La Entrada al Pacifico", or transportation corridor between the West Coast (Sea of Cortez, Port Topolambo, Sinaloa, Mexico) through this part of Texas to points beyond. I'd attended numerous local government meetings in El Paso that were partly concerned with this very issue: 18-wheelers making over-the-road hauls or such transport occurring on railroads, or a combination of both. In either case, massive construction and renovation of transportation routes would be required.

Should this actually take place through Brewster County from Presidio, the initial economic benefit would be immense, but the residual effect would be a loss of the peaceful serenity as well as an ecological upset. The much more logical route for increased train and truck traffic seems to be through Juarez-El Paso, where build-up and renovation has already begun.

Often, I was the only vehicle on the road; the BNSF tracks paralleling the Northside was just as bereft of (train) traffic. For an hour, I practiced a rarely used maneuver of on-off pedaling. Generally, it can be best described as inefficient, erratic, and certainly exhausting. I'd push-really-hard-on-the-pedals-and-get-moving-really-fast-then-stop-to-coast-while-catching-my-breath. It is not unlike being in a paceline except no other bicycles were involved and instead of continually gaining speed, I became progressively slower.

Completely out of breath, I stopped at a pair of historic markers in front of a fancy new solid structure that opened to the South. Though many roadusers would whiz by these markers as fast as possible, I, of course, could not do so. Not that I wanted to anyway; the compensating factor (even when my bicycle is fully functional) meant I could "see" the area, which included reading these summaries of significance.

The first plaque, erected by the Texas Historical Commission, noted this location as home of the Marfa Army Air Field, and was constructed during World War Two as a training station for multi-engine aircraft. Also noted was the increased visibility of minorities; women, African-Americans, and Chinese all received billeting here although it was likely not equal to that of white men. After completion of the substantial airfield by 1943, it's stature strictly depended upon the war. Upon victory in the European campaign, renewed stimulus came from the emphasis given to the Pacific front. However, once that war ended, the base was abandoned, leaving an economic and social hole in Marfa and the surrounding area.

The Marfa Army Air Field had been a boon, bringing employment and diversity to a remote area transected by an exceptional road and railroad. I understood that—my (limited) experience had been that wherever the military established itself, prosperity came along with it. The reverse is also true—if the military leaves, so too will benefits. Probably the Marfa bike shop went then, too.

I knew wind was another decisive factor.

I remembered decades ago as a signalman, high atop my ship, that the prow was *always* turned into the wind for underway replenishment operations. Likewise, wind direction and speed dictated a carrier's heading when launching or landing birds (Tomcats, along with other warbirds). While I had not seen the alignment of the runways, had they been constructed to consider the precarious winds?

Yesterday it was a sapping headwind from the South; three days ago and today, it was a huge tailwind out of the West; tomorrow, would it be out of the North or East? That uncertainty could have doomed the Marfa Army Air Field, regardless of it's progressiveness.

Or was there some obscure connection to a much more well known feature of the area, the world-famous Marfa Mystery Lights? When I first saw these phenomena, I recalled the viewing area to be no more than a large pullout, but now it is a veritable parking lot, with a well-built concrete structure of gender-specific restrooms, a large viewing platform to the South and descriptive markers. The adjacent plaque was the only thing unchanged, a bronzed tablet describing their actual sightings and lack of any scientific explanation.

I palmed the Sun, and knew I couldn't stay for this night's showing. I had a broken bicycle and the only bike shop around was still a few hours away. If I continued to take advantage of this tailwind, I could make it before dark.

I hadn't gone far when a large truck stopped in front of me. As per my usual practice, I passed it and parked in front, returning to the driver's side. The window rolled down, and I had the pleasure of seeing a young man, cell phone in hand. Smiling broadly in appreciation of the fact that he is separating the complex act of operating a motor vehicle from the distraction of dialing a cell phone, I began to return to my Doublevision.

"No, wait, dude," I heard him call out, "let me get your picture. I'm going it to send to my buds. They'll never believe it. You are one wild dude...."

"And crazy, too," I finished his sentence. "I haven't had a chance to get out pedaling like this for over two decades. Now that the children gone and with my wife's blessings, I'm going to Louisiana...."

"No way! You are a *crazy* dude!' he echoed back. "How..."

Again anticipating the question, I answered, "I'm a teacher with one of the best school districts in the world that is still on a traditional track, so I have a block of time to rejuvenate from the school year. I left four days ago from El Paso on June eleventh at two in the afternoon, after graduation and project celebration. My turnaround date is the thirtieth of June so I can be back in time for three workshops on the eighteenth of July."

"Dude, that is so crazy! Do you take hotels? Where do you eat? How can you do this?" he pilloried me with questions, still dumbfounded that anyone might be outside in this wind and heat.

"I carry two to three gallons of water, sleep wherever I end up at night, pretty much eat all the time when not pedaling or sleeping, and," pausing for dramatic effect, "I do this because I *can*."

"Dude! You are wild! They call me 'Steelman Mike' because I sell steel but I'm not as strong as you. I hope all goes fine for you," and the window silently rolled back up, then the truck roared back onto the roadway, literally leaving me in the dust.

While I always welcome the chance to help fellow roadusers, I regretted stopping this time.

As soon as I started pushing, the pedal fell slack and my foot slipped off, nearly causing me to obey gravity—again. The chain had broken where *another* outer plate in a link had opened up. It was becoming a ritual as I put the Doublevision on its kickstand, pulled out my breaker kit, and worked the chain. I was slowly pedaling within a few minutes, the chain frequently skipping between a few cogs.

It was tempting to turn out to the Paisano Baptist Encampment, but I am neither Baptist nor desperate enough to convert. The strong tailwind was a blessing—it kept me going—until ascending a small hill. With the added pressure of climbing, the chain came apart. I repeated the ritual, shortening the chain by another three links. Winding through the hills of Paisano Pass, this occurred three more times before the Sun dipped below the horizon. Now I hoped to make it to Alpine before pedaling out of chain.

Instead, I ran out of Sunlight while passing a picnic rest area.

Ahead, I saw a vertical string of red lights topped by a white light, all blinking, and knew that was a radio tower; Alpine surely couldn't be too much further. But lights at night can be deceptive and the rest area looked really good for my tired body. I turned around, pedaled into a picnic shelter, completely satisfied with this location for my overnight. I turned on my cell and began with a twitter message, but the signal was blocked. I attempted to call Ellen—the signal was still blocked. I walked out to the roadway—no signal. I walked up the roadway—no signal. I walked down the roadway—no signal. Regardless that I could see the flashing lights of a transmission tower, I concluded that the T-Mobile signal in this location was blocked. I returned to my bike and was soon asleep beside it after a quick MRE—my sleep was not blocked.

Overnight Five: US 67/90
Paisano Pass picnic/rest area

My waking early is a long-established habit, and this morning was no different. The difference was location. Only six days into my bike tour and, despite some exceedingly challenging problems, I was making progress, albeit slowly. Laying there, I initially could hear the silent dawn, then a few birds, which were drowned out by the coarse sound of a diesel engine starting. I heard the truck driver easily go through at least nine gears as he drove toward Alpine, a sure sign that I, too, would have no trouble going through my one gear.

I opened my eyes to a still world, looking on my right to see a cement picnic table bench, on my left a heavily loaded Toyota-white Doublevision tandem, minus my Z-rest pad, sleeping bag and an MRE. While taking a swig of fresh water, I reflected for a moment about my recent past, how the lack of this most precious liquid nearly terminated my tour before Border Patrol agents Lily & Jay literally saved my life (and bicycling goal) when they replenished my buffaloes; that the strong tailwind which had helped me achieve Van Horn in two days was the same Westerly which had decimated my derailleur yesterday and bringing me to this point; that the wind had been a Southerly which limited my distance two days ago. I speculated that soon I'd be in Alpine, at Bikeman John's shop, changing the derailleur and quickly being on my way. I'll make it to Marathon, maybe even Sanderson or possibly farther, since I do need to make up for lost time. Excited, I arose, finished off the MRE, and got underway.

I saw why no signal was possible last night. I had camped at a scenic view of the Eastern end of Paisano Pass, where the topography rose on both sides hemming in the roadway and eliminating any cellular communication. It was beautiful enough, but as soon as I had descended into open country, I stopped and sent my archived texts in addition to calling my wife and son. I left a message for the former, but spoke with Erik, who gave me detailed information about Bikeman John's shop: "Six zero two West Holland Street isn't going to be difficult for you to find because it's also US ninety."

I was a bit dismayed to discover that the downhill and tailwind put me in well before his opening at ten a.m. After filling up the sidewalk and part of the stoop with my tandem, I sat on the bench to construct a plan of action.

Besides the specific directions, Erik had also told me that he was listed as "cash only." I needed to replenish my larder of potable water and foodstuffs. Undoubtedly, I could find obtain both within walking distance. I squeezed my bike more into the porch off the sidewalk, locked it up, and walked toward downtown.

I noted a stand-alone ATM at the TransPecos motor bank along the way, then stopped to talk with first responders Tim, Mike, and Border Patrol agent Miguel. Amazed that I was bicycling and the tale I told, Miguel felt obligated to continue the tradition, giving me a bottle of water. Not in competition but not to be outdone, Tim and Mike also gave me a frigid bottle of water, along with directions to the best foodstore in town, Porter's Thriftway, "...just down there, past the road construction and streetlight..."

The street may have been in reconstruction, but it was pleasant to stroll along this older section of town where a veranda-style covered benches and planters add to the pleasure. I crossed the street around the roadworks and entered the store, easily finding gallon/3.79liter jugs of potable water, a yoghurt, and a few bananas. What really made this a comfortable event were Christine and Dennis, who were intrigued with my wheeling tale and went out of their way to help me. I also appreciated the cash-back on my VISA debit card, although I anticipated my bike repairs may cost as much as two hundred dollars—far above the maximum allowed. The two jugs of water were the heaviest of my load as I slowly walked back, but I still needed to add a minuscule amount of weight—folding greenbacks from that motor bank ATM I had passed a half-hour ago.

Actually, that withdrawal made me feel *lighter,* because concern about how to afford the soon-to-commence bikework was relieved.

I moved my bike back onto the sidewalk, sat myself down on the bench and leisurely enjoyed the just-purchased brekkie. Digging my cell phone out of my red camera bag, I tweeted current events, still discovering shortcuts that were new to me. Maybe I was inventing a new code of some kind that was barely comprehensible to me, much less any reader. Regardless, this was rapidly becoming my substitute for writing down information in my logbook. Surely the little snippets would be the only reminders I needed when I wrote the story later?

It was well after (10:00) when I began to wonder why Bikeman John hadn't already flipped his sign to "OPEN" when I read the fine print: "**or call**". I was perplexed for a split-second when I remembered my cell phone. Unfortunately, the El Paso area code is 915 and Alpine is another, but what is it?

Close to an Amigos Gasmart, I smartly figured that the cashier there could easily give me the Alpine area code. I was rather proud of myself for devising a clever method for obtaining those crucial three digits when I saw a man walk out of Big Bend Paper.

Why should I walk ten or fifteen steps more when I can just ask him?

Upon hearing my question, he looked at me curiously, looked behind at the Big Bend Paper marquee, loudly displaying the numbers, returned his now-belittling gaze to me, and replied "Four-three-two. Do you want to know what state you're in?"

Perhaps I was in a tired state? Possibly I was eager to talk with someone, anyone; or maybe unable to focus on anything other than Doublevision repair. But in any case, I meekly accepted his withering comment with "oh, thanks, eh", returned to the storefront and dialed the posted number.

To my consternation, Bikeman John did not answer, so I left a message on the machine, describing myself, my situation, and the high recommendation by Al of Marfa. No sooner than I had spoken the last syllable of "Marfa" than came the sound of a latch being thrown and the sign flipped to "OPEN".

Going inside, I met Bikeman John. No wonder Al of Marfa thought we were related—we *do* look amazingly similar. He was a lighter version of myself, although slightly balder and immensely more knowledgeable about bicycles—and a great wrench.

The closest he could come to my busted-up fragile Deore Shadow 9-speed derailleur was an 8-speed Alivio. It was love at first sight; I knew a good fit when I saw it—a massive (compared to the Shadow) derailleur of hefty construction that could hold up to strong winds, spokes, or just about anything else encountered while touring.

Since I'm a rather decent wrench myself, Bikeman John allowed me to perform the necessary work on his front stoop. I was quite pleased, especially with the shade and access to needed parts, which included three new 9-speed chains (ironic in that he didn't have any 9-speed derailleurs) and two bottles of White Lightning Clean Ride.

"That's the best stuff I've ever used on my chains," he told me, then gave me several quick links. "These should take care of all the chain problems you had getting here. Instead of using a chain tool, just pop these in. Works like a charm and you shouldn't have anymore problems, but if you do, there's a good bike shop in Del Rio. In fact, it's the only shop after this one on ninety."

"Gee, thanks," I genuinely replied. "This looks far better than the old stuff. Let's get a photo together before I take off. I hope to make it to Sanderson tonight."

Bikeman John looked at me with skepticism, adding, "Maybe so, maybe no. You've got a headwind out there that'll slow you down, and it's heating up again. I'd say that you ought to stop in Marathon and stay at La Loma del Chiva. You can't miss it, just turn right on first street, go six blocks, turn right and go another six blocks and you'll be there. It's really unique, and since your traveling cross-country, you might get to stay free."

"Well," I corrected him, "I'm not sure that I'll get much beyond the Sabine River into Louisiana, but maybe this ordeal of crossing Texas will suffice."

With a laugh and a hug between cycling comrades, I pedaled away, going East on U.S. 90, retracing my earlier path and beyond.

Bikeman John and BIKERJOHN sitting in front of his shop, 602 W. Holland, Alpine TX USA (www.juanitohayburg.com)

I slowly passed a delicious smelling Chinese buffet, which normally would have drawn me in like the flies on the dead hog carcass I had passed at the junction of routes 505/166 a few days ago (perhaps not the most appetizing analogy), but I was more hungry to get underway! That is, until I pedaled up a slight incline and nearly passed out with hunger pangs when my sinuses detected the superb La Tratorria Espresso Bar & Ristorante. I veered left into the parking lot, going around the stand-alone twice before finally yielding to my stomach. My 13-foot (4meters) long Doublevision took up the space of a motor vehicle in front on Holland Drive, where I locked the back wheel and seat tube together.

It was pretty difficult for me to be discrete. In fact, it was obvious to anybody that I was not nearly as well dressed as any of the other diners. But, I was enervated, unable to even pedal up across the street to my all-time favorite eatery, Subway. I was beyond the point of caring—I needed to eat and La Tratorria was my choice.

Some diners did put on airs; they would be speaking loudly enough for the rest of us to hear how important he is because of his connections to big-wigs at the Federal level, or her significance because of her amazing ability to write grant requests that are always fulfilled.

I cared only for the gazpacho soup, crackers, cheese, anchovies, and a *grande quesadilla*. Not quite ready for the headwinds and heat, I nursed my meal, eating ever so slowly, with Keith and the waitstaff tolerating my presence very well. Heck, they even re-filled my water buffalo bladders with clean, cold ice-water. I'll be returning here, and recommending this to all my friends!

Facing the inevitable, I did return to the pedaling East on US90/67, stopping only to talk with ex-Marine Javier, Robin, and others, all of whom marveled at my courage—or fool hardheadedness—to be out biketouring in this extreme weather. Though some rolled their eyes, all were supportive that I was able to do something I loved dearly; after all, I *had* waited two decades.

I slowly arrived at the diversion of US 67 from US90 and the adjacent picnic/rest area. Despite having eaten a substantial meal not too long ago, I found myself hungry and mostly tired. I was grateful for the roof and wall that gave me both shade and wind protection.

Most motor vehicles sped past. I could tell which were going West and which were headed in the opposite direction without rising from my prone position and putting on my spectacles. The former moved along relatively quietly, something akin to coat zipper being pulled down with little strain. The latter, however, were more like the zipper being pulled up, which had rusted, needing jerks and sharp tugs. The reason had everything to do with the wind speed and direction. Westbound vehicles were being pushed by a strong near-gale strength steady wind—little energy required for the car or truck to move along. Eastbound vehicles, though, were wholly different for they were motoring *into* that same force and required much more energy. The motor would strain and complain about its mechanical duty, growling louder as the lower gears were revved to max, keeping the vehicle moving. I could even *smell* the direction of the vehicles—those going East had a lot more fuel pouring into the overworked engine, increasing the foul exhaust.

Then I heard one vehicle pulling into the parking lot, its engine gurgling in neutral gear. I leapt up, thinking I was going to help a distressed motorist who had pushed their car too hard. It turned out that the motorist was stopping to help me. Although I was already plenty happy, my heart gladdened to know that many people besides Border Patrol were willing to help me if needed. I waved him off because, at that moment, I wasn't in need of assistance. Just rest.

Returning to the road, I groaned as pedaled into the wind, counting down in Spanish as I approached each mile marker, and caught up in a bizarre mind-game that I was speeding along. Behind me, I could see the Sun continually narrowing the gap with the horizon. I finally was able to make out buildings in the distance. It had to be the community of Marathon—nothing else could be out here!

The headwind made for incredibly difficult cycling.

The closer I got, the farther away it seemed—my mind-game was seriously malevolent.

At long last I pedaled into the small community of Marathon, and went to the advertised French grocery store, on Fourth street, one block North of US90. My body was in desperate need of chocolate milk, energy drink, coffee, anything that could quickly rejuvenate me. Parking on the dirt road, I took my red camera bag, which contained my money, ID, and cell phone as well as the camera, inside the well-lit, *wind-free* and *air conditioned* space!

I couldn't have asked for better. Well, maybe I could have, but I sure couldn't think of what it might have been at the moment. All I knew was no more pedaling into the wind tonight, and that was good enough for me.

College-aged Kyla was running the store, and it was inevitable that we had conversation about her future. She is an exceedingly adorable young lady, but it was her intelligence which convinced her she needed more than a high school diploma to have a secure future. As is true throughout time, most young people at that age cannot quite grasp much more than tonight, almost certainly never tomorrow and especially any consequences. Thus, she had set her sights on higher aspirations, that of becoming a Veterinarian, which necessitated attendance at Sul Ross University in Alpine.

"I really like it here with my family, though," she said wistfully, "and that job will allow me to stay."

In between gulps of chocolate milk, I casually quizzed her about preparedness for such an undertaking.

She spoke with wisdom that belies her youthful age, knowing exactly what was entailed; "I'm getting my 4-year Bachelor's degree, followed by grad school, and then" she caught her breath before continuing, "the ponderous task of actual employment. While the post-graduate programs are restrictive, successfully obtaining a position is even more difficult, not the least of which is the little demand for vets in Marfa."

"But there's lotsa' demand further out in the region," she continued, with zeal. "I can wait!"

Walking back outside, I switched on my lights, and slowly pedaled toward US90. Turning left, I stopped in front of Guzzi Pizza, 103 Main Street, (Yes, the only paved thoroughfare, U.S. 90, is also the main street.) and was welcomed by owners Michelle and Ron. This became my evening meal stop (the Calzones are best, along with more chocolate milk.) for another hour, until closing time.

"How do the authorities feel about people staying at those picnic tables overnight?" I asked Ron.

"Won't do at all for you to be there," he replied, "but if you take that street over the tracks an' go to G street, then right for six blocks, you'll find the hostel 'La Loma del Chivo' is a good place. Lot's of bikers stay there."

He reminded me of what Bikeman John had also told me earlier today and I knew that was my place for the overnight. I slowly moved outside and pedaled over the tracks, slowing down even more upon feeling the gravel road, scared that this path of what amounted to ball bearings underneath my wheels, would topple me. A pick-up truck began to roar past me, stopping in a skid beside me, and I heard the driver call to me in a slur, "Goin' t' th' host'l?"

"Yes," was all I had the strength to say.

"Jes' follow me, I'll git ya' there," came the reply, and he roared off.

Of course I'll follow, but not if I lose sight of him.

I could see the rooster tail around his tail-lights, kicked up by both the rolling truck wheels and the skid of his stop while he waited for me to narrow the gap. I was almost touching the pick-up when he roared off again, this time turning right.

I couldn't believe how far he had gone until I saw the brake lights shine red.

A guttural noise arose from within me, and I followed. I had to follow; I knew of no where else to go, nor did I want to go anywhere else. It was just so dang far...!

It seemed to take forever, but I came to where the pick-up had stopped, and passed through some sort of portal, whereupon I immediately felt at home. I was motioned in by a figure in the shadows, who also motioned no payment needed after my inquiry. I surmised that to be Gill, the owner.

Pleased to not be pedaling, much less in the dark on a doubtful road surface, I was given a choice of places to lay my head for the remainder of the night. I parked my Doublevision onto a smooth surface, then ascended to an open balcony with my Z-rest and sleeping bag. Tired as I was, the view was amazing—on an overlook covered by the bright full-moon-whipped starry night.

OVERNIGHT SIX: MARATHON

As usual, I arose before the Sun, and crept down the outside stairwell to my Doublevision in an eerie atmosphere. After making use of the bathroom, I discovered what was so strange: there was no wind! Dumbfounded by this, I **had** to take advantage of it.

Completely alone in the quiet morning gray, I scurried around, putting my personal cards all around in logical places to be found, each with a hastily jotted note apologizing to Gill that I "had to go, NO WIND!"

Pushing the Doublevision underneath the arch, I saw that scary gravel road from last night's pedaling in the entirely different light or early morning. Heck, it wasn't so bad after all, though I still had to be careful—one big rock could easily dump me.

I was gleeful about no wind, but I was also aware of stomach pains—*hunger.* Back on pavement, I glided across the tracks to Main Street (US90) and headed toward a cafe I had seen last night, Johnny B. The sidewalk table was occupied by a quartet of guests, to whom I indelicately intruded and elaborated about my Doublevision and odyssey. They seemed to be politely annoyed. Going inside, server Adriana, who commutes here from her home in Alpine, helped me understand the menu, then served me an interesting dish: the Garbage Can—a combo of everything edible. Not only was it interesting, it was perfect! Remembering my hunger after the Food Shark in Marfa, Maybe I should double the order?

The risk would be doubling indigestion, but my hurry was to get out riding before the inevitable wind. It took very little effort or distance (two blocks) before reaching the edge of town, where a visitor's shelter and a gas station exist. I was impressed with the shelter; blocking the Sun helps but the lack of circulating air made it uncomfortable. However, I liked learning more about Marathon and the picnic table could easily do as an emergency campsite—*if* one didn't know about La Loma del Chivo. Gasoline wasn't needed, especially at over four dollars per gallon($1USD/liter), but my upset stomach ensured I needed the toilet facilities. Clearly a case of "garbage in, garbage out".

The wind was rising, as was the temperatures when I stopped a bit further on for a remote coffee shop. It was closed, but the nearby plaque awaited my inquisitive eyes and inquiring mind. The Colonel Harmon information was remarkable, further evidence about the hardy immigrant souls who carved out a life in this harsh land and are remembered for it. Unintelligible graffiti covered part of the sign, put there by the lamebrained few, hoodlum(s) who have been unable to distinguish themselves in any way other than defacing this nice road feature.

Or the graffiti could be the result of adolescents, given the power of a motor vehicle to convey them on a nonsensical mission that partly involved such vandalism. I'd seen this kind of decoration in many places around the world, but in the USA there is often an no rhyme nor reason behind it, a classic hormone-driven to act before thinking—if any thought process, other than spontaneous gratification or wanton destruction, was used.

My belief to get underway as early as possible was validated as the wind did indeed arise. Headwinds in the morning may be fresh, but they become stale and tiresome in the afternoon. (And, really, they quickly become tiresome in the morning, too.) My practice of a reverse countdown in Spanish upon seeing a mile marker continued, although my progress was not nearly so challenging as it had been last night. Mostly, I felt kind of bad about leaving La Loma del Chivo without visiting with anybody there. But, I was on a crusade and my timetable dictated that if Louisiana was going to be entered, more time on the bike was required.

The contradiction, of course, is that while pedaling in the headwinds and heat definitely retarded my movement, I also spent a significant amount of time stopped, usually resting in windblocked,

Sunblocked spaces wherever I can find them. The other reason for stopping was usually for a photo of a plaque or road cut or some other feature, besides food and water. Anyway, I wasn't putting in as much distance as I'd like, and was becoming concerned that my goal of crossing the Sabine River might not happen.

I wearily pushed myself along, hoping to make good distance-time yet, ironically, always looking for a chance to stop. And, sure enough, upon rounding a bend, I came to a plaque noting the Denuded Quachita Rock Belts. These roadcuts were stupendous, sharp and clear examples of ancient, highly deformed vertical strata, overlain by less-ancient horizontal sediments laid down at the bottom of ocean. Looking around at the dry scrubland, had it not been for that plaque, I would have never guessed that *any* kind of water, much less an ocean, other than rare precipitation, existed here.

It seemed slow as I would reverse countdown mile markers. So slow, in fact, that in order to say "Zero" when passing that green vertical rectangle, I had to start adding "*punto nueve, punto ocho, punto siete, punto seis, punto cinco, punto quatro, punto tres, punto dos, punto uno, y zero punto zero*". Satisfied that I had finally figured out once again how to accurately countdown to zero—I was getting plenty of practice. I was also pleasantly surprised to find out how fast I was moving—until I realized that only the *even* numbered signs were on the right side of the roadway. So the question became, was I really going twice as fast? Ahhh, whatever; I was still just as tired, regardless of the signs.

The scenery, albeit desert, was ever changing. Sometimes US90 would quickly ascend, descend, or bend around a hill, while the railroad tracks carried on through a cut or fill. The mountains, which always seemed to be in the distance, constantly reflected the Sun as it traveled across the sky, giving mirages of rainfall or sandstorms or forests or tomorrow, creeping ever closer.

Rounding one bend coming out of a gully, I found myself staring at a water hole. It was partly covered with green slime, not yet evaporated because of tree shade. In it stood several buffaloes, nonchalantly snorting and wallowing in the ooze—until I stopped. Apparently my Doublevision was just as startling a sight to them as they were to me. The water, however much I wanted to immerse myself, was too sickly looking. I did, though, take advantage of the shade, resting a good long while, snacking some on an MRE.

Later, along one long stretch of fence, I had to look twice at the gate, which announced: **BRUCE RANCH.** Just beyond, I saw a near full water tank, it's side painted with **BRUCE'S** and a few palm trees. Since this obviously belonged to one my brothers (Bruce, of course), he probably wouldn't mind my climbing over the side for a much needed and refreshing dip. Unfortunately, as brother Bruce resides in Florida with his wife, I came to the rather quick realization that this was *not* his property, nor would I be welcomed for neither the fence nor the gate were receptive to trespassers.

However, I was refreshed when *la familia Ureste* stopped their motor car to give me two liters of exceptionally cold Evian bottled water. Shortly thereafter, another motorist, David Avila, gave me a bottle of the liquid. "I saw you back in Fort Davis—you're really moving along in this weather. I'm on my way back home to Del Rio. Maybe I'll see you there?"

"Sure," I nodded eagerly, gulping down the elixir, "I'll probably be there in two days or so. See you then, and thanks!"

I resumed pedaling, battling the headwinds and heat.

I did some quick calculations; make Sanderson tonight, Dryden the next night, Comstock the third night...! Two days to Del Rio? "...or so" became a much more realistic approximation of when I might see David in Del Rio. Maybe I should have asked for his phone number or address? No matter; I soon found myself in another cool culvert underneath US 90 for a short nap.

Back on the road, a motorcyclist came toward me, then swung around beside me, motioning to stop.

I was only too happy for another break.

After taking his helmet off and we shook hands, he told me that he was the unofficial Mayor of Sanderson by virtue of his name: John Sanders.

Chuckling, I said with a deep bow, "Well, it is indeed my great honor to officially be in his most honorable presence, even if unofficial."

"Thanks! As part of my unofficial duties, I had to check on you," he continued with sincerity. "I passed your parked bike earlier but didn't see you and was concerned. I would've done this anyway—can't be too safe out here."

"Well, Mayor Sanders, perhaps you are familiar with a person who was born here but now lives in El Paso," I said while fishing a personal card out of my pocket. "His name is Al Flores, married to Elizabeth, also from around here, and they own the Postal Annex shop which made up these cards for me."

Taking my card, he commented thoughtfully, "John Eyberg aka Juanito Hayburg aka BIKERJOHN. Bit of a mouthful, but covers all the bases. I don't know them personally but my wife is a teacher and I think she's mentioned them from a long time ago. Anyway, it's another ten miles to my town, and I'm glad to see you're alive."

"Thanks," I said appreciatively. "Hey, is there a good place to eat in town?"

"Sure! The Eagle's Nest Cafe, and a Dairy King across the bridge," he replied.

We shook hands and both began moving East on 90, he roared off, going much faster than myself, merely puttering along. I looked at the Sun, a little over four fingers high—about an hour before arrival. I hoped the Mayor was right about Eagle's Nest—thirst and hunger had become my missing companions, and their safety frequently occupied my thoughts. Grandpa Wolf on a tandem recumbent bicycle, I am.

At least the somewhat winding road had a descending grade, with the tracks sometimes very close and sometimes not, depending upon the easiest route over Sanderson Canyon, courseway for the intermittent Sanderson Creek. I cruised into town, and my hopes were greatly encouraged by a brightly lit Stripes gas station. Literally going downhill, I then noticed numerous abandoned shops and other derelict buildings and my hopes faded along with the Sunlight.

My goal was Eagle's Nest. It was a nice enough building but I had arrived too late, it was closed up tight, not a light nor hint of any life. Disappointed, I coasted downhill, across an exceptionally nice bridge anticipating soothing ice cream at Dairy King, only to be frustrated again. I continued pedaling to the neon lights of a motel, where my hopes were dashed a third time—no restaurant! I turned back to the only shop open, a C-store where I met two upstanding young men, undoubtedly products of the noted Sanderson educational system.

"Hi, guys," I started affably, "are there any other eateries beyond?"

"No, Sir," replied the skinny tall guy, "and you're too late here— they just closed."

I grimaced at the thought of pedaling back uphill to the Stripes station, but was gladdened when the other individual asked,

"Excuse me, but what kind of bicycle is that?"

I gave both of them my personal cards and launched into my oft-told story. When I stopped for a breath, they politely excused themselves and walked off.

A few streetlights and the luminescent moon showed me a clean route back uphill, and my well-lit Doublevision kept the moderate amount of motor traffic alert to my presence along the side of US90. At least I had a tailwind. All the same, it seemed to take forever, and was exhausted by the time I parked my bike alongside the curb booths. I remembered the Stripes in Marfa, and knew this would certainly keep me alive.

Going inside, I first sought out Muscle Milk, opening and drinking it in two gulps while looking over the remains of the deli—all fried. I didn't care; I just wanted something, the sooner the better. Okra, chicken, burrito, ice for my water bottle, a Skor candy bar, and another Muscle Milk.

"Is there any chance for a reduced price as this must be day-old?" I asked the attendant.

"Wait 'till mornin' if you want it fresh," came his bored reply.

I shrugged and gave him my VISA credit card.

It was refreshingly cool inside and the large interior seating area was unoccupied, the perfect place for me to rejuvenate and keep an eye on my tandem at the same time.

Once I had finished, this was going to be a similar overnight to Van Horn. Many 18-wheelers were parked in the lot out back, engines running while the operators were off the road as per D.O.T. rules. I was too unsteady to pedal and walked the Doublevision to a darken cement pad next to the dumpsters. I started to set up, which is nothing more than putting out my Z-rest, when the breeze gave me a whiff of the grease pit. One of the huge tractor-trailer rigs pulled around the corner, momentarily putting me in the glare of headlights. Another rig ground through the lot, and I figured that maybe this was not such an ideal campsite.

Leaving my bike, I walked toward the end of the lot, to a break in the bushline, and, by my helmet light, walked an overgrown back road. Exploring it for a short distance, I found another even more isolated patch that appeared quite suitable. I retrieved the Doublevision and made a campsite. Finally down for the night, I placed my glasses inside my bike sandals, next to my helmet and water bottle for a good night's rest, the sleeping bag haphazardly pulled over me.

I rolled over and several needles pierced my arm.

Jumping up, I found that I had inadvertently put my bedroll on some kind of cactus.

After correcting the problem, I laid down again and was nearly asleep when an ominous buzzing sound invaded my ear. Groggily, I thoroughly sprayed myself and the zone around me with OFF. Peace at last!

OVERNIGHT SEVEN: SANDERSON

Some peace! Three, maybe four times, or more during the night, BNSF trains would rumble through, giving the ground beneath me vibrations of a Richter 4.0 earthquake, accompanied with a long, sonorous, exceptionally loud air horn blasts.

Bleary eyed at the gray dawn, I pulled myself and bike back to the front of Stripes. Sure enough, there was freshly fried food being distributed in the hot display counter. It was delicious and filling and... well, I quickly developed a yen to visit a more private space. The bathroom, like the Stripes station itself, was immaculate.

Gravity was wonderful as I coasted down Oak Street (US90 East), seeing Sanderson in the new light of a rising Sun. The dusty, shuttered buildings had a different kind of sparkle, although still dusty and shuttered.

I hadn't gone far before seeing the Eagle's Nest Cafe, which appeared to be opening up.

Good! I was not so much hungry—I did just have some excellent victuals at Stripes—but was feeling that my body required more energy. Besides, having access to other food supplies meant not having to eat more MREs—those were emergency rations. Despite my initial reluctance, I had become sure that I would need them over the next several days, at least until I was pedaling in the East, where towns with eateries were reasonably close together.

Stopping in the parking lot, I parked the Doublevision and dismounted, preparing to enter. A middle-age man approached me, waving a "go away" signal, then told me, "We're closed for the week to remodel."

Crestfallen, I explained "John Sanders, you're unofficial mayor, had high praise for your establishment and I was looking forward to eating here."

"Yeah—I haven't seen him for a while so he must not know about our renovation," he replied. "My name's Perry, the owner, an' I can see you're lookin' forward to eatin' here, but it's not possible right now. I reckon the best you can do is keep on goin' downhill, an' just after the bridge, go to the American Legion hall. They've got an all you can eat pancakes every Saturday mornin' for a real good price of eight dollars."

I thanked him and thought he must at least be somewhat amused by the sight of me, looking ratty, disheveled, as if I had slept among the cacti, wearing a rather rank UBS T-shirt, and traveling upon a strange looking bicycle. Now I was salivating at his description of the meal awaiting just downhill. Heck, I could taste it!

Despite my ravenous appetite, I could not pass up the Terrell County Visitor's Center. It was closed, but a cactus garden around the side was well-worth my time and gave me a deeper appreciation of the area. The vertical limestone slabs were the tablets for which area pictographs and pictograms were replicated upon.

After having pedaled for a week, it was interesting to learn that Sanderson is at the convergence of the Chihuahua Desert, the Southern extreme of the Great Plains, and the Edwards Plateau. And I thought I was just traversing the desert, not such distinctive biomes. I did actually recognize a few differences, such as arboreal growth, but that was usually dictated by altitude—or the presence of water. Too bad Dr. Paul Hyder, my friend, former colleague, and specialist in the Chihuahuan Desert wasn't with me; he'd certainly know all of the flora and fauna distinctions. Lastly, due in part to the aforementioned unique junction, I was not shocked to find out that I was in the "Cactus Capital of Texas". As I recall, I attempted to use some of that prickly plant for an arm rest last night!

I coasted downhill, crossing the bridge, passed Dairy King, the RV park, and started to turn on Legion Street to the hall when I heard that deadly *hisssssssing* sound, filling me with fear, trepidation, and aggravation. The rear tire was going flat! I pushed the few paces to the American Legion hall, and parked it in the shade. I'll be able to deal with the problem *much* better after a substantial breakfast.

This was the right place. Several cars were parked around, with a few people hesitating for a minute to inspect me and my Doublevision before opening the wooden doors. When no one was present, I quickly took my bicycling UBS T-shirt off, replacing it with my non-bicycling UBS T-shirt. Both are yellowed and stained, bearing different emblems: one a Priceless blood donor card and the other a US flag free to donate. I keep the latter in reserve. It doesn't have the stink of the former.

Inside the air-conditioned space, the breakfast aroma of griddlecakes, bacon, eggs (any style), coffee, juice, milk, biscuits, gravy, hashbrowns, hot and cold cereal was overpowering. My salivary glands went into overdrive. And it was all made to order. No early start this morning—I was staying 'till closing time, at ten. Only two hours left!

Maybe I had just become disoriented and exhausted from the sleepless night or that mouth-watering, near-ether like scent, but Wanda guided me through what seemed an intricate process of filling out the order blank. Apparently putting one big check mark across the entire chit wouldn't do.

"Oh, you'll be able to fill out others, dear," she said softly. "We get a lot of people coming through on bicycles, stayin' at the campground. Sometimes they'll spend an extra night or two here when they learn about this breakfast. People, not just riders, come from all around for it."

I could see that; singles and families piled out of cars to sit at the long tables. At one table sat a squad of Border Patrol agents. Did I know any? Without a trace of shyness, I ambled over to them, exchanging a handshake with each, saying, "Thank you; you are doing a super job. You're overworked and underpaid—as long as you're not making over a hundred thousand a year—a plank in my platform that NO person receiving money from our pocketbook, which includes all those people in DC and their aides—get more..."

I stopped myself upon inhaling, then sincerely continued, this time off the soap box.

"Anyway, thank you. You're always ready to help me, especially giving me water. If it hadn't been for Agents Lily and Jay refilling my water buffaloes just South of Valentine, I wouldn't be here now. Thank you all."

They smiled and nodded, role-modeling what I needed to do: eat.

Wanda also allowed me to plug in my cell phone—I'll leave an extra tip to pay for the recharging. The added bonus to that was, while waiting for the first of my orders, I called brother Bruce in Florida. Having free long-distance weekends was nice! It was delightful to speak with him—he was infinitely jealous of me. He himself had bicycled much like I am a couple of decades ago in California and knew the utter joy of propelling oneself across landscapes, camping, coping with the demands of solo touring. But, now we are both much older, and I have maintained something of a cycling regimen while he had not. Even I was having some difficulty pushing the pedals, so he would likely not be able to push very well at all, if that. Cycling long distance solo *is* a challenge, to say the least, but at least my legs were used to the repetitive motion. Bruce had not been cycling regularly, and, he confessed, "I don't think I could make it—how 'bout I just be green-eyed over you?"

I told him to not be too upset—I had nearly quit after the third day, that it was the Border Patrol that saved my life with fresh, clean water which enabled me to keep going.

I promised, "Hey, I'll send you postcards!"

"Gee, thanks!" he replied sarcastically. "You got a good job that gives you the chance, but me, I haven't had a regular job in years..."

It was time to end the conversation, and the easiest way was "Bruce, you and I both know what a gifted carpenter you are, but you're in *Florida*, one of the hardest hit states by the housing bubble. Hey, I'd love to continue talking but my breakfast has just been served up..."

I wasn't exactly thrown out later, but it became pretty obvious that it was time for me to go when all the tables had been wiped down, including mine except for the space I occupied, and were being folded up for storage. Rather stuffed, I sort of rocked while walking back outside to find the Doublevision no longer in the shade, but the in full shine of a mid-morning Sun.

I inspected the rear wheel again; it certainly didn't *look* flat, but felt like silly putty upon squeezing. Sighing, I off loaded some of my gear and removed my Topeak JoeBlow floor pump, which I kept securely stowed inside the rear seat mesh fabric. (I also carry a smaller pump, but when going far, have learned that the bulkier floor model is far easier to use, particularly since I don't care about excess weight—another element in my "trouble-free touring" philosophy.)

Back on the 10th of June, while doing the final prepping of the Doublevision, I had replaced the tire with a new Schwalbe. Regrettably, I also tore the bead from the sidewall, rendering the moderately expensive tire worthless and useless. I rushed to Crazy Cat Cyclery and, taking a chance on this Kendall tire, successfully installed it. I had become impressed with it for not having flatted any before, despite derailleur and spoke breakage. It hadn't even lost any air!

After attaching the nozzle, I pumped it up to the max psi, 70/5bar. I heard no *hissssssssss*, and the tire remained solid. Raising my eyebrows in mild surprise, I figured to go as far as possible because this was a Slimed tube, and the pinhole had been sealed. Repacking the Doublevision, I pedaled off, officially beginning a long day of cycling.

Going over a small rise, I descended into the floodplain of the Sanderson Creek, stopping at the rest area on the Western edge of a magnificent concrete post-and-beam bridge. Dismounting, I checked the rear tire—still holding air. Pleased with the effectiveness of Slime, I walked underneath the bridge into the dry riverbed for an even more alluring pix: sleek AMTRAK locomotive units pulling eight haze-gray wagons Westbound on a railbed just above the dry channel.

How fascinating that kind of travel *can* be.

Why, Katy, Erik, Ellen, and I had taken a similar train several years ago from El Paso to St. Louis, plus a quick trip to Chicago. In fact, it was the East-bound version of this same train, the *Sunset Limited*, a good first (and last) family railroad experience. I regret to say that particular trip was the spike that killed any future AMTRAK travel ambitions lurking in my future.

We had arrived at the classic Union Station (NRHP), El Paso, via a SunMetro bus (which had been late) and I was concerned about missing the AMTRAK connection. I needn't be—it too was running late. Quite late. The first clue was the movie shown in the waiting hall: *The Music Man.* I guessed that was likely close to the last time (1962) the train ran on time.

The next clue to the retardation of the Eastbound *Sunset Limited* was the next movie: *"It's a Mad, Mad, Mad, Mad World"*. Undoubtedly, trains ran on time then (1963), too.

All four of us we're exhausted and hungry when this train finally came to a stop at the platform, nearly **five** hours after the original departure time of (14:00). We lined up outside with numerous other passengers, waiting for directions to our assigned cabins or coach seats.

I knew our festive ride-upon-the-rails was going to be long, easily figured from looking at the time schedules, but I was just beginning to perceive exactly how long and laborious this trip was going to be. The more we waited, the more I found myself thinking: maybe we ought to seek an immediate refund, return home and motor to Missouri?

No. That wasn't in the plan.

I was determined that all of us should know the joy I knew of train travel, albeit most of mine had been in Europe or much shorter journeys stateside, which included the *Southwest Chief, Coast Starlight, Lincoln Service,* and a now-abandoned Chicago-D.C. route, that dropped me and my Stumpjumper (after pedaling Big Bend National Park with brother Nils, December, 1985) in CrestlineOH. (Ellen and I were then living closeby, in Mansfield, and she motored over in the wee hours...) Anyway, the point was a fun-filled family holiday—and it started out very poorly indeed.

Once ensconced into our sleepers, we again waited, this time for our (late) evening meal call out. The porter, a jovial sort of fellow, kept us entertained as well as informed regarding how much longer before the delectable meal. As it turns out, the lengthy delays—train arrival was due to collision with a motor vehicle that tried to beat the train to a crossing, and the meal was due to a change of chefs/ restaurant crew.

Once fed and in bed, the *Sunset Limited* slowly left the station and the four of us enjoyed a vastly different perspective of El Paso. While passing through the East-side container terminal and crossing Chip-Chip Road, I proudly pointed out where my school, Riverside Middle is located. We settled in for a restful night when the train gathered speed leaving the city proper, but within a short distance, we came to a stop.

The porter came by to explain that Southern Pacific owns the tracks, and we were on a siding to let a freight pass.

Ah! That explains it. Apparently, there are numerous freight trains using this Southern route because we spent much of the night starting up, gathering speed, then stopping on a siding. I suspect the AlpineTX must have a notable station as we spent several hours there, though I didn't deboard to verify.

Or so it seemed, because I dozed off, waking only to see the trestle girders while crossing Lake Amistad in the gray dawn. The Del RioTX station was a quick stop, but we were thoroughly awakened with a delicious breakfast. The steady Eastward movement of the train had a decidedly somnolent effect upon me, especially considering how poorly I had slept during the night. Everything was A-OK!

Mid-morning, the train once again slowed down to an almost-flat-tire pace, but this time we were in the metropolis of San Antonio. While waiting at the unique station (NHRP) that could be mistaken for a mission, an ominous sign arrived with the *Sunset Limited*: heavy rain with hail! Unfortunately, we had missed the connection with the *Texas Eagle*, but not to be concerned. We were transferred to Greyhound buses, which delivered us out of the storm to a dry Union Pacific station in Dallas—*five* hours later!

We waited, not unlike the previous night, except this time there weren't even movies available to distract us. We made do. Instead, we walked around to visit the site of JFK's assassination, seeing the building where Oswald was presumed to have made the fatal shot, getting excited about every train that pulled through, even though most were part of the Dallas Area Rapid Transit (DART) system and much too small for our continuation to St. LouisMO.

This was just like El Paso with the all waiting. Determined that this was *not* going to be like that, we warded off fatigue with Subway sandwiches from a nearby shop. With the dusk approaching, the *Texas Eagle* also approached. At least we weren't famished!

Apparently AMTRAK had a higher status on these tracks, for it was a restful night of continuous movement. The observation car became our hang-out during the day, though it was incredibly small considering the large number of passengers who likewise wanted to hang-out there, too. It was a bit unpleasant having to let them know that "my wife/my daughter/my son is in that seat, and coming right back"—especially when a movie was playing.

Initially, the trees and scenery were verdant and quite gorgeous, but it all started to have a blurry look after so many hours. My mind began to wander, unable to concentrate on my reading book or logbook. During one particularly long spell in which one of my beloveds were absent, I nearly gave that spot away; then I caught myself, declaring, "But your not the Man from Seat Sixty-One!"

Then the *Texas Eagle* had stopped a short ways West of Little RockAR, due to an engine problem? At least, that was the rumor whispered among the passengers. I didn't take the bait to go find out for myself, an act that would give my seat to someone eager for such a prime location. However, much later I did learn that engine trouble was the *raison d'être* for this and two more stoppages, close to Popular BluffMO and St. LouisMO. It was a long three days; at least I had a comfortable bunk bed.

"I'm so glad to be *flying* back to El Paso," Ellen had recently started saying, not without a smirk, "and I'll be sure to pick you up at Union Station when you and the children return from Chicago, in two, no, three weeks...!"

I grimaced because, to retain the real flavor of train travel *sans* Ellen, I had booked our return in *coach* class.

Swinging my right leg over the Doublevision, I pushed the pedals, ascending along the Southside of Sanderson Canyon as US90 peeled away through the rugged topography with no shade. Regardless of the relentless headwinds and heat, my legs enjoyed a small pleasure in stopping at another Texas Historic Marker, where I learned about how this kind of desolation has differing appeal to different persons, depending upon their interests.

The marker bore text about the Baxter's Curve Train Robbery, 1912, in which robbers were specifically interested in stealing money and valuables from people who had been interested in earning such commodities the old-fashioned way, with work. The criminals—Ben Kilpatrick and Ole Hobeck—had apparently boarded the train at a waterstop in Dryden and commandeered it to a remote (more remote than here?) place slightly more West known as Baxter's Curve. There, they proceeded to uncouple the engine from the baggage/mail car in a manner learned during their apprenticeship with the Butch Cassidy & Sundance Kid gang.

Another individual was Wells Fargo Express manager David A. Trousdale whose interest was to do his job and prevent the robbery. Mr. Trousdale thoroughly and completely ensured the safety of the passengers, crew, mail, and money when he "...bludgeoned one with an ice mallet and killed the other with the first robber's rifle." Manager Trousdale received accolades and a reward for his actions, while robbers Kilpatrick & Hobek were buried in Sanderson. I felt relief that the stops which AMTRAK had had a decade ago during my family's adventure were never the result of robbery, but possibly to keep the tradition of unanticipated stopping alive.

This stop had my interest, but I was able to keep moving.

Within a few hours, the terrain had leveled out and I stopped at another marker, Dryden Intermediate Field Site 29. This airfield was first plotted in 1919, when aviation was still in it's infancy but of considerable interest by the military. Their interest waned and much activity ended during WWII, but civilian authorities assumed control. Currently known as the Terrell County Airport with two mile-long runways built atop impregnable caliche—the same clay that has made kept my trees from growing because the roots can't penetrate it.

Remembering another airfield back at the Marfa Lights pullout, it made sense. All these landing strips were within the safe distance such that a tank of AVGAS wouldn't be depleted. It was no different for train stations, which, during the steam era, had to be relatively close so as to supply water and wood for the locomotives. Indeed, in the early decades of the motor vehicle, towns with gas stations, lodging, and food were located relatively close for the same reason. Alas, I feel the non-motorized aspect of transportation (bicycles) is not a strong enough market to keep these small communities alive.

A motor car whizzed by me, stopped, then backed up to join me at this marker. Tim and Pat, geology professors at UT-Austin, weren't so much interested in the marker, but in me.

"Got to admire, you, Juanito, out here pedaling in this headwind and heat," said Tim.

"Yeah," added Pat, "I'll bet you could use some water."

"You bet!" I enthusiastically replied, and drained an proffered waterbottle. "This is great! It is unbelievably cold!"

"We've got more, if you'd like," replied Tim.

He already knew my answer; opened the tailwindow and lowered the tailgate of his Toyota LandCruiser. Within easy reach were two large round coolers, one of which he unscrewed the cap to bring my water buffaloes to full.

"Seeing your Toyota with all the camping gear almost brings me to tears," I said, and continued:

"I loved my ninety-three FourRunner. It had almost a quarter-million miles before dying five miles South of Johnson City while taking my daughter to college. All that remains is the white of my tandem recumbent, which Advanced Transportation Products, the manufacturer, said they could match to my 4Runner."

Wistfully, I continued, "it was so reliable! It got us—my two children, wife, and I—to all four coasts and everywhere in-between. The only thing I didn't like about it was the technology; it was so computerized that about all I could do was change the oil and gas it up."

"I know exactly what you mean," Tim replied. "This is a bit older, before all that, but I can make most repairs anywhere. It is really wonderful, especially having the four-wheel drive out here, or anywhere off the road."

I nodded in agreement, then added, "Unfortunately, it is not seaworthy, otherwise I'd be driving across the oceans instead of flying."

We all had a good laugh, then Pat asked, "So where have you gone overseas?"

"Wow!" I took a deep breath and began: "A lot of places, starting with when I was in the Navy, and caught my first ship in Karachi, Pakistan. During my five-year tour, I got all around the World, but not everywhere. One of my brothers and I biketoured Western and Eastern Europe in nineteen eighty-one. Neither the Soviet Union nor East Germany allowed us in, but we went through all the other countries behind the Iron Curtain. My wife and I taught in Medellín, Colómbia, for a year, then, a few years later, I escorted my mother to the Panama Canal and Mexico City for a week."

After another large breath, I continued, "Seven years ago, I received an inheritance. I took all of us to Europe, which Ellen had to return stateside after three weeks from Amsterdam. Being a teacher in the Ysleta Independent School District—still on a traditional calendar—and with our children in the same district, we had another five weeks. The three of us took the train onto Berlin for two nights, then a thirty-two hour train ride to Moscow for two nights before a flight to Beijing. After a week there, we luckily snagged three bunks in the first-class section on an international train back to Moscow. After a frustrating day of procuring tickets, we slept on the overnight train to St. Petersburg. From there we went on to Scandinavia, and back here. I hadn't squandered all of my inheritance and was able to take the three of us Down Under two years later—Ellen couldn't go due to opening up a library in El Paso. Two years after that, I took the kids, and my then-seventy-eight year old mother to Caye Caulker, Belize, so they could get scuba cards at Belize Diving Services. Now I'm biketouring to Louisiana and back, *and* I'll be able to visit my son in Houston and my daughter in Austin."

"Wow indeed!" exclaimed Pat. "What an education! And you've got the career to be able to do that. Not many people have such an excellent opportunity."

"That's for sure," I agreed with him. "Some people have disagreed, telling me that I should save it for retirement, but I know travel is too important. What's more important is that I was able to role-model for them *how* to travel, that, despite the fact that the World runs on the legal drug of alcohol, it is possible to get around without imbibing. Additionally, I beat into them that nothing but prison or even death comes from running illegal drugs or guns. Fortunately, our greatest challenge was language, and that was only in a few places—like buying train tickets in Moscow. I firmly believe that 'You don't known until you go!' "

"Right on! More power to you and your family," said Tim. "Caye Caulker is an interesting place, isn't it?"

"Oh, yes, but a week just about exhausts all you can do there," I replied. "Next time I go, I'll spend more time on the mainland, definitely go to Tikal or to El Salvador or Coast Rica or the other Central American countries."

Nodding his head, Tim laughed, "So true! So true!"

Pat spoke up, "We better get going; we're on our way to our cabin in Dryden."

"Dryden?" I raised my eyebrows. "Last time I went through, there were only two buildings with ninety going between them. Is there a new suburb?"

"No, no," he said with a smile. "It's actually off the road, kind of close to Mexico, with pictographs, and text-book geology."

"It's rough," added Tim. "Our wives prefer more refined lodging, if you know what I mean."

I replied with a laugh, "I sure do! Hey, maybe I'll see you when I pedal through Austin?"

"Maybe," said Tim. "Maybe. You know where we work. You just be careful out here—this is the hottest on record."

"Well, so far so good. I've been lucky because so many good people like you and the Border Patrol along the way have been giving me way. I'm very grateful. Thank you!"

"We carry plenty whenever we come out here," said Pat. "So it was no problem to help you out. It has been a treat to speak with you. Take care."

I watched them roar-off East on U.S. 90 in that beautiful Land Cruiser. I swung my leg over the Doublevision and pushed off myself.

I would have been successful had the surface been solid blacktop, but the gravel was a slippery surface of ball-bearing like sand grains and without traction, I fell over. Picking myself up, I embarrassedly looked around for witnesses, shrugged my shoulders, walked the Doublevision to that excellent shoulder and began the same scenario again. This time I was successful, and pushed against the torrid headwind.

Within an hour, I stopped in the shade of a former gas station on the South side of 90, DrydenTX. Last year when I came through, by motorcar, the doors were rolled up and I bought cold treats. Now, to my dismay, it was closed and my thoughts of anything cool dissipated.

Then I saw a quad scramble from the other side of this forlorn building across the road to another newer structure, with the driver disappearing through the front door. Then a old, weathered pick-up truck stopped there, it's driver disappearing through that same door. Within a few minutes, he emerged carrying an armload of mail and a soda. Problem solved.

I pedaled across 90, swerving when the wind almost knocked me over, parked underneath an overhang, changed UBS T-shirts, and went through that door.

I nearly fainted.

The cold air, dim interior, and shelves laden with basic rations of food and gear was such a radical change from headwinds, blazing heat, and intense blue sky I had known all day. It was overwhelming, and virtually identical to, strangely enough, to a scuba dive, when plunging into the water and the body gasps. I sat down, unable to move except to observe more clearly my surroundings. Instead of coral and colorful fish, I saw not only a store, but also a home. Half of it was reserved for essentials needed by area residents, including a postal stand, while the other half had a big-screen TV, couch, and computer area.

A young lady was studiously keyboarding and checking her notes, giving all of her attention to her schoolwork, with no more than a slight tip of her head to whomever should enter, whether they became seated, purchased supplies, or checked for the mail. Once composed, I immediately went to the refrigerated unit, removed a can of V-8 (daily vegetables), a Mountain Dew (sugar & caffeine), a gallon of potable water (don't get caught in the desert without it), and a large Twix candy bar (more sugar and a comfort food) off a shelf.

"Is it possible to get a cup of ice?" I asked hopefully.

She silently rose, went to a refrigerator that was on an invisible border between store and home, broke cubes from an ice tray into a cup, and went to the cash register. I gave her a twenty dollar bill, and after receiving a few coins for change, I thanked her. I was exhausted and beyond caring how much anything cost.

I must've sat there for an hour, basking in the cool air, slowly eating my food so I wouldn't get kicked out. I slowly became aware of my intrusion—it was Sunday afternoon, but if they were closed why were other people randomly entering, buying something or picking up mail?

A memory flashed into my mind's eye, that of Dunkie's Dry Goods & Mercantile Store, Lake SpringMO. Even though I was a twig of a boy then, that place is forever etched somewhere into the far reaches of my brain. Surprisingly, or perhaps not, I remembered an icy-frigid day outside, but inside a hot pot-belly stove with a steaming kettle of coffee atop it warmed the rectangular room with fogged up windows. Several, equally pot-bellied, or razor-thin scrawny, worn-faced farmers in their faded blue overalls sat around it, cigarettes (either roll-ups or commercial) in one hand or hanging on a lip, cups of coffee in the other, discussing the markets, their animals, and, inevitably, the weather. There was a card-table in the back room for us youngsters, where we were out of the way and out of trouble, where we could sit mimicking our elders, holding horehound sticks in nearly the same way. Eventually, Dunkie went over to divided shelf and handed various individuals pieces of mail while they started filing out. I can remember the gruff voices calling out a generic, "C'mon, good for nuttin' " and singly we'd leap up as if each unique voice was like a fishing line and we fish were reeled in.

That ended the similarity—the individuals entering and leaving were of a different generation, healthy and vibrant, dressed in refined work clothes of brand name denims, with faces rarely showing the wear of a physically demanding up-before-sunrise, down-after-dark employment.

Still, they *did* depart. *I,* however, was becoming a fixture, another part of the bench.

Now uncertain exactly how long I was there for only empty wrappers lay in front of me, but an older woman approached me as if the bench needed to be dusted off. Even my rarely-used UBS T-shirt carried a fine amount of dirt which gave it a brownish-white appearance.

"You're probably not used to people coming through here on bicycles..." I began to say, hoping that she'd kindly say, "It is unusual and you look exhausted. We're closed now, but you can lay out on the couch for the night and start fresh in the morning."

What she said instead was, "Yeah, this is a regular stop for bikers, except they never come through in this kind of weather. Don't stick around too long, neither."

"Fact is," she continued without emotion, "there aren't many travelers stopping here now anyway, and if you leave now you should be able to get to your next stop. You'll find two rest areas East, one eleven miles the other twenty miles. West is Sanderson, with a campground and hotel, twenty miles."

I felt bad for monopolizing the premises, and almost apologized.

I slowly rose with a groan and stepped out into the headwind with my gallon of water. Changing back into my biking UBS T-shirt, I topped off my water buffaloes and poured the remaining water over my head, soaking my hair and t-shirt. The several degrees shaved off made the next hours bearable, even pleasant until...

While ascending one hill, the chain fell off. Keeping my pride intact, I caught myself before falling. I was not ready for this kind of problem again; it was too soon after having spent almost two hundred dollars for new parts at Bikeman John's shop in Alpine!

Subsequent examination revealed a different problem, and a potential end to my Trans-Texas Bicycle Odyssey. The chainrings had become loose and wobbled, with enough movement that the chain would slip off the still-new teeth. The particular culprit was the outermost ring, the one upon which the forward chain looped around and the ring of the forward bottom bracket to which the crank I pedal is attached and carries my energy for propelling the Doublevision.

Remembering a well-used tactic from over thirty years ago (when I was pedaling between Escondido and San Diego), I began the difficult task of pushing the Doublevision uphill, envisioning those pedestrianized uphills and rapidly coasting downhills. I disavowed the memory almost immediately—these legs are built for bicycling, not walking, and the Doublevision for pedaling.

I pushed the Doublevision into a skinny area of shadow on the shoulder. Unstrapping the tool bag from my Blackburn spring-clip rack, I placed it close to the crossover bottom bracket and squatted beside it, keeping myself in the safest place possible—between the bike and drainage ditch. After analytically staring at it for a few minutes, I grimaced upon the realization that I had to remove each of the chainrings and reseat them. This is an arduous task back home in my shop, but out here, it is phenomenally challenging, made even more so by the lack of a chainring nut wrench.

This specific tool looks like an exceptionally broad tipped flat screwdriver with a blade that can span the slotted flange of .95cm/.375in wide barrel nuts. These are mated to equally precise fine-threaded 1.3cm/.5in bolts, driven with a hexagonal wrench. Using dedicated washers, five of these bolt-nut combination secure chainrings onto the spider, itself a part of the bottom bracket-axle-pedal-(long) chain system, which turns the rear wheel and moves the bicycle forward.

Lacking that tool, I instead use a standard-blade screwdriver (see previous paragraph) which isn't quite wide enough to span the nut, and have to wedge it against the downtube, another chainring, or the spider in order to gain sufficient grip against the bolt.

I can say with a great deal of accuracy that rarely is such a joint extremely tight, but in my thirty-five years plus cycling experience, I can also say with a great deal of accuracy that this is an extremely rare problem.

Unless I decide to improve it before a long journey, such as this one.

While working on the chainrings back home in preparation, an error I made while "improving" my Doublevision became evident: instead of using Loctite on the bolts, I chose to wrap them in Teflon tape.

What could I have been thinking?

The chainrings needed to stay on, not fall off.

Fortunately, I had included a small tube of Loctite in my portable tool bag.

Then I figured I could make the needed repair without removing the chainrings completely from the bottom bracket-spindle setup. Anything which reduces the amount of labor involved is definitely an improvement, because that means a reduction in the complexity of the task.

Working each of the five connections, I carefully placed the bolts, nuts, and lockrings in a sequence of small nests that would neither blow away nor roll down the hill and facilitate the reassembly.

Except for one bolt.

For the life of me, I could not gain any leverage on that infernal nut, and the whole combination would spin in the hole. I hoped that at least it wouldn't come apart, knowing that this amazing trip would be over if that was the wiggle that caused my chaindrive to fail.

An hour later, I was downright pleased with my successful reassembly and with the chainrings lacking that destructive wobble. After repacking and restowing my tool bag, *I* wobbled while pushing the pedals uphill. Insufficient momentum, uphill, flat, or even downhill, guarantees my falling. In those microseconds prior to dumping, I was able to gain enough velocity to right myself and keep going. Infinitely better, the chain didn't fall off; my fix was working.

Exhilarated, I found renewed strength to take on the headwinds, heat, and hills. In fact, I upshifted on one long descent, ready to enjoy the fastest cycling I'd known since Alpine. I heard the chain gnashing through the rings, catching the middle range and onto the high range.

Then my foot fell off the pedal—it had seized up and I could not push it. A sickening feeling began to overcome me when I realized that I was still moving downhill. Braking at the bottom, I analyzed the latest Doublevision problem. Putting it up on the kickstand, I was relieved to see the derailleur still intact and the chain was not broken. With my hand, I pushed a pedal and the rear wheel spun easily enough.

I continued to hand-pedal, when suddenly the pedals locked up. The problem was immediately obvious: when I rebuilt the chainrings on the upside of this hill a half hour ago, I had reversed the crossover ring, (the outermost one which carried the driving energy from my body and legs pushing the front pedals via a separate chain) narrowing the gap between it and the largest sprocket/highest range, thus locking up the two chains.

Frustrated that I had overlooked this seemingly minor detail during the re-build, I once again considered the circumstances. There was no way I was going to perform another rebuild; the Sun was sinking closer and closer to the horizon, and exhaustion was taking root. There was no way I wanted to walk this behemoth again, especially going up this hill.

During this thoughtful gaze, I was enlightened: I didn't need to use the high range *anyway*, and manually put the chain on the granny sprocket.

I also saw what had become an all-important blue information sign: "PICNIC AREA, ½ MILE". Elated to be so close to camping, I had a jolt of energy to pedal, albeit slowly. Once I was at the site, an adjacent sign carried an even more satisfying message "ACCESSIBLE" which meant a ramp into one of the picnic areas. I carefully parked on the lee of a wall, which effectively blocked that ferocious Easterly headwind.

Following an MRE, I laid down and was ready to fall into much needed sleep.

Except an incredibly irritating screech that pierced the air.

The sound was like that of fingernails across a chalkboard, except it was constantly rising and falling. Wearily, I bent the flagpole from rubbing the shelter to underneath the handlebar, and all was quiet except for the wind whistling through the trees.

Laying back down, the much needed sleep was an excellent place to fall into.

Overnight Eight: US 90 rest area

The sharp whoosh of Maxi-brakes followed by the steady rumble of a Mack truck woke me. The massive dump truck had pulled onto the shoulder beside me, but I couldn't smell the noxious exhaust. The wind, already ferocious when I laid down last night, had only increased, with sound rivaling that of the motor vehicle and with a force that sent the oily diesel scent West quickly enough to not alert my nose. I was glad to be protected by this low wall; while I may have stabilized the pole, the pennants on it were parallel to the ground, held there as if in a magical trance by the all-powerful gale.

It seemed odd that he—or she—would be stopping now, at the beginning of the day, when every trucker I've ever known would be well underway by daybreak. But what did I know? Maybe they had driven all night and was now going to get Federal/DOT-mandated bunk time? Or possibly their holding onto the steering wheel while driving into the wind is almost as tiring as my pedaling into it? Could it be that the uninterrupted landscape that was interrupted only with the topography had caused highway hypnosis? Whatever the reason, it was an excellent alarm clock for me.

After my morning ritual, I had a couple of used MRE containers which had been breakfast. After carefully placing a rock inside a billowing plastic bag to keep it inside the trash can, I deposited them into it, comfortable with the knowledge that they would not become debris fouling the landscape. A final bike check—the rear tire was still holding air—and it was time to get gone.

I struggled briefly to cross 90 because of the powerful sidewind. Once on the Eastbound shoulder, it was easier for me to stay upright in the even stronger headwind, although I had to gear way down and go slow. I remembered the first time seeing this: my first ship, the USNS Marias (T-AO57) was an oiler and our sole job on the high seas was to refuel other ships. Rare was the time that refueling/replenishment-at-sea didn't take place, and if there was a high wind (or any kind of wind), the ships always steamed into it. And now I was practicing the same as my control was infinitely better, despite the labor of pedaling against the wind.

What a stiff breeze! If I opened my mouth for a second or two, it would dry out and I'd have to suck more on my water bottle. My ritual now was to breathe in through my nose, out through my mouth. I was glad to have on both my prescription glasses and welder's safety glasses on top of them as little chunks of sand would pulverize my cheeks. I thought of the fairing, leaned up against a wall in my work area back home, and wished I hadn't removed it eleven years ago. The improved aerodynamics of it would cause such particles to pass over me instead of getting lodged in my gums and teeth.

Within an hour, I felt that stiff headwind temporarily subside and an invisible hand at my back with an unmistakable push forward. I knew what was happening, all too familiar with what happens when those big 18-wheelers blow by me. The brief vacuum was created by a draft of air following every vehicle; the larger space occupied by the rig, the more wind interrupted. This moment of luxury can be made even shorter—the greater the velocity of the machine, the quicker it passes thus the time inside this warp becomes an evanescent snap.

As it blew by me, I recognized the red lettering that jumped out at me, Mesilla Valley Transportation. Instinctively, my hand shot up in a wave to the driver, who could now only see me in the rear view mirrors. The air horn let out a long, loud sound that even penetrated the howling winds.

I am most partial to MVT because they've always been an excellent source of over-the-road information as well as potential training and employment for my students when they turn 18. The DOT regs forbid under-21 year olds from driving OTR but that is what makes MVT such an important resource—the younger drivers can gain experience as local operators, which are invaluable and essential skills needed for international truck driving.

Besides MVT, I recognized other trucks, specifically Danny Herman. The kinship I felt with these professionals was that many years ago, while Erik was a Cub Scout in St. Raphael's Pack 86. I was both Den 9 leader and Assistant Cubmaster. The dispatcher for Danny Herman Trucking was also Cubmaster Dawn, and DHT had provided significant in-kind support to Pack 86. I had endless gratitude for both Dawn and DHT, and could see the high-caliber of drivers privileged enough to be driving the dark-blue rigs bearing that name. It was an honor to think that my closeness now—a few feet(one meter)—had its genesis back then.

I must be getting in better shape, both physically and mentally, for my pace was steady (albeit slow), and I wasn't as fixated upon only fresh clean water—I also remembered food. Resisting the temptation to stop and eat the rest of my MRE's, I only stopped to take an occasional photo of debris flying low to the ground. I looked up to see if birds might be following or leading me while I pedaled, but apparently they knew better. It was just me, 18-wheelers, and mile-long(1.6km) trains out in this desolate landscape. Perhaps I was becoming delirious—now I was waving to anything out there, moving or fixed. I needed every friend I could get!

Rounding a bend I came across an abandoned tavern, itself seemingly blown apart by the constant wind. Pulling completely off 90 onto a now trashy parking lot, I found a spot both protected from the wind and the Sun for a short nap. It was not quite as good as in a box culvert, but I was tired and needed rest, and anything that met those two requirements would suffice.

While tempted to consume an MRE, rest was my greater priority and only ate a power-packed, 280 calorie Oatmeal cookie. That was enough; my stomach must have been full, which was just as well for I pulled off my Shimano sandals, put my glasses in one while using the other for a pillow. As with all of these episodic moments, I quickly passed into sleep for 20 or 30 minutes. I reckoned this time based upon the movement of the shade, which had given way to full Sun upon my face, waking me. I felt rejuvenated, and returned to my task at hand.

My only task was at foot: continue pedaling East on U.S. 90.

After experimenting with a with a reasonable range of effective gearing, I had settled upon the low, or granny gears. In the lowest gear, which is the chain running between the 34-tooth cog on the rear wheel cluster paired-up with the 25-tooth chainring in front. This is a 19-inch/48cm gear, which is a fairly easy push. It means that, for one complete revolution of the pedal crank, the Doublevision would roll 19 inches/48cm. For comparison purposes, "easy" means an adult can walk faster than I can pedal in this gear.

Pedaling, from the lowest gear to the highest gear is the epitome of bicycling. However, other functions seem secondary but are no less important, and one is hearing. Anybody who pedals extensively on one bicycle will learn to intimately recognize their two-wheeled horse by it's sounds. Besides the wind screaming in my ears, I listen for messages from my Doublevision and my pushing the pedals revealed a dreaded sound, a "click" that meant only one thing: the bearings in the forward bottom bracket needed tightening. What made my knowing the problem worse was I knew exactly where my BB tool was: back home. Without it, I had no choice but to keep pedaling and hope that the BB didn't fall apart on me before Del Rio. However slowly I moved, I heard that click. Not wishing to jinx myself, I refused to think about it anymore—though every revolution of the pedals was renewed torture.

Of course, another pain was the headwinds, which retarded forward movement, keeping me moving slowly anyway. The aforementioned fairing would have helped here, too, buy pushing the wind up and over my head. Instead, the headwind was hitting my faced so hard that any minute amount of dribbled streaked from the corner of my lip straight back to my before evaporating, leaving a tell-tale clean mark on my dirt encrusted face.

Mid-day, I came to a junction with RR1865, which goes North to Pumpville. The thought crossed my dried, fried, and sky'd brains to check it out—after all, it had replaced Langtry as a stop when the railroad re-routed—surely there must be a store there? But my body needed an immediate break from the wind and absolutely nothing, other than the skinny roadsign and a historical plaque, offered anything. The plaque revealed the likelihood that Pumpville was now a mere shell of a once prosperous railstop, that my pedaling there, fast as it might have been with the tailwind, would have cost me dearly in terms of strength and frustration when returning to this point.

I looked around. It was bleak. No windbreak, no shade, nothing that offered any respite. I pushed on, fatigued, ready to capitulate to gravity, when around the curve, a miracle appeared.

It was a rest area, with shade over a picnic table!

With small surge of adrenalin, I was soon reclining on the table, out of the bucking wind and intense Sun. Like my last stop, it was the heat on my face that woke me up. I knew I had to keep going; Langtry couldn't be that much further.

Remounting the Doublevision, I began pedaling, straining against what seemed to be an even stronger headwind. And it hurt—my lower back kept rubbing on something incredibly hard. I stopped, readjusted the seat cover and began pedaling again.

To my disbelief, the pain became even worse. This was unbelievable; had my spinal chord been dislocated? I couldn't go anymore, and had to stop to make another serious adjustment of the cushion.

Lifting the seat pad, I was shocked to see that *no* seat cushion existed. Other than the pad, I was sitting on a thirty foot ⅜ plastic-covered cable, coiled on heavy metal plates and former Stumpjumper tubing; hardly a seat.

Looking about me, the fiberglass pole holding the flags was bent sideways by that hurricane-like wind. Not only did it blow the pole parallel to the road, but my large seat cushion, which had been encased by Mina, was now hurtling West. I walked several paces back, hoping to find it lodged somewhere, anywhere, but to no avail. It was gone, gone with the wind.

This was a new, very disturbing predicament, another which could easily terminate my pedaling. What made it worse was the utter remoteness. I was totally alone—not a single motor vehicle had passed for the longest time.

No time to waste belittling myself for not anchoring the cushion better and I began to search the surroundings. I was pleased to find two useful items: a ragged, Sun-bleached shirt, and a pair of long, plush Pooh Bear socks. How nice—until I saw that they were a repository for sand burrs and cactus spines. Delving into my tool bag,

I use the perfect extraction tool—needle nosed pliers—to remove those undesirable nasties.

It was the first time since leaving El Paso that I appreciated the headwind. Every time I pulled one out of the cloth and flicked it up, the wind whisked the skin-piercing thorns away, probably into that fine encased cushion Mina had made for me.

After folding all three items into a square pad, I positioned it atop the coiled cable and sat down upon the Doublevision. This time, pain didn't consume my weary body and was bearable enough to pedal. I'll add more padding which will surely be found along the way.

I thought I was slow before, but now I was even slower, having to downshift into the lowest gear of the lowest range so as to not aggravate tender body parts. Moving slowly did have one advantage: I was able to scour the roadside for any more potentially useful debris.

Later, in the vain hope that I could find any such items, I parked the Doublevision on the shoulder atop another culvert. It did serve a useful purpose, I rested from the headwind and heat. Emerging from it, a familiar looking white pick-up with its green stripe stopped beside me. Using my my hand to shade my eyes, I saw the rooster tail quickly fading in the wind and noted that, when viewed closely, there was a light coating of brown dust all over it.

Agent Hernandez stepped out of the cab, saying, "Word's out on you—we know you're restin' underneath when your bike's parked on the shoulder."

Smiling with pleasure that I was acquiring a reputation, I replied, "That's great! What makes it even better are all of you. I wouldn't have made it this far if Agents Lily and Jay hadn't recharged all my water buffaloes with fresh, clean, and cold water..."

"I'm about to go off duty," he politely interrupted, "an' I have some fine Del Rio water, like what you've described. Could I interest..."

"You bet!" I enthusiastically interrupted him. "Meet you above. And, thanks."

While it was business as usual for Agent Hernandez—the Border Patrol's job, essentially, is to take care of everything, primarily people—along the border. On the shoulder beside my Doublevision, he saved my life by refilling my water buffaloes with fresh, clean, cold water.

"Yeah, that's the word—an' you're always thirsty," he said. "I've never seen a bike like yours, even though I bike a bunch when off duty on a Stumpjumper."

I made a connection upon hearing that. "That's pretty incredible, Agent Hernandez. I had a prototype Stumpjumper for fourteen years—a great machine that lasted longer than any of my bikes. In fact, part of my seat," I said, pointing to an exposed white tube, "is made from it."

"Sounds good to me. I'm ridin' mine hard but takin' real good care of it, always cleanin' it an' havin' regular maintenance at the bike shop, replacin' parts on schedule."

"Is it a decent shop? Do you know if they carry foam padding?" I enthusiastically asked. "I had a great cushion, but this wind blew it away back at the Pumpville picnic table. The bottom bracket needs tightening and now I'm riding on an improvised pad from stuff I find on the shoulder."

"It's Lakeside Sports and you can't miss it in town," he replied. "It's on ninety. There's a lot of stuff in there besides bikes, probably includin' paddin'."

"I was pretty upset about loosing my seatpad. Mina, my seamstress back home, encased foam with a heavy-duty green canvass-like fabric. This wind just plain took it." Then I added hopefully, "If you happen to see it..." and took a large gulp of that refreshing water.

"Ah, that is good. Now, if I just had a steak for it to wash down..." I said wistfully.

"There's a Sirloin Stockade on ninety, too, before you get to Lakeside Sports," he interjected. "It's all you can eat and I always go there after riding."

His words caused my mouth to water and my brain to forget. I forgot my exhaustion, forgot that I hadn't even gotten to Langtry yet, much less Del Rio. I couldn't even conceive of the distance. I could only see myself in Sirloin Stockade, gorging on plateful after plateful. No more MREs, no more old, ambient temperature water, just a lot of good old fashioned food.

Back on the road, the reality of headwinds and heat snapped me back to the present. I saw in my rear view three lone trucks passing each other at regular intervals as they roared up to and past me. It seemed funny because each were competitors—DHL, FedEx, and UPS—but they were really helping each other. The drivers were using the same principles of a paceline, each drafting off the other, each alternating in responsibility for breaking the wall of headwind. Of course, my benefit lasted but a moment when they passed me.

It was during that windfree second that I spied a long, blue tube of closed-cell foam laying far off to the side, caught between some rocks. That renewed wall of wind after the trucks passed stopped me instantly. I had to get that swimming pool noodle—a completely abstract object in this waterless, dry environ. I seized it with glee, folding it into thirds. Delving into my calefactive tool bag again, I pulled out a roll of sticky gray ductape and secured it as another layer between my bottom and the blunt seat frame.

What an improvement! I couldn't believe my good fortune. Had those world-wide deliverers somehow dropped the package that would enable me to successfully continue?

Naahhh. I had found it far off the road. But it was a nice thought anyway—they are such good companies, having effectively made beneficial deliveries for me in the past. (Notably, FedEx brought me the rear wheel which I am now pushing from Tandems Limited three weeks ago.) Why not give them credit, even if not deserved in this instance? All too often, they don't get acknowledged for the marvelous, time-critical work they do accomplish and blamed for rare instances of mis-delivery. Heck, my Doublevision wouldn't be the durable machine it is without the wheels, tires, and other components they have left at my front door.

After another hour of much less-bruiser pedaling, I recognized a sign not too far away and became over the top happy. My previous experience told me that the color and shape advising me of Judge Roy Bean's Jersey Lily Saloon, Langtry, was only a mile away. Relief was nearby.

When I got closer and could actually read it, I felt betrayed, angry, and sapped of energy.

Two miles! Every such sign I'd seen until now were ALWAYS only a mile to the attraction. What gives...?

Of course, it did me no good to get upset; I was already exhausted. All I could do was push. I stopped beside an old gas station and eatery, the Wagonwheel. The scent of a delicious meal in the air teased me, only exacerbating my punishing fatigue and hunger. I couldn't get past the locked door and wasted too much time searching in vain for access. At least state highway loop 25 to Langtry was downhill, despite it taking a huge amount of my strength to pedal against the wind and park at the entrance to the Judge Roy Bean State Historical Site and Museum.

Pushing the door open and walking into the thirty-degree (19C) cooler museum time-wharped me back to 1982.

In mid-July, Brother Nils and I were on a biketour and pedaling the Icefields Parkway when we overnighted at the Mosquito Creek Hostel for two nights. During the first night, cold and snow had blanketed the area with white, and Route 93 had become impassable with 2-wheeled vehicles, necessitating a second night. Since we had no particular schedule, another hosteler, Wisconsinite and chocolatier Cheryl, offered us a visit to the Jasper Tramway in her car. Since we couldn't pedal, why not a preview? Her generosity (especially with the Andes chocolates.) was much appreciated, but later I took advantage of the sauna and nearby frigid Mosquito Creek. After heating my body to the maximum extent possible in the enclosed space, I rushed out with brilliantly rose-colored skin and plunged into the icy water, returning to the sauna after turning blue. This alteration between intense heat to intense cold was amazingly rejuvenating, and I repeated the process much of the morning.

Twenty-nine years later, that kind of intense temperature differential was still amazing, albeit not nearly as rejuvenating—the change was still immediate, but this time it effectively drained all my remaining strength. I slumped down into a cushioned chair in the darkened video room, dazed and zombie-like.

Marsha and Susan, curators, paid scant attention to this smelly, scraggly bicyclist. Later, after ingesting water and some MRE parts, I revived enough to formally introduced myself and learned that their museum is a standard stop on the Southern tier of an Adventure Cycling Route, as well as many other people pedaling through, like me.

"We weren't ignoring you," Marsha said lightly. "We're used to it. I think everybody biking through does exactly as you, they enter and collapse in those chairs."

"Except it's a bit warm to be out, mind you," Susan half-chided me. "Anyway, you've got fifteen more minutes before we close up. Use the bathroom now—it'll be closed too."

"There's a free camp for you at the community center, where all the bikers stay," offered Marsha. "Just past the post office and first house on your left. They've got free water, too."

How can I turn that down?

My bum was having a delayed reaction to the earlier abuse when I tried to pedal without the padding and now my snail-like cadence to the free camp was constantly fraught with falling. Following the directions—not too difficult in a small town like this—I found the place, but a pay-pipe indicated that a $2 donation would help cover maintenance costs.

I was mystified—this gravelly patch needed maintenance?

Well, there really are no freebies in the World, especially if it comes with fresh water. After anchoring the Doublevision kickstand on some broad rocks, I put my money in and went for a walkabout.

I admit, it was felt nice to not be pedaling.

I stopped at the community building and read the historical sign, which explained that is was originally a schoolhouse from 1934. It is named "Vashti Skiles Community Center" for a beloved teacher who apparently spent his entire career enriching this once-thriving village. When the railroad moved location, the population dwindled and the academic instruction went onto Comstock schools with this building converted into its present use.

Initially shocked by what looked like a snake, I quickly realized that it was a hose and source for my free water. Turning the handle, I slaked my thirst.

Gagging, I spit it out.

It was warm, as expected, but it also had the distinct taste of salinity which only locals or desperately thirsty individuals might savor.

I was neither, and continued my exploration.

Moving back to Torres Street amidst several fixer-uppers, another marker noted the road's namesake: the Torres family. It was interesting to learn that they were the primary landholders who were skilled with irrigation. They donated land for the railbed as well as employing their skills to make water available for the steam locomotives. Their life-long efforts were to improve the region by increasing commerce that would arrive with the Galveston, Harrisburg & San Antonio Railroad in 1882. Even the settlement's name was changed, from Eagle's Nest to Langtry, which was possibly another enticement to the then-latest mode of transport. George Langtry was in charge of putting the tracks down. Mr. William H. Dodd was a transplanted limey who had also been, along with his wife Lula, staunch supporters of early Langtry. He served in several official positions, while she promoted various festivals and events that increased the town's visibility and desirability. Besides the attraction of clean, dry air for health benefits, Langtry also assisted Mexican revolutionaries due to it's proximity to Mexico. Robert T. Hill was another person who helped put Langtry on the map, when, in 1899, he a five others made the first recorded float of the Rio Grande. After a put-in at Presidio and detailing their route along the way, Langtry was the take-out.

I walked on this rough road toward the river to the last marker. This one noted a sleight-of-hand by one of the most, if not the most, shrewd individuals to ever claim a stake in Langtry: Judge Roy Bean. In 1896, he sponsored a heavy-weight title fight (illegal in Texas prior to 1933) here. Bean arranged for the media and the law to arrive via railroad/horse/buggy, then had the fight take place on a sand bar in the *Rio Bravo*—in Mexico. Since no authorities South of the border were available to stop the fight, and the Texas authorities had no jurisdiction in Mexico, the fight went on—Robert James Fitzsimmons KO'd Peter Maher in 95 seconds, but evidently it was Bean who got in the final punch.

I returned to my campsite, put out my Z-rest and rested beside the Doublevision, finishing off an MRE. It was good, but my belly still felt empty. "Empty" is an accurate descriptor for my condition throughout much of this biketour, but at least I had fresh, clean though not always cold, water to drink—most of the time. I lay back, shutting my eyes for much needed sleep.

It would be difficult for me to guess how long before a raindrop splattered upon my head, followed by another, then several more, but no matter. I opened my eyes to see lightning filling the skies over the USM with occasional spitting upon the USA. The tallest structure in this small plain was close to me, none other than the fiberglass pole jutting up from rear of *my* Doublevision. That lightning was menacingly moving North, and fear of a "quick fry" of my brains by night, as opposed to the "slow fry" I endured by day, motivated me into action. I quickly put on my Jox Sox and Plantation swimsuit (I'm *always* ready to get wet!), gathered up the Z-rest, strapped it onto the tandem and wheeled it all back to the paved road.

The whole area was brightly lit from security lights, and frequently by the even greater brilliance of lightning, but I didn't care about that. I just needed to find a place where my bike would not become a lightning rod. I analyzed possible options, even pedaling back up to the junction with 90, but the rain increased to leaving splats of wet on the road amongst dry patches. The most promising was the thin shelter provided by the overhang of the building opposite the Travel Center which housed the Lillie Langtry convenience store and a US post office. After moving a bench over, I was able to tuck the Doublevision beside the outside wall, securing the *Ming Tay* U-lock around the down tube and through the rear wheel. Satisfied with these emergency response procedures, my next task was to figure out how *I* was going to rest.

The drops had become larger and pelting me more frequently. I knew it was going to be a long and possibly very wet night—maybe I ought to set up the tarp-tent Mina had made for me?

At least I was comforted with the knowledge that my Doublevision was no longer an easy target for Zeus' arrows, so I sought refuge inside the post office—always open for boxholders. Regretfully, it was as brightly lit inside as the street and would surely keep me from resting.

Another distraction, though, was the ad for flat rate boxes. One price to mail for all that fits inside, no matter how much it weighs. It put me to thinking; if there was anything that I was pedaling with which was absolutely worthless, it was my ⅜ inch, 30-foot cable. It provided only marginal comfort as a seat, and was incredibly heavy. That weighty coil and I were parting company tomorrow morning, courtesy of the USPS.

I returned outside to find that the squall had let up significantly. Accepting that some dampness was inevitable, I posited myself across the street, underneath a cement picnic table at the travel center. It seemed as good as anyplace, and I could monitor my bicycle as needed. Laying face down upon my pad and bag at an oblique angle, I was able to limit the amount of ambient light and shut my eyes.

Overnight Nine: Langtry

Some rest is better than no rest was my solace when I woke after what seemed like mere minutes, and very uncomfortable minutes at that. Looking across the road in the early morning gray at where I had strategically placed my Doublevision a few hours ago, I was pleased to see it had not moved. I didn't expect it to anyway.

Rising with the stiffness that comes from contorted sleep, I collected myself, bag, and pad, refastening them to the Doublevision. Hunger gnawed at me, tempting me to eat an MRE, but I resolved to hold out until I could buy a more substantial meal in the Langtry Lillie or the Wagonwheel, just uphill.

That's it, that's my answer!

I unlocked the Doublevision and the wind pushed me back up the road, along with my short-term memory of the delicious smells of yesterday. Wagonwheel, here I come.

Disappointment washed over me when I parked in the same place as yesterday because none of the evocative scents nor an open door were now present. Resigned to temporary starvation, I remounted the Doublevision and pedaled downhill, back toward the post office.

I knew I was exhausted, but was it really this far? I struggled against the headwind, pedaling in my lowest gear, feeling as though I was going to be flung backward. I rarely have pedaled against such enormous headwinds, but remember those few occasions well—now including this one.

The first time was in 1979, when I had just separated from the Navy. I and two companions pedaled from San Diego to San Francisco, paralleling the Pacific. At one point, we overnighted at Gaviota State Beach and Campground, but to get there we had to overcome a super-stiff headwind, which made our meal that night well earned.

The next occurred while an undergrad at Mizzou in the early 1980s. I had cycled the 30 mile/48km to Jefferson City, where I overnighted with a friend. I was in remarkably good shape then, pedaling it in an astoundingly fast 71 minutes, or 36mph/68kph. Of course, I did have a 40mph/64kph tailwind! Unfortunately, the wind hadn't diminished overnight, so it made for a somewhat slower return—4 hours, or 7.5mph/12kph. So much for being in good shape.

Of course, neither of those memorable events stacked up to what I was now encountering. Besides the steady onslaught pounding my frontside, I was significantly older and had had arthroscopic surgery several years ago to remove an annoying sliver of meniscus that had been torn asunder in my left knee.

My re-arrival at the post office was perfectly timed as Postmaster Neal greeted me. That space had not changed from last night when I sought refuge from the impending storm, except now his window was open. Following a bit of guesswork, I stuffed a Priority Mail Medium Flat Rate box with my cable, Ft. Davis T-shirt, small cloth bags, and some of the documentation I managed to pickup in the travel center yesterday. Paying with my VISA debit card was delightful as I was able to receive a bit of cash back—very important when at a cash only establishment.

Though still famished, I did feel better (because I was lighter?) and walked around the corner to the adjacent Langtry Lilly store. It was a cornucopia of regional interest material which took up most of the interior space: The Jersey Lilly; Rio Grande/*Rio Bravo*; Billiard Hall; Roy Bean's Opera House Town Hall and Seat of Justice; Judge Roy Bean; Law West of the Pecos; Western lore; the Galveston, Harrisburg & San Antonio/Southern Union; gifts; more books; crafts;

picture postcards; knick-knacks, and numerous other souvenirs. However, most vital to me right then, were snacks of candy, ice cream, chips, anything that can help fill the pit between my innie and spine. Once I had quieted my growling stomach, investigated the wide assortment of practical and off-beat stuff, and purchased several postcards, usually the first item I buy anywhere—unless feeling peckish.

Returning to the travel center, Marsha and Susan knew exactly why my greeting was so brief. Re-entering the travel center from the loo, I perused the exceptionally fine displays and diorama. Much of it was devoted to Mr. Bean, his exploits and reputation as the "Law West of the Pecos". Apparently Mr. Bean couldn't make a go of it in numerous previous locales (including the Cactus Capital of Texas) before finally seeing success in Langtry. Perhaps he is most well known for his iconic behavior as a magistrate, dispensed from with his courtroom-saloon, The Jersey Lily (named for a British actress, whom he had a crush on), where his shingle proclaimed him to be "Justice of the Peace Law West of the Pecos".

Unfortunately, when GH&SA was acquired by the Southern Pacific in the 1920s, the track was re-routed a short distance away from Langtry and the inevitable decline arrived. It was not unlike a few decades later in the 1900s, when interstate motor routes were built. Fortunes of a community often teetered upon whether or not the new road went through it, or bypassed it. Langtry was such a place.

Without a doubt, anyplace, whether a large urban area (like El Paso), or a small village (like Langtry), it's vibrancy depends upon many factors, the most important of which is the community members. Regardless if they are the founders such as the earnest Torres family or immigrants such as the virtuous Dowds or the questionable Judge Bean, all have had and continue to play a dynamic part in the success of that community.

Ironically, when the railroad left town taking jobs, careers, and money, it was the reputation of the (in)famous Bean which is the current mainstay of Langtry. And who am I to knock it? Texas historical plaques are present all over, as is the glorious travel agency and park, built around the grounds of Bean's courthouse-saloon.

This shows that a close relationship between the ethical entities of businesses, governments, and communities is beneficial to the general population as a whole. Yes, some segments do benefit more than others, but that is in direct proportion to the risk of failure. The greater a chance of going into the red means a greater chance of going into the black, and most anybody willing to stick their neck out is counting on black, lots of it.

It is a lesson not only throughout history, but of the future too. Anybody who does not understand it is merely occupying space which cannot be sold, rented, or even legitimately used. Such people might get headlines but risk fines, jail, or worse. The only reasonable remedy to correct any abusive or unethical collusion between the public and private sectors is through the democratic process, the ballot box. Inability to recognize that thwarts democracy, ultimately denying a hard-won voice to deserved citizens while alienating the many.

Back outside, while I was readying myself to pedal again, a young man, Alex, roared up on his crotch-rocket. We both eyed each other; conversation was inevitable, and we extended our hands to each other, properly introducing ourselves.

"So you're a petroleum engineer from Pennsylvania?" I asked. "Drake's Well, eh?"

"No, that one's been dry for a long time," he replied, "but you came close. I'm fracking in the area."

"I've heard about fracking. Isn't that dangerous? I mean, doesn't it pollute the water supply?" I asked.

"You're not a tree-hugger are you?" he rhetorically asked with a smile. "That's not a proven fact, but I can tell you, as a fracking engineer, the gas is thousands of feet below the drinking water supply. Anyway, tell me about your travels."

After giving him the barest of details (neither of us had all day for my elaboration) and my personal card, he was suitably impressed, but wanted more information.

"I have a week left and want to get into Big Bend National Park. Do you know anything about it?" he asked.

"I'm quite familiar with it—I pedaled it with one of my brothers in nineteen eighty-six, and have since returned a few times with my family. Your biggest challenge is time; I don't think there's anyway you can take in Big Bend adequately *and* make it back to work on time. You could be in the park if you leave right now, continue West on ninety to Marathon—be sure you gas up there because it's quite dear in the park, drive South on three eighty-five and camp in the backcountry—Paint Gap primitive camp is great, not too far off the paved road. You can take the paved road into the Chisos Basin, Los Boquillas on the Eastern end, and Santa Elena on the Western end, but for me, the real highlight is the river road, fifty miles of rugged terrain, going through deep sand arroyo and over igneous sills."

I looked over his motorcycle, noting the tires.

"You don't have gnarly knobs, but it's light and you're strong enough to push it when needed. My brother and I spent two days driving from Missouri, and the Dfifty we drove in died at Paint Gap. We biked from there for four days, two of which we spent dealing with the river road. With my family many years later, I drove a FourRunner with four-wheel drive and we were able to get through. The key for being out here is having enough fresh, clean water to drink and its even more critical in Big Bend. I took my chances once and even drank out of the Rio Grande."

"Anyway," I continued authoritatively, "you could spend of couple of days in Big Bend, just ensure that you leave the park on US sixty-seven, going North to Marfa. From there, go East on ninety about twenty miles and camp at the world-famous Marfa mystery lights turnout. It's free and well-worth your time, or, once you've been amazed by the lights, you can keep motoring East to Alpine. Stay on US sixty-seven to DFW, where you can catch the interstates back to Pennsylvania. It's a hard trip but entirely doable, especially traveling at night on pavement—these daytime temps are murder, more so if you have a headwind."

Alex was wide-eyed and nodding, taking in everything I was saying. After I had rattled off the information, asked, "So that's what you think I ought to do?"

"You're still going to be pushing it, Alex, to make it back to work within a week. As long as you don't have engine problems or try to go to El Paso or Guadalupe Mountain, too, I think you can make it."

"Well, thanks for the help," and he began to mount his motorcycle.

"Hey!" I called after him. "I know what happens when solo touring, but would you take my picture on my Doublevision?"

"You're so right," he replied. "And here's my camera, so you can take a photo of me, too."

After watching him mount his motorized two-wheel machine and roar off, I followed suit, mounting my own two-wheeled machine and barely rolling off, with groans as I got my exhausted body into the familiar actions of pedaling.

Altering my parking spot only enough for the Doublevision to be in the shade, I was finally able to enter the Wagonwheel. There were the usual sweets and candies, but I had had plenty of those downhill and now it was time for something more substantial, something that will give me the energy needed to buck that rising headwind. The BBQ pork sandwich was just what I needed, and being inside, out of the wind, didn't hurt, either.

By mid-morning, I felt sufficiently nourished to continue my push into the wind, stopping briefly on the US90 bridge over the bone-dry Eagle Nest Creek. It was, in a contradictory way, pleasant to pedal in my low gear against that blasphemous breeze. I was still getting just as exhausted as ever, but was my body getting used to it? I kept on pedaling, stopping whenever a culvert was available to shelter me from the headwind and heat.

I pedaled off US90 onto a decent gravel sidepath, which led to my next stop, an overlook for the Pecos River High (Railroad) Bridge. After parking my Doublevision in the shade of a picnic shelter, I ascended a few steps up to a gazebo-style structure that provided decent viewing of trains slowly snaking their way through the desert. Interestingly enough, I looked the opposite direction and gazed into Mexico, which was actually closer.

Three historical markers provided a glimpse of life in the late 19th century and the challenges of transportation during those times. The lower Pecos River was an exceptionally difficult barrier, not only because it contained water, but primarily because of the enormously deep gorge it had created. Crossing it was of paramount importance to the Southern Pacific railroad in order to provide a second transcontinental crossing that was free of the ice and snow which hampered year-round movement on the first, more-Northerly crossing.

The initial Pecos River railroad crossing of 1882 had tracks descending and ascending the canyon walls, crossing close to the water level, where the railway town of Vinegaroon was established to support construction of those first tracks. The base camp must have been located on the Western bank of the Pecos because opposite was a sheer escarpment. And it was intriguing to learn that Mr. Roy Bean of Langtry fame had been a presiding judge here, part of his court circuit. After all, he claimed to be "The Law West of the Pecos" and Vinegaroon was on the West bank of the Pecos.

I imagine this temporary establishment consisted primarily of tents or possibly even shanties, though unlikely the latter because practical lumber is scarce in the desert. And a few seasonal floods would certainly stimulate discussion of alternate routes, the most likely and reasonable being that of a viaduct spanning the gorge, which is exactly what had happened nine years later.

At the time of its construction, this second bridge was the highest in North America and third highest in the World. By the Second World War, it needed to be replaced to meet the demands of heavier rolling stock, as well as increased train traffic. The third crossing continues to serve as the mainline for the Southernmost transcontinental railroad, and AMTRAK still stops midway to allow photos and gawking. I remember doing exactly that when returning to El Paso from Chicago years ago with Katy and Erik. What I remember especially well is not being able to see the storied structure because we had stopped on top of it—maybe a photogenic view of the canyon, but not of the bridge.

From the gazebo, I looked once again toward Mexico. In the closer distance, I could make out the faint disruption of earth that partially showed the original path of the first railroad. How handy a pair of binoculars would be to see both routes, old and present. Then I realized that, unless planned for, I would have put them in a flat-rate box back home, along with the cable. It made no difference—railway construction so long ago doubtlessly must have been extremely arduous and difficult. Heck, any kind of construction out here in this remote area must have been exceptionally demanding.

I tried to identify with it, believing the slight bike work I'd done qualified, but there really is no comparison. All I had to do was pedal into that consarned headwind on the smooth pavement, which had laboriously been put down by sweating and swearing road crews in the 1920s. Some of the South-of-the-border laborers might have had parents or other relatives who laid the railroad tracks 40 years before and were known as *traqueros*. Just thinking about their work made me tired, and this was as good as anyplace to rest from taxing my brain and body so much. I arose a short time later, refreshed and pedaled back onto 90.

I hadn't gone far before stopping on the shoulder to readjust my makeshift seat pad, when another Border Patrol truck, this time a Chevy Tahoe, pulled up alongside me. Agents Stovall and Mark stepped out with the offer of cold fresh water. I was starting to get spoiled, but I didn't refuse. I emptied the water buffaloes onto my head, shoulders, and body; even though the water was hot, the wind evaporated it and cooled me off. Besides, I felt related to it, laboriously carrying it through pregnancy, childhood, adolescence, into adulthood and now disliking the 'empty nest'. While they refilled the bladders, I praised the agents and all their colleagues:

"Yes, you two are lifesavers," I said, "just like Agents Lily & Jay a week ago just South of Valentine."

"Saving people is one of the many expectations we meet out here," replied a smiling Agent Mark.

"Yeah, everybody thinks all we do is interdict illegals," added Agent Stovall.

"Don't I know it! Actually, a year ago, I took a short five-day cycle North of El Paso and camped between fifty-four and the fence thirty-five miles into New Mexico; must've been in the Alamogordo sector, but four squad cars stopped to check me out."

Now grinning, I added, "However, I'm legal and I've got the papers to prove it!"

The wind blew those papers (my logbook, in this case) out of my binder. As if in a catatonic stupor, I couldn't move, but Agent Mark rushed after them, grabbed them before they sailed off to join my seatpad, and returned them to me.

"*Thank you!* Now you've also saved my documentation about this biketour." I gushed. "Border Patrol does *so* much more than just guard the border!"

"You bet," agreed Agent Stovall. "We get called upon for everything that happens along the border. It's been real nice to help you..."

"I'm so appreciative," I said, then got up on my mock stumpspeech: "However, one of the planks in my platform is that no one who receives a paycheck from us taxpayers will get over a hundred-thousand per year, although there can be a ten percent bonus..."

"I wish we got paid that much," Agent Mark replied, with a smile.

"...which you have certainly earned by stopping for me," I finished.

After a pause, I continued, "I know the Pecos is close as is Seminole Canyon State Park, but can you tell me how far it is to a restaurant?"

Agents Stovall and Mark in turn looked at each other, then at a bearded bedraggled me, my fully loaded Doublevision which had become coated with the light brown haze of dirt, and Agent Mark gently spoke, "I don't want to burst your bubble, BikerJohn, but it's gettin' late and if you started at at Langtry this mornin', you're only about halfway to Comstock—another fifteen miles. The wind is gettin' worse, which'll slow you even more."

"And," added Agent Stovall, "there's not much there—our section station, a gas station, a remodeled hotel, one cafe that doubles as a bar, which closes around dark."

"OK, ok," I replied thoughtfully. "It sounds like I'd better get a move on, then. With this fresh water you've given me, I've got new energy. Thanks so very much!"

I slowly maneuvered back onto that fine paved shoulder and saw the Border Patrol truck in my rear view mirror rolling away on a gravel road, the rooster tail blown horizontally. The headwind whining in my ears blocked all other sounds.

I was exhilarated to see the magnificent Pecos River High Bridge for US 90; this was progress. I pedaled as quickly as possible across this OK bridge that towered over the Pecos River. It was only OK because during the entire crossing, that fine shoulder became non-existent, thus I was forced to take a lane on what had become a narrow 2-lane highway. It really bothers me when I have to do that because, as professional a motoring community as the 18-wheelers are, they have the same relation to me as a long train does to a motor vehicle: in the event of a collision, woe betides the lesser-massed.

As soon as I crossed over, I pulled onto an overlook on the left-hand side. From where I stood, an additional walk/bikeway could be attached alongside the bridge and serve as a viable means of crossing for non-motorized traffic. I know that US90 is regularly used by bicyclists, although not always during the headwindy heat like me, but it would be tremendous safety enhancement, possibly encouraging more bicycling. Gazing below at the attractive water, a desirable quick dip in the Pecos seemed to be unreasonable—I *was* almost 300 feet/91 meters above the water. Gazing above, I saw that the Sun was now four fingers above the horizon, or about an hour of light to go.

I was in familiar territory, that of hunger.

Seizing the opportunity for some kind of real food, and pushed into Seminole Canyon State Park. Delirium took over my brain when I saw the sign for edibles inside the office, and eagerly parked the Doublevision before I scurried up to the door.

Dang! It's closed! I moved around to the backside, only to find that door locked as well. Looking around, I saw no person anywhere, no indication of other life, no vehicles besides my own Doublevision, nothing. Severely distressed at the prospect of no food, I was overheated and exasperated.

I had to resolve the most pressing issue first, that of being too warm. I am all too familiar with heat stroke, having suffered a bout of it in the early 1980s while an undergrad at the University of Missouri, Columbia. I saw a desert garden, which, ironically had a water hose laying beside it. Following that hose back to it's source, it was connected to an above-ground cistern. Well, I figured, if I can't go inside a cool space for some decent grub, I'll just turn on the tap, use a little water to soak myself and eat some indecent grub.

Sprawled out on the sidewalk, I checked out the remains from my MREs, which was not much. Jalapeño ketchup, bar-b-que sauce,

Nescafé Tasters Choice Coffee, sugar packet, crackerjacks, Tobasco sauce, dainty toilet paper sheafs, and matches. The latter two items were not digestible, but the first six had great possibility. In fact, they were the *only* possibility to keep my body going. If you're starving, you're not going to be squeamish about what (no Tobasco, though) goes down the gullet.

I returned to US90 and pedaled furiously with the Sun on my back. I **had** to get to Comstock before dark or have a very hungry night! The headwind hadn't abated and the terrain was rolling. I was able to speed downhill, but only crawled uphill. My focus was very directed, gleeful on the descents, but gloomy on the ascents. In fact, during those slow moments I confused "Comstock" with "compost", which was more indicative of my up-and-down attitude.

Creeping up what had to be the last hill, I stopped at the drive of an RV park, and was offered a site for only five dollars.

"But do you have a restaurant or store or someplace I can buy some food?" I asked.

"Nope, that'd be in Comstock—another mile on," came the reply.

I cursed myself for stopping, and now it's another mile to compost.

Climbing another short hill, I parked at the first lit-up business, Jim Holley's Place.

Entering, I saw three men puffing away and playing pool. I went into the restaurant portion, whereupon Jim (I assume he was the owner) came in and went behind the counter.

"Are you closed?" I asked tentatively.

"Not while you're in here," he rasped. "What can I get you?"

"*COMSTOCK!*" I fairly yelled, elated that I had gotten here in time for a meal.

Jim backed away, somewhat alarmed.

"I'll have the burger with fries!" I finished my answer.

"No you won't; that's for tomorrow, when the Julie opens the restaurant," he said.

"*COMPOST!*" went through my mind, then asked, "Well, how about some of that stuff which doesn't have to be cooked?"

"Now you're talkin'!" he exclaimed. "Whaddayou' want?"

"Well, since I can't get any real food, and I'm powerful hungry, I guess I ought to buy enough to get me through the night 'till tomorrow, when you're open," I replied.

Luckily, I was able to buy a several nut rolls, besides a caffeine- and sugar-laden Mountain Dew.

"I think I should buy that jar of peanut butter, too," I said. "I ate up the last of my emergency food back at Seminole Canyon, and I *don't* want to get caught somewhere without anything to eat!"

While nodding, Jim took my payment and motioned for me to leave. As soon as I stepped outside, I heard the door latch clunk and the lights went dark.

I sat down at the table, spread out my meal and slowly devoured it—maybe I will survive the night? With that thought in mind, I started looking around, considering my options for a sleeping spot. Being ignorant of the area and mindful that I'm going to be trespassing wherever I lay my head until morning, my choices were limited—especially since I didn't want to be far from breakfast. An adjacent cement pad had possibilities, except for the substantial amount of broken glass covering it.

I returned to my next nut roll and began thinking that, actually, right here might not be too bad, when I heard the door open. Two of the pool sharks walked out, passing me silently, dragging on their fags as the door latch gave another definite "clunk" of being locked. Nobody can enter, and now I hoped the third man, Jim, was staying because his exiting would interrupt my repose on his porch.

I hadn't much settled in before a couple walked across 90 directly to me.

"Hiy' there!" came her cheerful voice and he said, "Ya' might remember me—I 'm Aaron and was one of the poolsters."

"Ah, sure...," I said slowly, reconnecting my short-term memory, "...you were the short guy with the cue stick, weren't you?"

I handed them each one of my personal cards.

"Yeah, that was me. Say, me and Whitney's got a proposal for ya'..."

"...I think it's amazin' that y're tourin' in this wind an' heat!" Whitney interjected. "We're motel sittin' for now, an' y're more than welcome to take the storage room. Get out of the wind, nobdy'd bother y' an' all, y'know. "

"There ya' go," said Aaron. "The other part of our proposal is we make ya' breakfast. Too bad ya' got here too late, we had a bang-up dinner earlier, lots of cheese an' pasta, real good for bikin'.'"

"He said the God's honest truth—say, what's y'name?" Whitney asked, holding my card up to the sky. "Can't read in the dark, y'know."

Puffing up my chest a bit, I responded, "My name's John, but you can call me 'Juanito', my pen name for two of my books, or 'BIKERJOHN', my pen name for an elementary school bicycle safety book..."

"Anyways, come on over an' stay in th' storage room in back, y'know," Whitney added. " 'Bikerjohn'. Cute. So, in the mornin' we'll whip together a great omelet for y'.'"

"Sounds too good to be true," I replied with a laugh, "but I'll take you up on it. Thanks!"

A few moments later, we gathered at the far side of the Comstock Motel, away from 90 and obtrusive lights. It was not such a bad place to lay down, just windy—I deferred occupying space in the storage room, instead preferring to sleep beside my Doublevision.

About to lay down on my Z-rest, I remembered that I my water buffaloes were short of water. I knew exactly where to get the freshest, cleanest, and coldest water anywhere, and that source was virtually within spitting distance—*if* with the wind, which it was.

The Border Patrol station was sharing a parking lot with the motel where I was now camped. In fact, the motel seemed to sited precisely between the station and another parking area as many agents were continually walking between the two, constantly passing in front of the motel. It took me very little energy to meet any, and one in particular, Agent Gonzalo, filled up my buffaloes.

"I heard about you—understand you made a huge pedal today, coming all thirty-seven miles/59kms from Langtry in *this* wind. Man, that's something, all right! I'm glad to help you out with this."

Border Patrol—they got my back.

Overnight Ten: Comstock

Even though it was as dark upon waking as it was when I closed my eyes, I had had a good sleep. So why am I so tired? I felt as if back to my third night, just South of Valentine, for the persistent headwinds had only increased! I groaned, but was relieved because this was Comstock, infinitely more cosmopolitan than that lonely camp between 90 and the fence, where my sole relief was fine T-Mobile cellular connection and salvation from of Agents Lily and Jay. They were doing their job, checking on this strange camper and giving me the most essential fluid for life anywhere, but especially in the desert: clean fresh water. They had set precedent for every fabulous Border Patrol agent thereafter because now they *all* saved me by giving me water. I remembered last night, when Agent Gonzalo was happy to not have to carry the heavy stuff any further than my buffaloes.

In every contact with Border Patrol, I felt a kinship, a bond wrought by slow movement along the border. I'm significantly older than most of the agents, that being one factor in my Eastern creep along US90. I'm also pedaling around 400 pounds/181 kg into incredibly strong headwinds under extreme high heat conditions. No analogy readily comes to mind which conveys the magnitude of my attempt, except that perhaps I am *muy loco*?

As the Sun started to break the horizon, I stretched, and soon found myself sitting in the very same seat I had occupied several hours ago when Whitney and Aaron had invited me to the wonderful camp behind their motel. Unfortunately, they were unable to follow through on the tantalizing promise of an omelet. Since they were no where to be found, I went to the next logical place, where Julie would soon be opening her restaurant to hungry passerbys like me.

Besides the scrumptious food, especially the nut-filled brownies, were other individuals who stopped in. One such person was a youngish man of Germanic or Slavic origin, and may have had a troubled childhood. He kept his face buried in a breakfast plate of eggs, bacon, toast, refusing to do more than grunt or speak a few words replying to me. Had I somehow alienated him? Was I too garrulous? As soon as he had completed dining, he made quick payment—plus extra for one of Julie's brownies—and geared up, Westbound in his dusty 18-wheeler.

I myself was about to gear down, Eastbound, on my dusty Doublevision 2-wheeler. Aaron and Whitney approached me in the same manner as last night, except now the Sun was on the rise and the wind felt like it was blowing bruising subatomic photons.

"Juanito," Whitney began, "we overslept. We can still put th' omelet together if you're willing to stay a bit longer."

"Just had a huge breakfast, including two of Julie's brownies," I replied. Raising my measuring hand, I calculated. "Sun's been up for at least two hours, wind's blowing harder, and I need to get underway."

"Well," said Aaron, "if ya're sure ya don't want more food, ya'know, t'fight the wind an' all..."

"Thanks, but there's only one way to fight the wind and that is to just grind away in lowest gear. And I do very much appreciate you allowing me to sleep back of your motel last night. It was great to be away from the road."

I swung my leg over the Doublevision and had a shaky start—all my energy seemed consumed instantly as soon as I pushed the pedal.

"*CLICK!*" I'd forgotten the bottom bracket needed attention, but now I was reminded of it, louder and more threatening than ever. But what could I do? I *had* to get into Del Rio today, to that bike shop. Would I make it? I didn't want to think it, but what else could possibly go wrong?

Then I was reminded of the headwind—it was ferocious! Maybe I ought to reconsider the offer of more food? However, there was something different. The heat didn't seem so hot. Doubtlessly, that was due to a cloud cover. It almost made the pushing pleasant, and I remembered to put on another layer of Sunblock—UV rays easily penetrate clouds and give a painful Sunburn.

So I slowly creaked on, became immune to the clicking sound, gaining enough speed for a higher gear and was soon moving steadily East on that fine shoulder. I might have been pedaling for an hour when my body demanded a break. In my now well-practised routine, I found a close culvert, parked the Doublevision above it on the shoulder, and picked my way into it, escaping the wind.

Not only was my routine putting me into a more ebullient mood, it was the feeling of getting closer to my destination of Del Rio and fulfilling my dream of transiting West Texas by bicycle. My body was telling me that I was close to ending the painful saga of the past week—it was more interested in the promised recuperation at Sirloin Stockade.

Evidence was abundant in the topography and roadworks that were much like of many other similar sites around the world I've visited. It looks almost recent, a nearly unnatural arrangement of scrub land occasionally bordered by dwellings hoping to have, or already have, docks with boats in the water. Graded roads, usually unpaved, cutting toward these structures, or toward where a developer anticipated new homes. The relatively "new" US 90 slicing through ages-old mangled layers of earth strewn as if un-topped pasta had been taken out of the fridge and dumped onto a plate.

Rounding a bend, I gasped at the sight of a beautifully long through-truss bridge that would be my crossing over Lake Amistad. Talk about magnificent structures! I was anticipating pedaling it when disappointment took over because AMTRAK was slowly moving on the bridge. *My* US 90 bridge, like so many before, was a simple post-and-beam construction, had been obscured by the beautiful trestle. A sign advising me (and everybody else) to neither park nor fish from the bridge were appropriate, but where are "Share the Road" signs, especially if this is considered a major U.S. Bicycle route? I was grateful there was little motor traffic on 90, because, like crossing the Pecos yesterday, it was unpleasantly narrow and lacked a shoulder for safe transit.

As soon as I had crossed, I stopped on the right behind construction cones, and got comfortable, removing my helmet and sandals. I had a very satisfying vision: soon, that fatal click would be remedied, I'd eat forever at the Sirloin Stockade tonight, and I'd have a great night's sleep somewhere.

With that dancing in my head, I extracted the peanut butter and a water bottle for a well-earned lunch on the brink of today's goal. The highly viscous peanut butter slowly gummed through my mouth, generously lubricated with ample hot water.

Looking at the trestle, I saw AMTRAK was moving very slowly, probably coming to a stop at the Del Rio station. I distinctly remember that event from our family trip so many years before; the only difference was that it was mid-day, not early morning. I smiled; No change there, either—the train had probably been on a siding much longer.

I already knew about Lake Amistad, its 1969 bi-national creation from damming the Rio Grande for flood control, irrigation, hydroelectricity, and recreation. But right now, as I sat on the cement curb behind a traffic cone savoring my sandwich seeing the water below, satisfaction began to well through me. This was my kind of recreation, pedaling, pedaling, and pedaling. I was not unlike a postman who always delivers the mail come rain or shine or gloom of the night, except my delivery was on a Doublevision tandem recumbent in horrific headwind, heat, and with bedeviling mechanical problems. However, without any kind of shelter from wind or shade from the newly shining Sun, I had to keep pedaling.

The desert scrub was giving way to increase plant and habitation growth. I could see a water tower. And there's a better place to eat—an isolated Exxon station/mini-mart. I parked underneath the generous overhang to enjoy a windscreen and Sunshade, but inside, well, that was heaven. Euphoria swept through me again as I began to enjoy the delights of a big city, after so many days of privation. And I was just on the fringes of metropolitan life.

I made friends with everybody present, including all who entered this fine establishment, regaling them with my trail-tales, handing out personal cards, readily giving comments about my Doublevision, the weather, or anything else appropriate. Following would be a summary of my speech.

"Yessiree, what a marvelous day it is, what a wonderful odyssey I'm having, but I've scarcely begun—on my way to Louisiana, I am, but now no more desert, only flatlands all the way from here," was my general announcement.

Most people were courteous, and most gracious was the receptionist, who not only allowed me to positively interact with other customers, but also permitted me to replenish my water buffaloes with fresh, clean, cold water and ice. Of course, I was constantly buying numerous food items, some of which I knew weren't overly nutritious but were so-o-o-o-o pleasurable to ingest. After an hour or so of this invigorating break, I had to get underway.

My enthusiasm was surely put to the test—again. The headwinds seemed stronger as I pushed on, but I was grateful because it could've been worse. Despite US90 being in a sort of trench—the land rose on both sides—it was greatly improved, with five lanes (the center turn lane separating two opposite flow lanes, while that great shoulder continued). On my left was obviously a small rise before the shore of Lake Amistad, while on my right were all the trappings of more city.

A street light served at the junction of US277, US377, both from the North, with US90 and all three routes combined to form a near-interstate quality, divided highway Southbound. I waved to a Del Rio police officer, patiently waiting in his squad car in a tree-shaded spot in the median. He cut his return wave short to gun the engine and race after an errant motorist. I suspect this area might see a lot of similar problems—the motor traffic has greatly increased.

So after a few more miles, I was not surprised to have to carefully take a lane upon seeing my shoulder lane fully occupied by another squad car and an errant motorist, the former issuing a ticket for an infraction to the latter. What did surprise me was that the latter was an 18-wheeler, life blood of our roadway system. I noted, when passing, no visible markings of major company, just the required information hand-scrawled on the cab door.

I couldn't have been pedaling for more than an hour when I surprised myself by stopping at another Exxon gas-mini-mart. The previous one had set a superb precedent and I expected this to be similar. It was busy at the pumps, but that was not my concern; I wheeled up to the mart and took an entire parking spot with the Doublevision. It might not be quite as wide as a motor vehicle, but it is as long as, if not longer than, many of them.

It was time for some more comfort food, and to refill both water bottles, but it was nothing like my previous Exxon stop. I didn't try to befriend everybody, I merely put fresh water & ice in the plastics, and got into line with a couple of candy bars (Kit-Kat and Skor). The cashier rang me up with another surprise: he charged me for the ice. This did not bode well.

Outside, a man was carefully examining my Doublevision, and greeted me cheerfully.

"Quite a recumbent you're pedalin'," he said, then offered his hand. "My name's Neal. I pedal a single 'bent, but this is the first time I've ever seen a tandem. You're not from around here, are you?"

"I'm John Eyberg aka Juanito Hayburg aka BikerJohn from El Paso, on my way to Louisiana," I said proudly, handing him my personal card. "But first I need to get to a bike shop..."

"Wow! That's some biking!" he said, and began manipulating his smart phone. "Lakeside Sports is where you wanna' go. You just stay on this street for about three miles and look to your left. There's a bike on the roof, you can't miss it. It closes in an hour, so you should have plenty of time."

Impressed with this 180 degree change from the cold (literally!) store inside to the friendly hot outside, I worked on a way to note the dramatic change between the two, and not just in temperatures, I connected with a sign I just saw.

"Are you the Neal who owns this station?"

With a laugh, he replied "No—you're not the first person who's said that to me. Anyway, BikerJohn, it's been a real treat seeing you and it's always a pleasure to help fellow bicyclists. You'll like Lakeside Sports. Tim's the owner, a good guy who has lots of information about the area."

With that, he motored off, North on US90-277-377 while I went the opposite direction, up a slight hill when I smelled it. Sirloin Stockade! I didn't see the distraction because my full attention was required for the heavy traffic. This city riding was so much more difficult than what I had known the previous week of rural landscape. I was multi-tasking—steering, pedaling, watching motor vehicles whizzing by in front, behind, coming off side streets, *and* looking for a bike mounted on top of a store. When I saw it, I carefully veered into the center-turn lane and waited for a break in the oncoming traffic.

An affable young man rushed over to hold the door as I began pushing my Doublevision into the standalone building. With nobody else present, I made a calculated guess, "Tim?"

"That's me alright," he affirmed. "And you are?"

"John Eyberg aka Juanito Hayburg aka BikerJohn, from El Paso on my way to Louisiana," I replied. "I've heard a lot about you, ever since Alpine, where Bikeman John told me you had the best—the only—bike shop around these parts."

"You're putting in some miles, I can see," he said, pleased to hear support from afar. "And you've got a ways to go, but you're through the desert with its few refueling stops. So how can I help you?"

"A quick fix—that bottom bracket needs tightening," I told him. "That's the thing about touring for me, I always think I've got everything then find out the one tool I need is the one I left behind..."

"Yeah, I know exactly what you mean, but its been awhile since I've toured," he replied. Giving his sprocket wrench another eighth turn, he announced, "There you go, good as new. But we've got a person who tours every Summer from here, who is a something of a celebrity. He's a retired guy named Dexter, and has lots of support. You might've seen it on the bank sign coming here."

"You know," I said thoughtfully, "I *do* remember seeing a marquee with 'Go Dex, Go!' on it. Now it makes sense."

"As old as he is, it's amazing that he can do it," he told me.

I was about to remark how challenging it is for me to do the pedaling *I'm* doing, and I must be ten or twenty years his junior as he continued, "His wife drives their motor home and they camp all the way. Everybody here tracks him."

That must be nice, I thought, to get that kind of community support. Maybe I ought to consider re-locating here....no, this is his

115

spotlight and there's room for only one. I'm plenty happy with what I've got.

"We get a lot of bicyclists coming through, but you're the first one I've seen on a tandem recumbent like this, or as heavily loaded as you are. Most of 'em have a sag, kind of like what Dex has. You must be working hard, riding into those winds," commented Tim.

I nodded my head in assent as I fished out a 5-dollar bill for him.

"No, that's OK, it wasn't anything..." Tim protested.

But I thrust it into his hands, "Maybe not to you, but to me, this fix is worth everything. I'll be able to keep on pedaling."

"Well, thanks. Also, it looks like you're going to be here tonight. The Elks Lodge puts up through bikers without charge—just continue East on Veteran's a mile or so to the first left on San Felipe Springs Road, after the country club, then go a long way back. It seems far, but there's a nice quiet pavilion where you're left alone and you can camp free!"

"I'm not ready to camp yet, still too much to do. I see an HEB over there, where I can get some cash and foam for my seat, then I've got to eat—I smelled the Sirloin Stockade back uphill, and I need to get another memory card for my Stylus Tough."

"Yeah," he said with a chuckle, "that's what all the bikers do when they come through—eat 'till their ready to pop at the Stockade. If you go back a little bit more, there's a Radio Shack which can help with the memory card. I'd advise you to take Avenue G which parallels Veterans and avoid all the cars."

I only followed half of his advice, escaping the traffic by pedaling Avenue E, which also parallels Veterans.

And why did I do that?

Because HEB was on the other side of Veterans, closer to Avenue E.

Stopping there was essential. In fact, when I am in Eastern Texas, HEB, along with Subway and Whataburger, became my most reliable means of continuing this Trans-Texas Bicycle Odyssey. All reliable sources of nutrition, I was also able to get cash with my VISA debit at HEB.

Feeling very successful, I pedaled back up the hill, with the scents of multiple restaurants filling my nasal passages, causing me to salivate like a leaky faucet. This time I saw the Sirloin Stockade across Veterans and it was maddening to not stop, but I had to get to Radio Shack before it closed.

My ignorance once again showed itself, as I couldn't quite figure out how to load the new 32-gig memory stick. Myra, the saleswoman-cashier handily flipped my Stylus Tough over, unlatched the bottom slot, popped out the filled stick, and inserted the new one.

After a couple of test pix, I exclaimed "Wonderful! This is a great belated Father's Day—not only am I getting half-off on the memory stick, but you also taught me how to change it out. It might seem strange, but part of what makes this day so fantastic is that I've pedaled across the most difficult part of my Trans-Texas Bicycle Odyssey, US90 from Van Horn to here. It's more like a 'Father's Month' because I couldn't do it without an agreeable wife and being a teacher that allows me this kind of time."

Then, in a boastful-braggart manner, I added, "My turn around is Louisiana—probably don't have enough time to do more than just cross the Sabine River, except this time I'll stop in Beaumont to visit my daughter's boyfriend's mother, into Houston to spend some time with my son and onto Austin for more respite with my daughter before making the return pedal to El Paso in time for workshops on the eighteenth of July."

She smiled, wished me well, and opened the door for me while turning the sign to "CLOSED" —about as clear a hint as possible that it was time for me to quit gabbing and get along. My stomach insisted that I no longer divert from the most important task, eating, I took the fastest way to Sirloin Stockade, East on Veterans in the setting Sun.

Once again, I locked the Doublevision to itself and went inside. Server Darrel welcomed me in, but had to add a small note of caution: "Glad to have you here, but we close in an hour. Help yourself to as much as you can before then."

He hadn't finished speaking when I had already piled my first plate full of perfectly cooked MEAT! My second plate full still included some meat, but I added more side dishes. My third plate full was almost entirely green, the leafy stuff full of vitamins and minerals not available that I had not seen, much less eaten for at least a week. I was also remembering what Ellen had verbalized sometime back in the desert—that I need to be sure to eat vegetables, not just MREs, snack food, and burgers.

By my fourth or fifth or maybe it was the sixth plate full, I don't remember exactly, I had pretty much sampled everything that was out, some items much more than once, and was finishing off with the desserts. It was a grand feast, one that I had earned and consequently was bloated, stuffed to capacity with it all, nutritious or not. I was power-packed and ready to roll onto the free campsite at the Elks Lodge.

Lights blazing, I did indeed roll downhill, past Lakeside Sports, past HEB, past a Valero-Subway and McDonalds, past a Sonic, onto a road of no cars, no trucks, no streetlights, a virtual wilderness. I had forgotten what Tim said, so I abruptly turned around, pedaling back past the Sonic, past the McDonalds, past the Valero-Subway, and into an opposite weight station lot. I'd become skillful at finding nooks where for a night's repose and was starting to lay down when the glare from headlights danced around me.

I looked up to see a green light reflected off the building that provided some privacy, and while watching it, that reflection turned yellow then red, causing the headlights to quit dancing. It turned green and the procession of headlights resumed.

It didn't take me too long to remember Tim telling me about the superb free camping at Elks Lodge, and it became my obsession. Still uncertain, I pedaled next door to the Tejano Shell gasmart for directions. The attendant must've thought I was from outerspace, Skid-Lid atop my head, but he knew exactly where the Elks Lodge was—turn left on the first road after the country club, about a half-mile past McDonalds.

Now reassured, I followed his directions, passing the Valero-Subway, McDonalds, and Sonic for a third time. This time I carefully examined the berm on my left, and took comfort in seeing a turnout for the SFCC. Then I got really excited at the next lane on my left—San Felipe Springs Road, and there is even an Elks Lodge sign.

I pedaled onto this isolated lane for what seemed a long time when I reached another sign that read "San Felipe Springs closed". I didn't understand; where is the Elks Lodge? Frustrated that probably it was no longer accessible, that Tim or the attendant hadn't been told of its closing, I pedaled that long distance back to US90.

I double-checked, and, yes, a very well maintained sign indicated this was the road to the now fabled Elks Lodge. I retraced my route to the San Felipe Springs sign, except this time I looked around. Aha! There is another road, less well kept, veering off to the right! I carefully pedaled upon it, coming abreast a large facility.

I carefully pedaled closer to it, until I concluded that it was a municipal water treatment plant, not a Elks Lodge with pavilion for free camping. Dismayed, I returned to US90. But why is that Elks Lodge sign there? Why? Why? Why? This *has* to be it; I'm simply not looking hard enough!

With new resolve, I biked a familiar path to the plant. This time, I gingerly went farther on an unknown beaten road. *At last!* I found a modest sized building that had to be my destination—Elk horns mounted on an overhang.

Exhilarated, but tired, I looked no farther. The clear night showed a screen of brilliant stars undisturbed by peripheral light. I put out my pad and doused my surroundings with liberal amounts of OFF. Completely satisfied and completely undisturbed, I fell fast asleep.

Overnight Eleven: Del Rio

Hmmfff! Hcckkff! Uugggghhhh! Bllluuukk! Hiiffff!

I startled awake, wild-eyed and gagging, coughing, choking, gasping for any breath I could get. My face was wet; was I being waterboarded? My sleeping sack, pad, Doublevision, the grass, and building were wet. I couldn't believe this—it was raining!

Moving quickly, I started throwing everything underneath a slim overhang beside me, the last item being my heavy Doublevision. Assessing the damp factor, I put the less dry things and my pad closest to the building, while leaving my Doublevision more exposed to take the brunt of the squall. Laying back down, I thought it remarkable; no lightning, no thunder, just a downpour, and returned to sleep.

"Excuse me, we've got a pavilion out back which is much better camping than here, where you are blocking our door."

"Uhhhh," I throated upon leaving a deep sleep. "What?" I asked from a daze, then collected myself enough to know that during the night I had sought refuge underneath the shallow portico, which had the sole purpose of keeping rain out of the doorway.

"I apologize for being in your way, Sir, but it was extremely late when I stopped last night and I wasn't able to make it any farther." Offering a soggy personal card, I went on: "My name's John Eyberg aka Juanito Hayburg aka BikerJohn and I'm pedaling to Louisiana before returning to El Paso for three workshops."

Raising his eyebrows, he commented, "A teacher; no wonder you can be out for so long. Got a good name, too—I'm John, secretary and I need to get into the office to wrap up some work. If you need the bathroom or shower, just knock on the door."

"Thank you very much, but I'll be out of here soon, having breakfast at McDonalds and using the bathroom there." I said. Then, before he disappeared into the building, I added sincerely, "Except for the rain, this is one of the best places I've ever camped. A little hard to find, but once here, fantastic. Thanks again!"

"You're welcome; come on by anytime," were his trailing words as the door closed.

The Sun was breaking the Eastern horizon while I collected myself and my gear. I gave a noisy yawn and stretch, noticing how hungry I was despite distending my gut last night with an abundance of delicious Sirloin Stockade food. Once my Doublevision was repacked, I needed to explore.

I was amazed at how large the Elks Lodge space really was; there was the actual headquarters, which I had camped beside, a large lot with electric hookups for RVs, and, behind HQ in the floodplain of the San Felipe River, was a beautiful large pavilion. I was a bit disgusted with myself for not going a little bit more for what would have been an excellent campsite, and rain-free. Next time....!

But this time, after several nocturnal attempts at pedaling in, I confidently pedaled out on familiar road feeling pretty darn good this morning. Its been a long time since I'd ever been in such thick humidity, and even some condensation was forming on my glasses. The best feeling, though, was a brilliant red Scarlet Tanager, flitting up, down, all around as I myself wove a pattern on the broken pavement.

Only one other bird could have brought me better good will: a Red-winged Blackbird, which had been a constant companion when brother Nils and I pedaled from Missouri to British Columbia in 1982. But that was long ago, back when I was at boot-camp weight, pedaling an upright, and, as I vaguely recall, the glorious Redwing ceased to fly alongside when that biketour ended. Despite numerous other cycle journeys, I've never seen such a beautiful creature since— until now. As if in a dream, the vivid Tanager flew away when my idyllic pedal gave way to conscientious roadwork —exactly when I reached US90.

Sitting inside the McDonalds looking out the front window while sucking down coffee, I could see my Doublevision right outside, then the US routes 90, 277 and 377. The former diverged from the latter two conjoined roads, which went South across a bridge; 90 continued East. Catty-corner, I could see the weigh station where I had attempted to camp last night—was I ever glad to not stay there. Directly across from me was an inviting park, my next stop after refueling my body.

After filling my water bottles, I pedaled across 90 and entered the attractive area (Horseshoe Park) which combined parking, walking, and getting wet—something crucially important during these hot days. It was built around the fluvial centerpiece of the San Felipe River; so many natural attractions always incorporate water, fresh or salt, moving or still, large or small, in some manner. The overnight showers had cooled things off, but this cloud-free day was resuming a pattern of heat—already a hot 90°F/ 32°C, and it was only (09:00). The shade trees provided a measurable degree of comfort as I read the always interesting historical plaques.

It came as no surprise to me that the clean fresh water became an early site for anybody in the area, and, as I had learned in Langtry (and anywhere out here!), this fluid was essential for for all life over the ages, not just the more recent arrival of explorers, soldiers, farmers, and businesses. All persons who could, made a claim upon the springs, and those who controlled it effectively controlled the prosperity of the surrounding area. Much of the water was siphoned off into irrigation ditches from this constant source.

A plunge into that water with other bathers was tempting, but my concern was not getting too comfortable so early—I had a long way to go and knew the day was just going to get both headwindy and warmer. I couldn't start out with the inevitable breaks now!

Pedaling along, I soon discovered that I had entered Del Rio from the wrong direction. A stout granite marker announced the city, founded 1885. Actually, several historical plaques arrayed around a simultaneously functional and intriguing entrance to Laughlin Air Force Base provided the meat of the information about this unique setting. The smooth entrance and exit to Laughlin AFB is a good representation of the beneficial relationship between it and Del Rio. Their mutual support has guaranteed each other's longevity and with the combination of a good climate and sure water supply, both have thrived.

This base had the rare distinction of being named after a person, native son Jack Thomas Laughlin, who was killed in action when the B-17 he was piloting over the Java Sea was shot down in 1942. Congressman Charles South and strong local support combined to earn the pergra for the renaming. However, the Army Air Base was closed in 1945, along with the end of WWII .

But once the connection between this base, flying, Mr. Laughlin, and Del Rio had been firmly established, there was no holding back the intertwining of the entities. In 1952, it re-opened as Laughlin Air Force base with a new lease on life devoted to U-2 reconnaissance, astronaut training, undergraduate pilot training, and other air-related tasks.

While this main access is attractively built, I was not passing through during rush hour. I imagine that at certain times, it is heavily congested. And, if a train happens to be passing through at that moment, the waiting cars would accumulate, along with operator angst!

But I was not troubled, although mildly irritated at my slow progress.

Ah, so what?

At least I was moving and, after all, it *was* a bit cooler from the overnight rain.

Personally, I could have spent another day, or two, or even more, exploring the dynamic bike-friendly area, but the open road was calling. I needed to get under way!

Within an hour, I stopped at another historical marker, this one pronouncing the effectiveness of US90 as a premier route connecting *Baja Tejas* through *Norte Méjico* as the "Chihuahua Road". It's importance was disrupted in 1877 with the completion of the then-newest technology through San Antonio, railroads, (including a far Eastern extension of the *ChePe*) which had a competitive advantage. Regardless that rail traffic is significantly more efficient, the road regained it's value within a half-century when motor vehicles (commercial and private) became the predominant mode of transportation throughout the USA.

No disagreement from me; whether called the *Camino Real*, Chihuahua Road, or US90, this highway is truly wonderful—regardless of numerous challenges to it's efficacy. Remounting my Doublevision, I felt it begin listing to starboard. Incidentally, I have become used to an inordinately large number of listings, and skillfully dismounted in a hurry.

Within a split second of beginning the free fall, it landed and a small angular piece shot out.   Retrieving it, I immediately knew what happened: the right-hand caliper of my new HS33 Magura Hydraulic brake had snapped off. Restoring my Doublevision to its upright position, I considered my next plan of action.

Is this the end of my Trans-Texas Bicycle Odyssey? Should I contact Ellen, or maybe Erik, and ask either to come this way to meet me? Could I continue with just one brake? What happens if the Doublevision goes over again, as it surely will?

My front Magura hydraulic was still functional and, really, the front brake *is* the most important brake. I'd just have to be more cognizant of increase stopping times and distances, especially since I am pushing some 400 pounds/180kgs. I've already completed what has to be the most difficult part of my bicycle odyssey, US90 Eastbound in tremendous headwinds and heat, and the rest of the odyssey should be relatively flat, comparatively speaking. Ultimately, I decided to pedal on; suspending my journey will happen only if and when my front Magura breaks—or I die!

So this is the trade off to finally arriving in East Texas. No rear brake but no more long, steep hills, regular eateries instead of MREs, no more wind, and—this is the prize—a large foam block, which revealed itself during my search for pieces. I folded it over to make for a long-desired and much-needed seat pad. My posterior was pleased!

With trepidation, I carefully set out pedaling East, frequently pumping my left hand, testing the brake for stopping distance and time. Throughout the next hour, I learned to approximate the minimum requirements for me to come to a full and complete stop. Successful stopping throughout the rest of my odyssey will require maximum planning and slower speed. The former would certainly depend upon my physiological condition while the latter was pretty well assured anyway because of the headwind.

I carried on, pedaling into the wind on a fairly level plain filled with more developed scrub trees, frequently sucking down fresh, clean albeit warm water, pleased with my progress regardless that my stopping ability had been cut in half. Then I saw a sign that lifted my spirits even more:

PICNIC AREA
HISTORICAL
MARKER
1 MILE

Exhilarated, I increased my cadence, as well as my heart rate and sweating, soon stopping under the shade of a superb covered picnic table. I didn't need a handicap accessible sign to see the cut curb ramp, and parked in the penumbra of that overhang. Removing my Skid-Lid, I laid on top of the table, closing my eyes while my leg muscles sagged against the radiant heated top.

Sufficiently recuperated, I ambled to the always fascinating historical marker and read about the ill-fated community of Dolores that had once been sited here 1834-6. Land baron John Charles Beales attempted to establish the Rio Grande colony in this area, naming the settlement for his wife. Unfortunately, Aboriginal American raids, drought, and revolution against Mexico concluded this venture. While this history was important, I am most intimately familiar with the current reality—the lack of fresh, clean, water—lose that, and everything is lost!

Knowing I wouldn't take my Doublevision on the gravel access road, I was still curious about the shade possibilities underneath the bridge and walked there. I caught my breath when I saw a large pool of clear water, fed by an intermittent Pinto Creek that had not yet evaporated. Without question, I knew what had to be done: the long practiced rite from my youth of complete submersion! After completing the displaced Ozark ritual, I considered myself officially baptized on transiting across West Texas to East, or wet, Texas.

Returning to my Doublevision more refreshed than ever, I resumed pedaling East from this fantastic resting area!

One to rarely throw anything away, I began planning the return of my broken Magura HS33 hydraulic brake. It was still not yet noon on Monday, and Bracketville was visible on the horizon. Remembering when I had shipped my heavy cable back home from Langtry, I could easily make it to the Post Office before closing time....

Hissssssssssssssssssssssssss!

The fix I had made several days ago with Slime in my rear tire finally quit holding air. I was rather pleased to have made it this far—all the way from Sanderson, Cactus Capitol of Texas. Stopping on the wide shoulder, I elevated my Doublevision by using two rocks from the ditch to prop up the kickstand, which facilitated the removal of the rear tire.

Not to brag, but I am quite experienced at this procedure of removing the wheel, prying open one side of the wheel, pulling out the flatted tube, installing a new replacement, inflating it, and ready to roll within 30 minutes. Throwing the stones back into the ditch, I sat down and rat-trapped my right foot. I pushed off, eager to make it to the P.O.

POIP!

This fix might have lasted a half-minute, a minute at most. Shaking my head, I pulled those two rocks out of the ditch to repeat my previous half-hour of life.

Did I mention experience?

This might be where I have gained my most experience, having to do over what I should have done right in the first place.

Stripping out the tube, Alex, another excellent wrench at Crazy Cat Cyclery, came to mind. He was warning me about this particular tube, that if I overinflate it, the result will be a loud "poip" as it goes flat. Funny, that's exactly what happened.

I grimaced at the memory, especially when I remembered thinking that it would be impossible to overinflate a tube inside a tire that was already stuffed with tiresaver and an old thornproof tube. I didn't take his word of caution seriously then, and now I was paying the price. If frustration and disappointment with my task could have discourteous nouns and adjectives, I surely uttered them.

A westbound car stopped across from me, and the electric window smoothly rolled down. The woman inside declared, "Darlin', it's too dang hot out here to be doin' what'yr doin'. Take this," and she handed me an ice-cold water bottle.

I gladly accepted, twisted it open and took a long gulp. All of a sudden, my task didn't seem so bad. I raised the bottle to her in thanks while bowing my head. She had already rolled the window up, but nodded back and accelerated away.

Looking at my underseat thermometer, I found it to not be all that hot—it was only 88F/ 31C, nothing as hot as yesterday, nor the day before, nor any day yet that I've been pedaling. But it wasn't so cool that I couldn't polish off the rest of that cold water in another long gulp!

While it is true that most bicyclists abhor my kit because of excessive weight, I take pride in knowing that I can almost always keep (solo) touring because of the extra gear. I installed a new BikeNashbar 26-inch self-sealing tube, and the wheel seemed better than original upon finishing. Happy as a lark, I rode away, confidently forging ahead.

It might have been the coolest day I've had yet on this biketour, but I felt hotter than ever. What gives? I saw Brackettville on the horizon, but it seemed to take me longer and longer to get to it, like Marathon. The water tower kept disappearing, and now I was ascending a long hill. Did I really have to go all the way up this thing?

US90 seemed to split into two roads going into Brackettville, with a narrower route 166 going straight at less of an incline while a newer, more spacious US90 veering right and, surprisingly, continuing up the hill. I opted for the easier route despite knowing that the usual eateries were much more likely to be found on the US route but maybe an independent restaurant was available. Thus I pedaled 166, or Spring Street, and it became readily obvious that I was my thinking was correct. I hadn't gone far before seeing local eatery Daddy's Grill, 301 W. Spring Street.

I quickly changed into my "clean" American flag UBS tee, and, while cleaning my hands in the bathroom, discretely disposed of my worthless tube in the trashcan. Of course, whoever takes it out later will know instantly where it came from—that guy on the super-long bike!

The food (including an extra-large Mountain Dew for that caffeine and sugar electrolyte!) was especially delicious, but the real delight was not being assaulted by wind or heat. As delightful and tasty as my respite was, I still needed to keep going. But, since I was out of MREs, my next task was to find a grocery store.

"Super S foods is a coupla' blocks over there," pointed the cashier when I paid. "Go left on Fritter, left on Anne, across from the high school."

I seemed surprised to notice large leafy deciduous trees crowding a number of substantial limestone buildings among other well-cared for wooden homes while pedaling the given directions. I didn't have to go far before seeing the busy Super S Foodstore. I made room for my Doublevision on the sidewalk, crowded with carts, tucking it out of the way beside the building. Going inside wearing my skid-lid, I drew a few stares, but quickly dispelled amusement or fear with my personal cards and garrulous conversation.

One of the interested people was manager John, who followed up the many queries about my situation while the others moved on with their own business. Deeply knowledgeable about the area, he was able to help me resolve my most pressing issue: is there a rest area reasonably close?

"Yes, Juanito," he replied, "an' from what you've been tellin' the others, you'll like this one. It's about five more miles from here on ninety. I think you'll like it."

"Yeah, you will," echoed the feminine voice of Maribel, the cashier. "And now that you've satisfied your immediate needs for now by eating at Daddy's, and since you're out of MREs which have kept you alive so far, you'll definitely need food tonight—there's no restaurant out there. Look at the powdered drinks and dry cereals. I wouldn't bother with anything chocolate—it'll melt into a gooey mess."

I made a rather critical analysis of ingredients, and gave priority to those water-soluble products which were high in calories, preferably composed of sugar/fructose, caffeine, carbs, vitamins, or protein. I returned to the register with Parade Cherry Drink mix, Golden Crisp cereal, Cracker Jacks, Jack Link's beef jerky, and two more gallons(7 liters) of distilled water.

"This'll keep you going," Maribel commented as she rang me up, "but I don't see a toothbrush or toothpaste. You'll get lots of energy, but this'll be rough on your teeth."

"I appreciate your concern, Maribel, but not to worry," I replied. "My teeth are top priority, have been for years, and I also carry floss!"

We both smiled while I bagged my few goods, and carried them, as well as holding the waters by the handles, out to my waiting bicycle. After recharging my water buffaloes, I pedaled as John recommended—East on US90. Fort Clark and Alamo village were both too far off the road for me to consider stopping at either.

I remembered having visiting the latter many years ago with my family, on one of our periodic journeys to Louisiana or Florida or someplace East. It was a film setting, created to reflect a significant event during the War with Mexico, 1835-6. The original site in San Antonio is currently surrounded by cityscape, something difficult to eliminate when attempting to accurately recreate that momentous battle.

The Sun was dipping below the horizon as I wheeled by the blue sign informing me of an upcoming picnic area. Turning left into the parking lot, I noted a compact car parked and, further in, found an amazing accessible double-pavilion, just waiting for me to become the sole occupant. It was so quiet and serene, broken only by the lights and rumble of a a rare motor vehicle passing on 90. True to what I had told Maribel earlier, I thoroughly brushed and flossed my teeth before laying down. My brain and belly were content; I slept.

Overnight Twelve: US 90 rest area

I had been wise in buying the food yesterday at Super S in Brackettville because that was one of the best aspects of my remote camping: the incentive to not stay too long, to keep moving on, always looking for some kind of an eatery for a better meal. And today I would surely make it to Uvalde early enough to mail my broken Magura hydraulic home!

Another positive aspect was the relatively cool early morning, but what was remarkable was the heavy fog. I wasn't concerned about speed since my velocity was already low, but I did stay much closer to the right hand edge of the shoulder, just in case a motor vehicle was wandering. Fortunately, none passed before the fog burned off to a bright day. Very nice cycling on these rolling hills!

An opportune stopping moment came within an hour as the fog lessened, at the historic Sparks cemetery, but what was of greater interest to me were the railroad tracks. It seemed strange that out here, away from any residential or commercial construction, there would be numerous tracks, including two level, signaled US90 crossings so close together. However, once I had read the posted information, it made sense; this was a "wye" or "triangular" junction that enabled trains to turn around. To limit the liability for persons or property, a remote location such as this isolated point was ideal.

It remained relatively cool when I rolled up to one of the biggest Border Patrol check station I'd seen yet. The agents smiled back after I complimented them on their fine building: "This sure beats your trailer I passed earlier!"

"Yep, this is the biggest you'll see to the border," he said, "but we still use the other."

Their smiles grew bigger after some small talk, which included my disclosure about their impending paycaps—should I ever get elected! It was a quick check, and my appreciation for our Border Patrol continues to grow. They are of inestimable value to the USA!

The divided highway sign meant that US90 went from being am excellent 2-lane, well-shouldered route, superior for all kinds of vehicular use, to completely segregated roadways, also very good for all vehicles—although I was very glad that few (motor) vehicles were Eastbound! This upgrade of the roadway was for the sole purpose of crossing the Nueces River and it's floodplain. With Sun high overhead, I felt inspired, even more stimulated to continue doing what I always do when solo touring—talking to myself—and, at this moment, about this remarkable road.

Interestingly, this magnificent piece of engineering had its genesis in **our** want of movement. Ever since we, as *homo sapiens sapiens*, regardless of whether we wanted to go next cave, get from one side of the river to the other, or off this Earth, have been infused with the desire to do so. The rise of industrialization and increased transportation possibilities also gave rise to a vast and complex structure of strategies to assist and aid in "figuring it out". This phenomenal intellectual growth is possibly one of the most documented yet came from one of the least recognized aspects for human advance ever since we have existed: that of getting from point A to point B in the easiest and most convenient manner possible.

Firmly rolling on Earth, I came to a through truss bridge over the Nueces River. In fact, it was *most* interesting! My comfort level increased significantly as I pedaled on this classic 1933 Depression-era project had not been destroyed; it had instead been converted into a one-way lane upon completion of a much more modern adjacent bridge for the Westbound traffic.

Passing underneath the "15FT 5IN" height sign was like pedaling backwards nearly three decades, to Sunday, 10JUL1983.

I was still a year away from earning my undergraduate degree at the University of Missouri-Columbia, and had decided to spend my last "free" Summer pedaling the perimeter of Missouri. On that day, I was Southbound on State Line Road, and had gone into Amoret for a much needed re-supply. As always, I happily discussed with anybody my actions, and, as always, I received much input from locals about road conditions, etc. In this particular instance, I received a dire warning to stay away from Worland, the implication being that I could pedal to there but I might not pedal away.

"Be sure t' retrace yer' route 'cause there ain't no way out," Danny told me through his mouthful of chaw. "Roads all fulla' potholes an' tore up. Be sure an stay off the leftside a' th' bridge, them boards all bad."

I knew what Missouri was like in the sticks, having spent my formative years in the fine state and now this kind of threat? I think not, and returned biking on my intended route, this time with a specific deviation: Worland! How could I *not* go there?

Wheeling on the road wasn't too bad—initially. The finely graded gravel road was easy, as was a well-built functional concrete viaduct over the Marais Des Cygnes River. Then, just as Danny had said, the roadbed degraded into crater-infested washboard. But that paled in comparison to a rickety iron truss bridge suspended over Mine Creek. I stopped to analyze this unbelievable structure, amazed that it was there. Equally astounding, in these remote backwoods, undisturbed by much civilization, resided a peacefulness, a quietude broken only by the herons wading below—and then by the railing squeaking and straining as I slowly pedaled across. Careful to follow Danny's instructions, I stayed to the right on the clattering boards—some of which didn't quite reach all the way to the leftside. The thought did cross my mind that I really am too young to die so far out, yet so close. I safely made it across, and camped the night in Worland. Obviously, if you're reading this, I must have biked out and lived to write it. The details of that episode will be written up in a future book!

So why would the Nueces River bridge even cause me to recollect the Mine Creek bridge, which has undoubtedly been replaced by now?

They are both bridges, with wonderfully strong truss construction of the miraculous building material, steel. While the Mine Creek bridge is likely gone, replaced by functional structure of concrete similar to the Marais Des Cygnes bridge along with road improvements, this similar Nueces River bridge hadn't been destroyed nor replaced. Indeed, big money had been saved by relegating it to a one-way road, for Eastbound traffic only—a common practice throughout the USA.

As soon as I pedaled under the last truss shadow and back onto the safe shoulder, I looked left and saw the new elevated bridge, a solid, functional, characterless concrete post-and-beam structure—very much like many I'd already had the pleasure of crossing, although displeased with the temporary loss of a safe shoulder. In my rear view mirror, I fondly gazed at a receding silver-painted truss bridge, a symbol of Depression-era employment and well over a millennium of engineering wisdom.

It was smart by not building two bridges across the Nueces River—recycle the then "shovel ready" project and pocket the savings. Unfortunately, whatever money was saved did not go into continuing the divided highway, and it wasn't long before US90 returned to a 2-lane, broad-shouldered road. Whichever route I pedaled was OK with me—I follow the rules of the road, and expect all other vehicle operators to do the same.

The Sun was back in full strength by the time I was rolling into Uvalde, much relieved that I was finally going reduce the weight on my two wheels by mailing the broken Magura hydraulic back home. US90 became an extremely nice 5-lane thoroughfare, the fifth lane in the center, designated for double left turns.

I was quite comfortable occupying the entire right-most lane until my stomach ordered me to stop in the driveway where I could buy fresh peaches. The homeowner not only offered me an low price on the succulent fruits, but also to blend them into a frosty drink for me.

"Well, the day sure has warmed up from the fog this morning, and I'll be happy to give you another buck if you blend it again." I told him.

"You deserve it, coming here all the way from El Paso," he replied. "Saw the weather report yesterday, and you guys are gettin' more rain than we are."

"I don't know too much about it—I've been gone for almost two weeks now, but I did get a surprise rain in Del Rio a couple of nights ago," I replied. "And when I crossed over the Nueces earlier, it looked bone dry."

Shaking his head, he added, "It's a real problem, this drought. We're just about to get into stage four restrictions, can't use no water for nothing, and it really hurts the peach crop. What's really aggravatin' is these big commercial farms are gettin' all the water they want. It's not right for us little guys!"

"I can understand, you're not happy with that at all, I sympathized. "But I am glad you gave me some water for this—it's super, and I'll buy another dollar's worth of peaches that I can eat later."

"Leaving out of Del Rio, I fell and broke my rear hydraulic brake. I saved it, but don't want to carry it any farther. Do you know where the post office is?" I asked.

"Sure, it's easy; keep on for another couple of blocks and turn right at the first light," he replied. "It don't look open because of some reconstruction goin' on right now but it is, and you have to go in on the side."

Thanking him, I pedaled away.

Finding the post office was as easy as he had said. I turned right onto South Getty Street, then another quick right on South Lane, where my Doublevision occupied an entire parking slot. Accessing the PO was mildly challenging because of the ongoing reconstruction, but after wending my way inside, I joined the window queue.

"Somethings really fishy in here! And you gotta' be the squid, wearin' that funky headgear!"

I turned to see a smiling, burly man, his ballcap showing that he was a VietVet.

Immediately, I bowed, showing deference and honor to him, declaring, "I'm so glad you made it back alive. I was a skivvy waver and was ordered to Karachi, not Saigon. I didn't get to the South China Sea until seventy-seven, and my only combat was with the First Class."

"Yeah, good for you, it was a real bad over there," he replied, no longer smiling. "I was a Marine at Da Nang in seventy, what a mess."

In my usual style, I attempted to deflect our downer conversation by injecting levity into a general discussion with the crowd around us. I will admit being a tad uncomfortable, and it was a relief to flat-rate my brake back home and get back on the road.

I didn't go too far before finding two extremely satisfying stops.

My first, and longest, was at Evett's Bar-B-Que. I couldn't pass it up anyway—the misquite & beef scent saturated air compelled me to stop. I couldn't believe my good fortune! Owner Janice even gave me a personal tour—her husband had lit off the small tight pit several hours ago. She also made specially prepared combo plate that satisfied my palate and filled my always-empty belly. For an added benefit, she allowed me to keep the Doublevision parked on the grounds while I made a quick run to the HEB across the road for cash.

"Before you go, Juanito," she said as I packed up, "you can mail your postcards up there on your right, by the bank, and you said you really like the picnic and rest areas for camping; you'll like the one three or four miles past Sabinal. Then in a few more miles, you need to stop at Bill and Rosa's Steakhouse and Saloon in DuHanis for a full meal. It's as good as here—I always stop there goin' that way, and it's the same if Bill come's this way. Tell'em I sent you!"

"I sure will. And I'll tell *everybody* about Evett's." I emphatically said. "Thank you so very much for everything!"

Passing by several other fast-food eateries, which would have been satisfactory but I was glad to have stopped at Evett's. Even though she was busy, Janice's personal attention made it worth it, and the BBQ made it even better.

I was surprised at the extended boundaries of Uvalde; it seemed to go on and on and on. But then, perhaps I was just tired out by the late afternoon heat and it only seemed to so. Fortunately, US90 continued to be a superior bicycling route, with all other vehicle users respecting me as I did them.

In Knippa, I found slight shade (any break from the intense Sun is welcome) on the shoulder to park under and consulted my map while munching down on two peaches. I stayed in this sparse community too long, but had good incentive: it was a level railyard, mainline bypass, and switching station. I eagerly bounded across the 5-lane road, Stylus Tough 8000 in hand, to walk and photograph amongst the various track repair and maintenance machines. It made sense to see that so many of these tracked vehicles, specialized for tie removal/installation/ballast tamping/rail correction, were built by Caterpillar—a name I had previously only associated with *wheeled* roadworks—but *railed* roads are the same kind of transportation systems, albeit confined to laid track. What's more, railroads are certainly one of the most effective and efficient carriers of persons and products around the world. Besides, I had been an enthusiastic HO-gauge collector in my youth, so this was a particularly interesting diversion.

Then came a rare delight: two mainline trains meeting headon. It was not a massive collision, but a gentle passing just East of RR1049, where the Westbound freight train yielded to the Eastbound freight train. It was pleasurable seeing this, but served to keep in mind my desire to keep pedaling.

Glad that US90 was still a very decent bicycling road, my joy was magnified at not having a strong headwind, although the heat seemed to be working against me. It took me a couple of hours to get here, only 11 miles/18kms, and I still had that much to Sabinal and half again to the rest area Janice had told me about. Despite my full stomach and peaches from Evett's, that was a long time ago. Even after the recent peaches, I still needed more. Consumption of beef jerky and a peanut butter sandwich put an end my craving, and I pushed on.

I arrived in Sabinal famished, and was overjoyed to find Dairy Queen. With the Sun four fingers up, surely the sugar and caffeine from Mountain Dew will give me sufficient power to knock out the next five or six miles? As soon as I entered, the sweet scents of ice cream, sodas, french fries, and cooked meats in the air overwhelmed me. Laughter and chatter had filled the air like the aromas, too, but all became quiet when I entered. No doubt, my strange appearance— undoubtedly my Skid-Lid added to the spooky look—made some customers step away. Then I took it off and flopped down into a booth, exhausted and innocuous.

After a few minutes rest, I ordered Mountain Dew in the largest cup possible because it came with a free refill, and, heck, I might as well have a meal, too. Before I knew it, the Sun was a half-finger above, and I still hadn't gotten the refill.

The happy banter had returned; apparently this was a girl's softball team who were celebrating an earlier victory. I certainly didn't want to spoil the festivities, but did engage in brief conversation with Karen, who is mom, head chauffeur and part-time coach.

"It's starting to get dark out there, John," she said, "and you may not want to pedal anymore on ninety. It's shabby in many places and there's construction."

"Thank you, Karen. Do you know of a place I can camp around here?" I asked earnestly.

"No, no, you need to ask a local," came her reply. "We're from Knippa and this is the closest ice cream stand."

Going outside and saddling up, I was surprised at how sore I felt, backtracking to the streetlight. A Subway I had missed earlier was closed, but the One Stop was still open, and it became my information point. Parking my Doublevision, I took an entire slot and entered the small store. For some reason, I measured myself against height tape on the jamb, then felt guilty shiver go up my spine.

"Can I help you?" came the cashiers gruff voice.

"Uh, yes, in fact, you can," I turned my attention to him.

His badge identified him as Jeff.

"Jeff," I asked, (he was a bit surprised and pleased to be called by name, something which I've learned is a similar reaction from many people) "is there a park anywhere close-by where I could crash for the night?"

His face brightened, and with a much different tone of voice, he almost sang, "City park? Crash for the night? Sleep? Of course! Take yourself six blocks North on Center Street, right there (pointing out the window) and you'll be there."

"Do you know if the police make wake-up calls during the middle of the night, Jeff?" I asked.

"I doubt it," he replied, "your rig out there looks like you mean business and if you aren't makin' any problems, they'll leave you alone."

"Thanks!"

"Have a good night's sleep, man," were his last words.

I slowly pedaled on Center Street, counting each street that passed under my wheels. At the corner of a expansive area, I continued past a lit-up basketball court and turned onto a gravel road leading into the park itself.

My first goal was to find a darkened area, away from the bright lights. I found a bathroom (always a necessity in the morning), and close-by were four large, heavy duty, industrial strength grills. While distinctive scents filled the air, the darkest area was between the grills on a cement pad. Looking around, I was too tired to go farther, parked my Doublevision beside the grills and put my Z-rest next to it.

While brushing and flossing, I watched a trio of adolescents playing a rough-and-tumble basketball game and was reminded of my own youthful attempts at basketball. I couldn't dribble or shoot, but I sure could stand underneath the basket and grab any balls that came toward it. Soon enough, they tired of the game and left. I, too, was tired and returned to my own campsite.

Laying down, I completed my last task—soaking myself and surroundings with OFF. This kept the carnivorous insects from checking out if my old meat was as delectable as that which had been grilled and dripped earlier. A toy Yorkie barked me to sleep; it'll probably be a horse if it continues.

Overnight Thirteen: Sabinal

Indeed, I woke to a ragged sounding *perro*; surely I was not the cause?! The park in dim morning light revealed much more than what I had seen late last night, which makes perfect sense. What amazed me was a near-duplicate courthouse of Judge Roy Bean in Langtry, also close-by. This version was similarly identified as "Law West of the Pecos", a serious mistake as it was quite far *East* of the Pecos—at least four days pedal away! However, it served other purposes, such as the Ranger Headquarters, possibly a clubhouse of sorts for the local youth.

It was very nice, but I had to get going—this was my opportunity for a good early morning start, and planned to pedal into San Antonio later today!

Unfortunately,when I weaved onto Center and began retracing my route back to US90, my nose, in collusion with my stomach, held me up. At the cross street of Peters, the smell emanating from Connies food truck caused such a rebellion against leaving the area that I could go no further. Making a huge 18-wheeler turn-around in the intersection, I parked beside her chorizo-scented wagon. She was happy to take my order, although I had to wait, my GI tract growling in anger at the delay of gratification.

All purchases here are "to go" and as long as I informed the intestinal rebels that chowdown was minutes away, it was easy to resume pedaling. I wanted coffee to wash the breakfast tacos down with, but it was too early for Subway to be open, so Jeff's Place (One Stop) was more than satisfactory. Not only was the java excellent, I went healthy with a Minute Maid orange juice while sitting in the booth. Now I was feeling quite good and spread bliss with kudos about the seating, Jeff's park recommendation, the DQ, and Sabinal in general.

Contentedly underway, I soon realized the wisdom of DQ Karen's words. US90 was not only shabby, it was downright dangerous in many places, where I had to swerve off the shoulder into the traffic lane—and still had to be conscientious of the potholes, cracks, chippings, and other debris.

The divided highway sign was an important prognosticator of improved roadwork, and I actually sped up—maybe moving along at a big 8 or 9 mph/13-14kph? Passing the last rest area in Texas on US90 Eastbound, the temptation to visit was strong, but, heck, my progress was good and I had ample water, why disrupt that? Besides, stopping would mean delaying entry into San Antonio, my goal for today.

My immediate goal, though, was Bill & Rosa's in D'Hanis, which Janice recommended. She had said their food was just as good as Evett's and my stomach is starting to express itself! On the edge of town, US90 East shrank from a divided highway into a 5-lane Main street and I slowed down, looking to both sides for the eatery—no way was I going to miss it after her glowing recommendation!

D'Hanis and Knippa are excellent representatives of how nearly all communities throughout history were founded: the ballast as a primary means for commerce, which in this case was the railroad. The traditional business district was aligned parallel to the tracks and US90, both crucial elements for transportation of goods. That single factor can make or break a town; it reminded me of Langtry or Dryden, which became more derelict when the railroad was re-routed away, in addition to the technological improvement from steam to diesel locomotives. Regardless that steam is now passé and no longer a critical and frequent stop, water is always required by humans. I pedaled by the still-relevant water tower, which provides the most essential part of any development at all: a reliable source of the fresh, clean, life-giving fluid.

Moving my eyes 180° to the Southside of US90 is the less business developed D'Hanis, although I did see Valero and Exxon stations. Looking left again, I saw the tracks and forest.

What?!

I can't be leaving town now, I have to eat at Bill & Rosa's. How could I have missed it? D'Hanis is tiny.

Confused, I pulled into the Valero station and parked alongside the Pico C-store. Not wanting to disclose my concern, I nonchalantly entered the store and discretely ambled to the reefer units. Maybe some POM wonderful was available?

But, no, too bad, I really needed to eat something more substantial, something from Bill & Rosa's Steakhouse.

"Anything I can help you find?" asked raven-haired Clarissa, one of the attendants.

Totally unlike my usual social persona, I stammered, "Uhm, well, uh, yes, do you know of a Bill and Rosa's Steakhouse? I've been looking everywhere..."

Clarissa, and her fellow worker, equally ravishing Virginia, burst out laughing.

"I know it's hard to find anything around here," Clarissa said between gasps of breath, "lots of visitors are always stoppin' to ask directions!"

Virginia, fairly well recovered from hysterics, said, "It's a half-mile back. Go to th' light, turn right, cross th' tracks and to your left. You can't miss it."

"Go all the way to the light," Clarissa said with a quivering lip and a tear of mirth dripped from her eye. "Be sure to not turn at the first right..." and then she lost it, giving a belly-laugh like I've never seen.

"S-s-s-o-o-o-o-r-r-r-y-y," she said, trying to regain her composure. "I'm not makin' fun of you, it's just that we get a lot of questions like that from out-of-towners."

"Nothing to be sorry about," I told her with a big smile. "It is kind of funny, but I'll bet it's also kind of a sad commentary on the visitors. So I sincerely thank you ladies. If you hear a two pipes from a whistle (I showed them the one strung around my neck) later, you'll know it's me."

Following their directions religiously, I stopped on Sacarosa Avenue in front of Bill and Rosa's Steakhouse and Saloon, gazing at the overhang, decorated with strands of icicle lights—I wouldn't have missed it at night! After parking the Doublevision in the shade, I met the scent of well-Q'd meat before meeting the exquisite waitress-owner Sharri.

I would have regaled her with tales of pedaling from El Paso, but my mouth was preoccupied ; she was busy helping other customers anyway. That didn't stop me from assailing an unaccompanied woman Jois, who had entered a half-hour after my own entrance and was now seated at an adjacent table.

She calmly took in everything I said, albeit my information was delivered more staccato-like between bites. Abruptly standing up, she nodded to Sharri, then said, "OK, Bikerjohn, it sounds like you've had quite an adventure. I'm with the Anvil-Herald in Hondo and we might be able to use it. I'd interview you now, but I need to follow-up on two stories, one in Old DuHanis—you do know you're in New DuHanis, don't you? This town was relocated to here in eighteen eighty-one when the railroad bypassed the original site a mile East. The cemetery is especially interesting, as are the ruins. Hondo's the next town you'll be goin' through there; take a left at the third light, cross the track for two blocks, we're on the corner across from the police station. Please stop by. But I need to go—I've already been here too long. Maybe I'll see you sometime, do take care."

Eager to not let this chance escape, I held the door for her, then confessed, "Not only am I a real gentleman, but my ulterior motive is to show you this, my Doublevision tandem recumbent. I'd give you a ride on it if you weren't in such a hurry and it wasn't already loaded down."

The heat didn't stop her icy reply, "I am not that much of a load. But I do have to go. Granted, you will be easy to see. Bye."

After settling my account inside, I returned to pedaling East, whistling as promised at the Valero girls. Despite my excitement about an interview, I slowly covered the 3 miles/5kms to Hondo, my sluggish movement due to digesting massive amounts of delicious Bar-B-Que! Slow as I was, being gorged was an excellent reason to pass several more fine eateries until I reached the third light, Avenue K.

I pedaled over the tracks and North to the Anvil-Herald office, where I introduced myself, giving out several personal cards. After a slight delay, Missy and I had a pleasant conversation; she took notes and a few photos.

"So are you biking for a cause or organization or, well, why are you doing this?"

"I'm not tied to any specific organization—too many variables that can knock me off a schedule—although, as you can see on my T-shirt, I'm a regular platelets donor to UBS and push donating to UBS, or Red Cross. I've a daughter in Austin, a son in Houston, and since I'm a teacher I have the time for this long journey, and, most importantly, my wife agreed that this was the year to go," I said, then continued. "As you saw with my card, I bicycle as much as possible but it's been two decades since I have had a good, long distance tour. What's important is that I can do it without hurting myself—so far! And this Trans-Texas tour is really part of my plan to pedal around the World."

"I've never seen such an unusual bike. Did you build it yourself?" she asked.

"Not hardly; it is a Doublevision tandem recumbent, built by Advanced Transportation Products in Seattle, but I bought it through Tandems Limited, Birmingham, Alabama. And, I did not pedal to or from there—yet—but picked it up while motoring through to visit family in Louisiana and Missouri. In two thousand, I was thinking that we—my son, who could pedal his own back then, and my daughter would pedal with me on this—would biketour the West coast, from Victoria to Tijuana. Unfortunately, those plans never came through, but this 'bent is too expensive for me to not use it. Actually, it's pretty good because I'm able to load it up with all the gear I need."

"Two more questions: how much did it cost, if you can divulge the amount. And it looks awfully heavy—do you know the weight?" she asked.

"It cost plenty—I had to go on a payment plan," I responded, evading a dollar amount. "And it *is* heavy—I've been on the scales at Jobe Concrete. I was surprised when they told me four hundred pounds (181 kgs), but I'm half of it. The rest of the weight is on the rear seat and rack. Missy, when it starts to go over, I've gotten sensitive enough to jump off and let it fall. In fact, a couple of days ago, when I was East of Del Rio, I was stopped at the Chihuahua

Road historical marker when I couldn't get sufficient traction to pedal and it started falling to starboard. You see, that's why I don't have any pride because..."

She rolled her eyes, finishing the well-known phrase, "...because you're always falling!"

"Exactly!" I exclaimed, "But this time, it landed on the caliper for my fantastic Magura hydraulic brakes and broke it right off. The last thing anybody wants is to be on the road without brakes, but I still had the front Magura hydraulic, and that really is the most important brake to have—as long as I'm careful! So here I am, and I'll look at getting another rear in Houston, which ought to be easy since it is a major port."

"Well, good luck on the rest of your journey, and we may be able to put this into the paper," she said. "I'd like to see how you're able to get started. Be safe!"

We both waved as I easily pedaled away, feeling quite good. Pleased with my first interview ever, I'm looking forward to seeing this article!

She had suggested that I go one block over to read a historical marker that summarized the founding of Hondo and exploration of this area. Although the marker was very specific, it occurred to me that it was not just a local story. It was an individualized but oft-repeated tale of how most places around the World became inhabited: opportunity convinced people to locate, endure hardship, prosper, and stay. Or endure hardship, suffer, and not stay, depending upon future events. In the cases of Dolores or Dryden, the events conspired to cause no or little residency. In the cases of Knippa, D'Hanis, or Hondo, the events combined to make stable, if not thriving, communities.

Scarcely outside city limits pedaling East, I saw a private road going North, not unusual, but under the tall gate, I saw farmer's stand. At last! Farm fresh eats, guaranteed to be good because the point-of-sale is so close to the point-of-production. I've always found these to be the best source of energy as well as information. I quickly pulled in, parking my Doublevision in the shade.

A young woman was busy delving out baskets of recent pickings: corn, chard, small peaches, and zucchini.

"Put nine in that one," I overheard an older man say.

"Why nine?" I asked her.

"Because that's what my father said," she replied, "and he knows the price exactly."

I looked at him, seeing a man who was perhaps about my age, looking at a sheet of paper then punching numbers into a calculator.

"It's nine because," he looked up briefly, "I know how much water has gone into producing the zukes, the peaches, lettuce, and corn. Besides our labor, that's the most expensive factor—there's just been no rain this year and the price for piped water has gone up. What you're seein' here is at the end of all we've got for now. So, if you want the box of zukes, it's two dollars. In fact, all the boxes are two dollars, but the amount in each vary dependin' on what it is. And I'm barely breakin' even."

"Two bucks is a great price for farm-fresh produce," I agreed, handing over the cash. Now speaking directly with her, "I see you've got a volleyball jersey on; play much?"

"Oh, yeah," she squeaked, smiling brightly, "I love the game and I'll get to play varsity this year!"

"So you're practicing, are you?" I queried.

"Yeah, all the time," she responded.

I asked, "And you're not violating UIL or anything?"

"Oh no, it's not regulation play or anything like that," she said without a hint of alarm in her voice. "Definitely nothing sanctioned by school."

"She's a darn good player," her father spoke up proudly. "Justine keeps up her good work, she'll get a scholarship. She's going to need it—if this drought keeps up, I won't be farmin'!"

"Family support makes all the difference," I said, "and it sounds to me like you're a state champ! You'll go far, Justine!"

"So how far are you going?" she asked me.

"I can't believe I didn't introduce myself!" I said in shock. "Here's my personal card; I'm John Eyberg aka Juanito Hayburg aka BikerJohn, a teacher, and I left El Paso on the eleventh of June, right after Project Celebration and some sleep. Some people have questioned my sanity—heck, Justine, there have been moments when *I* have questioned it—because I began this solo bicycle odyssey across Texas in the *afternoon of a triple-digit day.* My original goal was to visit with my son in Houston, cross the Sabine River, turn around in Louisiana, and pedal West, overnighting at the home of the mother of my daughter's boyfriend in Beaumont, spending Fourth of July holidays with my daughter in Austin, visit with a friend in Wimberly, and return to El Paso. My intention is generally staying parallel to eye ten, South of it while Eastbound, North of it while Westbound. But I now may have to revise my route because I'm incredibly slow—I've had lot's of mechanical problems, the unbelievable headwinds, the heat, and the dryness."

She stared at me as if I was crazy.

It was time for a bit of levity.

"In other words, Justine, my brains have been dried, fried, and sky'd by the headwinds and heat. But I persist because my legs and knees are cooperating. It's been a good twenty years since I've had a decent long-distance biketour and I'm proving, to myself if nobody else, because *I can still do this.* All too soon, I'll get really old and may *not* be able to pedal. Do you understand what I'm saying?"

"She might not," her father spoke up, "but I do. I congratulate you, and hope you make it!"

Justine looked at me blankly, then said, "Good for you, and I hope you make it, too."

"Thank you both," I replied. "And I know you'll become a top vollyball champ and even be a great representative for the USA at the Olympics!"

She beamed while we waved to each other as I returned to pedaling East on 90.

My enjoyment of cycling across the mildly rolling terrain was heightened when I was able to do what I do best: assisting another person. I stopped to render aid to a lone motorist, who had parked his SUV straddling the paved portion of the shoulder where I pedaled and on the outer graveled portion. With the rear door raised, he looked fairly comfortable lounging in the shade reading a textbook.

"Interesting place to read a schoolbook..." I began, when he clarified,

"Out of gas, so I figured might as well make good use of my time."

Extending a hand, he continued, "My name's Steve, and I'm a student at St. Mary's."

"My name's John Eyberg aka Juanito Hayburg aka BikerJohn," I clarified, "and I'm a teacher from El Paso, pedaling to Louisiana and will see my children in Austin and Houston before returning. I sure wish I could help you out, but the only fuel I'm carrying is for my personal engine."

"I've got it covered, my uncle's coming out soon," he stated. "That's quite a machine your powering; I can see it's a tandem, but it doesn't look quite right."

"Oh, it's plenty right, all right," I said. "It's a recumbent with underseat steering—lot's of people are confused by that. I'd give you a ride on it, but, as you can see, your seat is occupied."

"Yeah, I can see, but thanks for the thought anyway," he replied. "And thanks for stopping—you're the first person who has."

"I've been helped by a multitude of motorists who have stopped for me," I told him, "and I will always stop for others. What goes around, comes around. Now I'll go! See you!"

"Yeah, that's right. See you, too," he said, with a wave.

The rolling hills had become longer and steeper when, upon cresting one, I looked out onto the town of Castroville. It was a rather steep downhill, and not one I was felt especially well-prepared to go down with just one brake at that moment. Much to my pleasure, a roadside park was sited on the North shoulder, surely just for me! The accessible cut-curb allowed my Doublevision a spot beside the picnic tables, and the historic marker gave me information about this unique town while I ate the last of my zukes, beef jerky, cereal, and cherry drink. More power to my left hand, which will be receiving much more use, especially when I brake going down the hill.

Coasting down, I was pleased to not be blasted by the wilting force of hot air which had been nearly a daily occurrence. The electronic marquee of the Broadway Bank showed a temperature of 95°F. Ecstatic about that good sign, I pushed on, crossing the Medina river and saw a most un-Texan structure, the Alsatian Steinbach house. Undoubtedly one of the building constructed to reflect the origin of the immigrants from the Old World, it was "A touch of

Alsace, France." Visiting that *région* will have to wait—my Trans-Texas Bicycle Odyssey has priority this year.

That visage tied right into the street names, which were from around the world. And if that wasn't pleasant enough, I crossed FM471 and was starting to ascend when my nose unerringly picked up the tell-tale scent of great eats.

As I continued to pedal, the scent faded.

NO! I had to find the source!

Careful as always, I signaled my intentions then wheeled around to another building, similar to the one before but larger, and the marquee gave it away: Haby's Alsatian Bakery.

So what if I had just eaten a half-hour ago at the roadside park?

That was just a snack, now it was time for some real food.

While looking for preferred parking, I found a beautiful mural, and obvious depiction of the founder and beginning of this gracious community. Finally, I parked my Doublevision in the shade and the air was filled with the mixed aroma of baked goods, sweet and serious. The atmosphere became saturated whenever the door opened and closed—which it did frequently. I saw concerned-looking people entering, and happy looking customers exiting, bearing bags of cakes, pies, breads, or whatever. I could hardly wait to get inside.

Had I died and gone to one of those rare places of supreme joy?

Not only was my smell assaulted by an distinct flavors emanating from certain sections within, but the temperature was amazing. It felt as if I had stepped into the Travel Center back in Langtry; all I could do was melt into a chair, suddenly exhausted but simultaneously excited. I had to investigate everything, compelled to find each unique treat shedding it's olfactory persuasion.

Ultimately, I gave into a loaf of pumpernickel.

Unfortunately, no meat was available to go with it, but I had seen a Super S store a short ways back, and knew I could get the filling there.

I started coasting through the adjacent Shell station parking lot when I saw a Subway shop tucked in the far corner. Already familiar with that fine restaurant and not particularly wanting to backtrack, maybe I'll just go there first...

Turning the handlebars, I leaned in that direction as well.

That eerie feeling of being out of control came over me as the Doublevision kept going straight.   Gravity rules, and I pitched over.

Gee, I hadn't fallen since yesterday!

Since my pride had left years before, picking myself up was easy, then my Doublevision. Fortunately, the fall was to the right, same side where the Magura was already broken. This time, though, the break had to do with the underseat steering column. Decidedly, I'll go to Subway first, pushing the Doublevision there and parking it for good visibility. Repairs can be initiated *after* a much needed, good meal!

Subway sandwiches are exceptionally good and nutritious meals, always fresh, fast, and inexpensive. Besides the superb food, another huge benefit for me is that the dispenser on the ice machine meshes perfectly with the orifice of my water bladder. This is fantastic! I filled all four bladders with ice cubes, topped off with clean, cold water—that irreplaceable, most intoxicating of any liquors, such an essential elixir of life!

Always a regular, healthy, must-stop—whether bicycling or not!
(www.juanitohayburg.com)

Mike and Connor were the young men in charge of this Subway, who, after expertly delivering well-crafted chipotle chicken & cheese sandwiches—one to eat, one to keep—with guacamole for an extra buck, went back to the constant maintenance required to keep the eatery open and up to the standards required to meet health department criteria. In my professional mode as a work-study coordinator, I not only praised them for their obvious strong work ethic, I also discussed their futures and paid employment. They were demonstrating what all employers want: reliability, competence, professionalism, and friendliness, which are keys to success, regardless of whatever position they pursue, whether continuing on here or other work. Both expressed a desire to taking on a new challenge, such as attending community college within a year or two, but the current need was to save money for tuition.

Then Mike gave me critical information regarding my immediate future: "Yeah, ninety gets really bad the closer in you get to San Antonio. You oughtta' bypass it if you're goin' to Louisiana—take Anderson Loop. I drive it everyday, an' it's really decent. Once on the other side of San Antone, take back roads to Gonzales to ninety-A because ninety runs into eye-ten an' you don't wanna' pedal that!"

"*You* are the reason why my bicycle odyssey is going so well," I replied gratefully. "I get far more pertinent information from locals like yourself than this general road map of Texas. Thanks!"

I turned my attention to the pressing issue of getting underway, currently not possible due to the handlebar slippage. Upon closer examination, it should be an easy fix: just tighten the bolt. Well, it would be an easy fix if the handlebar was *overseat*, but these are *underseat*, with access greatly reduced by the closeness of the Maxxis Hookworm to the handlebars. Sure, I could take the wheel off, but that means deflating the tire, popping the Magura brake from the mounting stud, removing the wheel, and finally using a 6mm hex wrench to tighten the handlebar.

I was in no mood for messing with the front brake—it has been performing exceptionally well since becoming my only stopping tool. And I for sure didn't want to mess with the front tire—it also had had no problems since that dastardly Milano flat back in El Paso, 13 days ago. Then there is the usual confoundedness of both removing and reinstalling the wheel to the fork; historically, it takes me longer to fit it correctly.

Aware that I could ruin my Park Y-tool, I carefully angled it into the bolt head, tightening right up to almost rounding the hex. Now for the test...

I sat in the thickly-padded sling seat, balancing with my right foot on the sidewalk and my left hand holding the single brake steady, I released it and pushed off. Turning the handlebars left along with my leaning, the Doublevision went exactly as I directed. Success!

Carefully watching the traffic, I crossed the Westbound lanes of 90 into the center-turn lane, and, when no other Eastbound vehicles were speeding up the hill, I took the right hand lane.

Traffic had increased in both directions, but the commuters streaming out of San Antonio were exponentially greater. Adding to my relief was the Sun's position—low on the Western horizon, **behind** me and other vehicle operators. All of us Eastbound on US90 would not be blinded by the Sun, but, I guess, it is possible that a Westbound operator could become disoriented and swerve wildly into oncoming traffic...! Anyway, despite bicycling during one of the two most dangerous times (the other is Sunrise), my route was safe and clear, but I needed to find a campsite soon.

On the Western edge of Bexar County, I took Montgomery Road exit, for the sole reason that it appeared to be quite remote and isolated because there was no gas station, no shops, no reason for other vehicles to exit. It was positively good in another way—once beyond the ramp Montgomery Road was little more than a gravel path, and there was only building present: Mr. W Fireworks, along with several closed stands.

It was better than good; due to the drought, burn bans were the rule, thus fireworks could not be purchased nor even made. The threat of a fire was too great in a parched region that had little water to spare for dousing a conflagration. Wheeling up to Mr. W Fireworks, I parked my Doublevision on a superior sidewalk and rolled out my Z-rest.

While brushing and flossing my teeth in the fading light of a red-tinted dark sky, I thought of the many, many similar Sunsets I'd seen over the previous decades, particularly when I was aboard ship. Yes, this was land and the horizon was not perfectly flat, but no matter; it was a glorious Sunset for an edge of the world, quickly racing into the shades of waning quarter-moon twilight before several hours of darkness. It occurred to me that the other half of the world was in daylight as that gray edge was receding just as quickly. Undoubtedly, there were people who, like me, were enjoying this inevitable physical process albeit they were seeing the beginning of day as opposed to the end of day I was witnessing.

Looking in the opposite direction, a similar penumbra of light rimmed the Eastern horizon, which I knew to be the peripheral lights of San Antonio. I felt relief at knowing that I wouldn't be pedaling into that crowded asphalt and concrete jungle, that, after discussion with Mike, Anderson Loop, 1604, was going to allow me to effectively skip around it. Sure, I might miss some decent eateries and showing off my Doublevision, but it was the 24th of June, six days away from my turn-around date, and I wanted to at least cross the Sabine River before going West!

According to my state map, I had about 300 miles/480kms to go; according to my Beta-1 cyclecomputer, I had pedaled 53.18miles/85kms today. Quick calculations proved that I could do this fairly easily—provided I get cool days like today and none of those vicious headwinds. I could do this! It is possible!

Mere words fail to convey the grandeur of the scene or the immense feeling of impending success that had swelled up inside of me. I laid down, closed my eyes and thought, "This is PERFECT!

OVERNIGHT FOURTEEN: US 90/ MONTGOMERY ROAD

Car tires crunching on the gravel woke me. Staying still, my hand slowly moved to my Shimano bicycling sandals, where I had carefully posited my glasses. Donning them, I raised my head enough to see an unbelievable scene. Judging from the running lights, two *big* cars, undoubtedly SUVs, had parked beside each other, positioned so that the drivers could roll their windows down for conversation that didn't include me.

I just hoped it wasn't *about* me!

Admittedly, I was tempted to rush over, offer my personal card, strike up a friendly conversation, ask them if they needed assistance, and just be me. However, this was something I'd only seen in movies or on television, which prejudiced me into thinking that perhaps I ought not make such an introduction. In fact, the chill that ran up my spine convinced me to continue laying low—I won't bother them if they won't bother me.

Of course I was bothered by that ominous scene, but what really bothered me was Mr. W Fireworks. Parked in front of a door, lights from inside squeezed out from around the jambs. Why on Earth would the lights be on? What is happening inside this building that required lights? Is somebody inside? Or is somebody, say, somebody in either of those cars, wanting to get inside, but a bicyclist and his Doublevision are blocking the way? Is this fireworks factory just a front for something much more deadly—like meth production—

occurring inside? Or was it going to occur? Had I, in my ignorance, interfered with some massive drug deal?

Suddenly, the cars roared off, spewing gravel around, some of which landed closeby. Still confused as to why the lights of Mr. W Fireworks were on, I carefully stashed my glasses again and fell asleep.

Gravel crunching under car tires woke me *again*. I couldn't tell if they were the same vehicles or not except they were similarly big SUVs, parking in near identical positions as the earlier ones but closer to me. The lights of Mr. W Fireworks behind me were still on as I grasped my glasses. Frowning, why didn't I move when those other cars took off, at least away from the entrance? I was certain that I was the topic of the motorists' conversation—I was really interfering with the drug operations now! I was keeping them from getting inside, where they could cook meth, yet here I was—*still*—costing them big, albeit illegal, money. Or maybe I was witnessing a drug hand off, though I didn't see anything, but they weren't going to take any chances and have to get rid of me somehow? After another tense hour, these two vehicles roared off into the dark night, gravel spewing, except this time a few little stones made it to me. I flinched, feeling something more like a mosquito bite. OFF definitely wouldn't work.

Wait! Maybe those were Border Patrol agents checking on me, making sure that I was OK? Yes, that must be it! They've been watching over me ever since I began this biketour...

No, I realized and became crestfallen, if it was Border Patrol, they would've already spoken with me, fulfilled their duties of investigating everyone and everything awry in the border zone.

Now's my chance to relocate, go somewhere that was more out of the way, somewhere that I won't block the entrance to Mr. W Fireworks, somewhere.... I fell asleep.

A distant rooster woke me. I wasn't ready to get up but had to after seeing a gray band on the Eastern horizon. It was time to go—still cool and there was no wind. After gathering myself up and having a small breakfast of cereal, beef jerky, and water, I resumed pedaling East on US90. This was a lovely, pleasant experience, few other vehicles Westbound or Eastbound, and I was anticipating the junction with 1604 and a food stop quite soon—hunger was starting to gnaw in my belly!

The expected road signs only served to whet my appetite:
LOOP
1604

Followed by:
Sea World
Fiesta Texas
NEXT RIGHT

Anderson Loop
EXIT ½ MILE

Towering overhead were high-voltage transmission lines, along with promising billboards, a subdivision, and the Texas Department of Criminal Justice: I was in suburbia!

Then the development seemed to disappear, and I was once again pedaling beside brown fields with intermittent trees scattered about. Delight should have filled my heart—along with food filling my empty stomach—as more road signs showed me that I could go North on Loop 1604 to Sea World and Fiesta Texas, and my actual route, South, on 1604, Anderson Loop.

This should have been a major intersection, but it was not; no truck stop, no food store, and no go at a red light! Skirting a gravel apron that had a few motor vehicles parked on in a semi-arranged order as if in an auto sales lot, I grimaced when at the thought of going seven more miles (11kms) junction with I-35. No matter; I continued to pedal, resolute in the belief that surely *that* intersection will yield what had been so sorely lacking here.

Fortunately, the topography was rolling, and 1604 was very decent bicycling—a very limited number of motor vehicles were on the road. There appeared to be more outposts suburbia, but, like my first encounter at the last intersection, they too disappeared.

Some development, as well as the obvious overpass, made it clearly unmistakable that I was approaching I-35. There, on my right, is a Valero Station. Food! But I smelled a breakfast that was not Valero. Passing underneath I-35, I saw an Exxon station and—*yes!*—Burger King.

Maybe I was wrong? I circled it twice; it looked too good to be true. Or was I delirious, having gone too long without a proper meal? I carefully took the slot beside the disabled space, using slow measured movements as if it, too, might disappear like the other faux suburbia sites.

Going inside, manager Priscilla greeted me royally. Apparently I was the first customer of the day, and I was ready to gorge myself! More followed within an hour: Kim and Troy; Lee and Andy with their son Ty. Not only was my body regaining vital fluids and nutrition, my brain and mouth also loosened up as I made friends with the passersby.

Sufficiently full both physically and socially, I set off once again. While 1604 remained a cycling treat, I had at least two times the distance already pedaled to get out and away from the sphere of San Antonio. Worse was that now I was *again* battling those horrid headwinds and heat.

Thank goodness I had low gears! I crept forward, observing the dry, mostly barren trees and shrubs. This scorched earth almost looked like El Paso, in the Northern reaches of the Chihuahuan Desert. At one point, I sought refuge under a broad Live Oak, its massive limbs providing shade and shelter. Ironically, pedaling out from under it, I hit a surviving mud puddle. Rather, my rear wheel slogged into the hardening muck, lost traction, and down I went. Checking the machine, I found all conditions A-OK and remounted to press on. The previously ice-choked buffaloes had long since given up all coolness, but I was glad to have fresh, clean albeit warm water to drink.

By early afternoon, the I-37 overpass loomed ahead; but it seemed to be awfully far away—I was pedaling steadily and slowly, incrementally getting closer. Much to my relief, to my left, like an orange-and-white lighthouse, was Whataburger. Even though I was most of the way there, it seemed to take forever to pull up beside it, park, and go inside.

It was all I could do to sit down and rest my head, gasping as if I had just pedaled a century in two hours, leaving my sweating body drained. The merry background music and din of of the other customers left my ears; I must've fallen asleep. Looking up, I saw the Virtual Tourist flag and other pennants on my fiberglass pole wavering perfectly horizontal in the wind. I groaned—the headwinds have gotten worse! And the heat! How could I got back out there, from this wonderful air-conditioned space?

It would take energy—a lot of it. I had to eat—a lot.

Desiree, Santos, and the dynamic Whataburger crew could tell what I was up against—they had seen me pedal up and park, come in, collapse at a table. I struggled to the register and placed my order: nothing less than a double meat with grilled onions & double cheese, onion rings substitution, and a super-thick vanilla milkshake—just like I like it. What was really nice was the special attention they gave me—not that they didn't give that to everyone—but they made me feel exceptionally welcome. I discovered something else that made this stop significant: like Subway yesterday, the ice dispenser fit the orifices on my water bladders perfectly.

Another must-stop—whether bicycling or not!(www.
juanitohayburg.com)

I was particularly grateful to them because every time I considered continuing my biketour, the wind appeared to gust so much as to bend the pole a bit more, and felt an unspoken encouragement to "stay a few more moments". They *knew* the challenge I was facing, especially after I gave them all the details about my Trans-Texas biketour. It was pleasurable to continue eating, as I attempted to slowly ingest and enjoy every bite. That was a futile effort—I was ravenous, with the only enjoyment being that of stuffing myself with meat, bread, fries, vanilla shake, and lots of water.

Unfortunately, the wind only seemed to increase, but, after a couple of hours respite, I felt recuperated enough to push off, albeit a bit unsteadily. Once underway, I could tell that my muscles and body had become more conditioned to the grueling work. The memory of my second day out, the century/160kms between Fabens and Van Horn now seemed amazing, and the reality of the third day, the scant 50 miles/80kms between Van Horn to just South of Valentine, seemed equally amazing. Headwinds and heat were now regular and even expected riding partners—tolerable as long as I had a mid-afternoon break with lots of shorter respites throughout the day. In East Texas, my thoughts were no longer absorbed with concern about running out of fresh, clean water or food, but I stayed focused on going forward, always forward.

I was extremely pleased with 1604. It is an exceptionally broad, four-lane road and I saw why: farm equipment such as the slow-moving combine toward me taking up most of it. Since I was moving in the opposite direction, all I needed was a slender amount of the pavement for safe passage, something readily available on 1604. I mention this because it was similar to a circumstance that occurred on a much smaller road when pedaling in Czechoslovakia in 1981.

I was on my A-D, brother Nils was on his Diamond Back, and, in an extremely dangerous maneuver, we both had to duck under an exceptionally wide, waving grain header that took the entire roadway and then some. How lucky we were to not get injured or killed.

Other than the combine and a few other motor vehicles, 1604 was virtually deserted. I enjoyed the rolling hills and surrounding countryside, much of tilled and waiting for desperately needed moisture. Stopping in the slender shade of a scraggly tree, I heard an ATV roaring in the field across the road from me. Looking toward it, I saw a light brown plume of airborne dirt streaking away behind its wheels with a woman and man hailing me from the seat, while their well-muscled farmdog barked endlessly.

I've grown accustomed to people (and virtually all dogs!) curious about this most strange contraption beneath me. They knew it was something on two wheels, but unsure of where the engine was and why there were no obvious emissions.

Indeed, it was that uncertainty that caused a motorist, Ms. Barbara Brown, quarter-horse breeder of AnthonyNM, that motivated her to pull over in front of me. She was Westbound on US62-180 when I had just finished repairing another flat tire (5 on the rear within three hours) some 35 miles/56kms East of El Paso when I saw her white, beefy, double-cab duallie pull over in front of me. I was on the second day of my annual Irene's Pedal, this time a vuelte este to Dell CityTX-Sierra BlancaTX-San EliTX-home. Much earlier today, while pedaling into the Sunrise, I had figured that the ancient tube-tire combo on my Doublevision was doomed to repeated failure from roadside debris and returning home was my best choice. However, the despised backtracking meant fighting a strong headwind and continued flats; if anybody stopped...!

I approached the driver's side to find Ms. Brown had rolled the window down to discuss my plight. But I already knew my decision, and literally told her that I'd hold my Doublevision in the back, could you please drop me at Montana and Global Reach? She initially thought I should ride in front along with her yappy dogs, but relented when I assured her that my riding in the truck bed was now legal. That hour-long ride was a blessing—it would have taken me 2 or 3 days return if I had to pedal into that wind.

A single recumbent is an unusual enough bicycle, but a *monotube* tandem recumbent, my Doublevision? People were intrigued by it and wanted to talk to me, not always the other way around! Am I lucky or what?

Of course I was going to speak with the ATV couple!

It was such a pleasure to meet these two farmers, who, like Justine and her father, are true dirt -under-your-fingernails, leathery-skinned individuals (not young Justine) with fine time-wizened wrinkles who have had a lifetime of working the fields. They displayed the honesty and wisdom that comes only from living the direct relationship between effort, food crop production, and animal husbandry.

"We saw the combine an' then you," Connie half-yelled.

"Yeah," Ed followed up with, "it's good to see you made it with no trouble."

"We've seen a lot of bikers on this road," she resumed, "an' you're the best yet. You really know how to share the road."

"Yeah, usually it's a pack of 'em an' they don't give nothin' to nobody, even if it'd be better," said Ed. "You're the first one who's not been obnoxious out there!"

"Well, you make a real good argument for why I detest riding with more than two or three other people," I replied. "I know exactly what you're talking about and I hate it. They have a mob-mentality and start breaking a few rules, then more and more. What's really infuriating is that because we have a right to the road, they don't understand that our right is to *share* the road because we don't stand a chance in a collision with a motor vehicle; it's simple physics. So while I take a lane, I'll be happy to give it up if someone in another vehicle is determined to take my space. Fortunately, most people using the road don't want to be involved in a crash, especially if it means someone gets killed, and knowing that can make some bike riders even more audacious."

They were shaking their head in complete agreement, but wanted to know more about me and, of course, the Doublevision. I enthusiastically recited my itinerary and the reasons behind it. Now it was my turn to be the curious one.

"Tell me," I asked, "how is it possible that you can have such brown grounds but I see those huge irrigation pipes over there, on your side of the fence?"

" You don't see any irrigation pipes because those are only risers for the water lines into the San Antonio," said Ed.

"It's big money deliverin' our ground water to all those water-wasters in the city," chimed in Connie. "an' bypassin' us completely. It's a crime. Why, if we can't use the water to grow our farm, all the water in the world comin' outta' their taps won't feedem'. You can live for a while, but not forever on water alone."

"Yeah," agreed Ed, "but their tryin' to make'em more careful—they're in stage three restrictions right now, but we practice economical water use all the time. That's the difference between bein' rural or city. It's hard work bein' out here, but we wouldn't wanta' live anywhere else."

With a wry smile, he added, "Yeah, it'd be kinda nice to be able to have a valve on those pipes to get a little bit of the water, but...!"

"I can understand what you're saying," I nodded with my head up-and-down, "my own city and area is about a million people, and the El Paso water department has claims on groundwater a hundred miles East in farming country. No thought whatsoever has been given to the people living on the surface who might need some of that water, too."

"Hey, why don't you stay the night here?" Ed asked.

"Yeah, it'd be real nice to have someone else around to talk with, like you." Connie echoed.

Holding my hand on the horizon, I shook my head no, replying, "Thank you so much, but I've still got at least two more hours of ride time. And, like I said earlier, I've had too many short days due to mechanical problems and now that I'm not having any, I've got to put in as much distance as possible if I want to get to Louisiana. So, thanks, but maybe you can tell me where the closest HEB..."

"Sure!" Ed spoke up. "It's about eleven more miles (18kms) after turnin' South on one-eighty-one an' you're there."

"Even better," added Connie, "there's a Whataburger in it's parking lot. If you liked the one back there with Desiree and Santos, you'll like this one, too."

I felt a pang of regret at leaving their amazing hospitality, and, even though the wind had let up a little bit, I simply had to move along. Louisiana was pulling me.

Impressed that I was making fairly good time, I turned South on US 181 and found this road to be just as bike-worthy as 90 and 1604. The broad shoulder was beautifully wide and I had no trouble staying far away from the motor traffic lanes, although I did have to exercise caution when crossing intersections—this was *not* a restricted access road.

A hulking pick-up pulled in front of me and a wiry young guy got out of the driver's seat to greet me when I stopped behind it.

"Man, yer lookin' fantastic! Tell me all about yer," he insisted.

Pleased to once again tell my story, I went through the well-rehearsed litany.

Then, out of nowhere, he began telling me *his* tale of woe, and woeful it was. Step-parent problems, his stay in a hospital, bouts with the law, and, yes, he'd like me to hear more of what he had to say. So we agreed to meet at the HEB, and his parting words were, "I'll be waitin' for yer, havin' a beer, holdin' yer seat. I'll clear the way, make sure nobody's gonna' give yer any problems."

No matter how much I gladly engage with people, something about this individual didn't feel right. The more I thought about it, the more concerned I became, when I realized that if I was going to have problems with anybody on the road, it was *him*. I resolved that upon seeing him, I'd tell him to go away, that my single greatest fear on the road are people like *him*, people who will have a bit (or a lot!) of alcohol in their system and perhaps not be able to respond appropriately behind the wheel of a motor vehicle. In fact, *he* could become a murderer—he could kill *me*—if intoxicated and/or under the influence of other drugs. I could not, would not, condone his actions.

I knew the risk of telling someone that *she/he* is the problem, that she/he cannot outsource responsibility for it to anyone or anything else. I devised a strategy: gain his confidence by telling him that I, too, had an alcohol problem when in the Navy, but I learned from my mistake and had been on the wagon for over three decades. It is possible to become successful in life. He *had* to do that, too, because boozing was not a solution to problems but only exacerbated them.

Or maybe my luck will continue and he won't be there. Wouldn't that be nice, not having to deal with this yo-yo at all? But, I'm ready for whatever awaits me. I turned on my head and tail lamps, then pedaled up another short hill into Floresville in less daylight because the Sun had descended below the Western horizon.

Connie and Ed were absolutely correct about the HEB and Whataburger, but they couldn't have known how satisfying it was parking the Doublevision on the South side of the HEB garden section. With a growing hunger inside me, I went inside to find Oscar, who expertly helped me buy provisions—specifically, in the deli section— and my to-go dogbox was filled with rice and chicken, along with more beef jerky, something easy to chew while I pedaled. Checking out is one of the most important parts of my HEB experience—using my VISA debit card, I maxed out cash ($50) obtainable.

Amply supplied, I returned to my Doublevision and pedaled around the area a bit, looking for anyplace with a bit of darkness where I might be able to rest undisturbed—by the authorities or the disturbed young man who was "holdin' a seat fer" me. I was greatly impressed with a neat little park area at the junction of US181 and Texas 97, and, despite a certain lack of privacy, the proximity to Whataburger more than made up for it. I gazed at the sign while my body appreciated the dogbox of wonderful HEB food I had purchased a short while ago, and was followed by mandatory brushing and flossing. This was as far as I wanted to go, even though the risk of disturbance was very real—more so than any other places I've camped so far.

OVERNIGHT FIFTEEN: FLORESVILLE

My slumber was not altogether so bad; the motor traffic really did dissipate through the wee hours and, shockingly, nobody bothered me. I had actually rested rather well, all things considered! Maybe my Virtual Tourist flag was responsible? Now it was time to cash in overcoming the potentially problematic circumstances—I pedaled across 181 to Whataburger. The outstanding service of this fine restaurant, under the leadership of Dean, Ignacio, and Norma, continued the model of efficiency, compassion, and effectiveness as I was ready to roll within an hour. I was fully energized from not only Whataburger, but also, as always, from contact with locals.

Specifically, I met fellow Whataburgians Linn & Sue, and regaled them, along with several other patrons, details about my bicycling odyssey. They, in turn, were able to advise me concerning East Texas. My original route had been to remain on US90/South of I-10 while pedaling East to Louisiana, but had altered it following discussion with Subway Mike in Castroville.

"And now that I've been able to circumvent the hassle and hazards of city cycling in San Antonio," I told them, "Subway Mike also strongly recommended that I could pick up a good road, ninety-A at Gonzales after taking back roads. On my map, I can see a winding ninety-seven is about as direct a shot as there is; can you tell me about it?"

"We aren't from around here...," Linn began.

"...but we're retired teachers and we travel these parts a lot...," continued Sue.

"...and Subway Mike told you well—it's a flat road with a few curves to there...," added Linn.

"...with a shoulder all the way, 'cept for a short stretch above Nixon..." said Sue.

"...where you can get a great lunch at the Taco Ranch Cafe, too!" finished Linn.

"Thank you so very much for telling me about the road." I replied, pumping their hands.

Without saying so, they had also told me that they'd been married for a very long time.

Pedaling Texas 97 East was not a bad road; in fact, the shoulder, as they had said, was outstanding; delightfully broad, debris-free, and safe for bicycling. However, when Linn stated that it was a "flat road", skepticism fluttered through my brain—"flat" to a motorist is very different from "flat" to a bicyclist! The road was reasonably straight, but it was more like Western Missouri, with long stretches of sometimes nearly imperceptible incline and decline, lots of passing possibilities—if in a motorcar. On my Doublevision, though, my legs signaled when going up or down as pedaling would fractionally become more difficult or easy, respectively.

At one point, I wanted to contact my wife, and stopped on a crest where visibility was unimpeded. When my phone wouldn't connect, I was surprised. Here I am, not 3 nor 5 miles(5-8kms) out of Floresville, where I had excellent reception, yet here I could not pick up a signal! And there is a cell tower within a stone's throw! I couldn't even send a text message, to neither Ellen nor Twitter! I was extremely unhappy with our carrier, T-Mobile. Maybe merger with AT&T will improve service?

After another hour of pleasant cycling, 97 merged with US87; the shoulder and roadway improved significantly, to near interstate standards. At Stockdale, I was sorely tempted to cycle into downtown, but it was Sunday, what would be open? Besides, I had plenty of food and water with me; stopping would only slow me down even more. Still, I'd never been in Stockdale, and if that well-kept water tower was any indication, it would be well-worth my time. So inspired, I turned on Main Street.

Then a triple-whammy. I saw a church parking lot jam-packed full of cars and knew downtown would be closed. I attempted another cell call, to no avail—T-Mobile reception was unbelievably terrible; it was non-existant. Then the windless early morning became a windy mid-morning. At least the partial cloudiness kept the temperature from soaring. Spirit sagging, I grimly accepted fate and made a broad U-turn, returning to Eastbound 97/87, looping around town.

About the time I reached Pandora, 5 miles/8kms further, the clouds had burned off, temps were increasing, cold water in my buffaloes had become hot, and I was fatiguing in mild but steady South wind. I applied extra Sunblock to the right side of my crispy body.

Six miles/10kms later, in Nixon, I perked up at the sight of the Taco Ranch Cafe. I really shouldn't have been hungry, but it seemed like a long time since the Whataburger in Floresville, and I had been pedaling pretty hard. Why, yes, food and a break, now that's the ticket!

I parked in the shade in the back, then entered the closest door. It was refreshingly cold inside but surprisingly snug. Seeing only one table, I took a seat and looked the place over more closely. Cigarette smoke lingered inside as other patrons arrived and carried on conversation between them-selves and the hostess. I guess smoke-free places are strictly determined on a local level. Apparently, the wait staff was on lunch, so I meandered over to the hostess and told her that I'd like to order the same sandwich she was having.

"You're in the wrong place, *Señor*," she said indignantly. "You need to go over one—and you'd better hurry; they're about to close."

"*Oh!*" I said in the biggest surprise of the day. I scurried out of the bar, going next door to discover closing wouldn't happen for another half-hour, and reparked the Doublevision in slim shade in front. What a huge difference as I put my Skid-Lid down on a table off to the side. The air was just as cold and bracing as the bar, but completely free of smoke. Numerous tables were available, each with a menu, and I hungrily anticipated joining what several patrons were already doing: eating. Ignoring the namesake, I had wonderful tasty enchiladas, chips, iced-tea, cake, and, of course, icy cold water—which also recharged my water buffaloes. I was extremely pleased to have the cash from HEB yesterday and not rely so heavily on my VISA charge card.

This fine restaurant was an unexpected benefit to my arrival in Nixon; my original intention was simply to find out why the name? Especially during August 1974? What were the repercussions, if any?

I turned left, off US87 onto state routes 90-97, I saw a mural that explained it all. A portrait of Robert F. Nixon, founder, along with that of a train, a longhorn, and a chicken. Although I saw no chicken farm nor cow, not even a railroad, and certainly no RFN, I understood it. Long before Tricky Dicky, RFN developed the area based on ranching and farming, along with a train service. Over the passage of time, motor vehicles became the dominant transportation scheme—I did share the road with 18-wheelers, trucks, and cars, while Nixon adjusted to the progress, it's population rising and falling accordingly.

One thing that continued poorly was the lack of cell phone coverage—T-Mobile couldn't even roam to pick up a carrier; very frustrating. Even when I pedaled a short ways out of town and parked as close underneath a tower as legally possible, I could not get a signal. I was beginning to think that perhaps my old snicker-style cell phone had finally lapsed into utter technological uselessness. Was I going to have make use of yet another flat rate box to mail the bloody thing home?

My annoyance turned to fear when Texas 97 split off from Texas 80 and I was pedaling a reasonably paved but narrow two-lane road with *no* shoulder. It was almost as bad as when I had cycled old US63 between ColumbiaMO and RollaMO, the difference being that 97 is not nearly as winding as 63. On the latter, I remember having to nearly pull into the ditch when any motor vehicle whizzed passed me, whereas on the former visibility was immensely better, thus allowing adequate safe passage. Unfortunately, because it was Sunday, there were far more 18-wheelers and fewer 4-wheelers, those operators probably cognizant enough to stay off this road and leave it for the big rigs to run. Fortunately, the tractor-trailer operators are quite professional and knowledgeable about road use, sharing it with a vehicle that is a minuscule 200 times less their mass.

This road remained a challenge until I pedaled into Cost, and, since I always stopped at historical markers, the brown sign beckoned me. Not expecting this at all, I was almost shocked, and I am a former Texas History teacher!

This is the gateway to where the world-famous, climatic Texas Revolution began—the shot heard around the World. A most massive sculpted granite marker reminded me of a mausoleum, bearing a copper plaque depiction of men bravely standing over a small cannon, ready for combat. Summarizing the inscription, locals defying a return policy by the Mexican government fired a cannon on 02OCT1835, beginning events which ultimately resulted in the juggernaut known as the USA.

What caught my eye were the first two words—NEAR HERE—I still needed to pedal 1.5 miles/2.4kms on spur 95 to the actual site. Despite the headwinds and heat, there was no way I was going to pass up the chance to see and be in *the* fabled place that has been such an enduring pivot point in history. That familiar degree of uncertainty and expectation, something I've always had from never knowing exactly what was around the bend, over the hill, past the bridge, river, or railroad tracks, grew inside me pedaling the pleasant blacktop downhill, passing a jogger and his daughter.

At the bottom, the road encircled another monument, this time consisting of a flagpole flying the national colors over the Lone Star flag with a granite stone beneath. The headstone had been inscribed:

HERE WAS FIRED THE FIRST GUN
FOR TEXAS INDEPENDECE
OCT 2, 1835

———

ERECTED BY THE
CHILDREN
OF GONZALES
CITY SCHOOLS,
APR, 21, 1903

Looking around, I saw a house—apparently a private residence—but was disappointed to not see a kiosk selling the usual kind of trinkets: fridge magnets, postcards, miniature cannons (especially since there was no cannon anywhere, and it's ownership was the contentious start of war), flags of Texas, and other relevant what-nots. I did see, though, where the pavement continued through a thicket of trees. Surely that must be where another marker, designated the Mexican position until the shot forced a retreat?

Passing a trash can (*not* for household garbage) and other large signs, I instead found a boat ramp descending into murky brown water—definitely not like the clear-running Pinto Creek I had immersed myself a few days ago. In fact, it reminded me of decades ago, when I, along with childhood friends Bubber and KJ, had innertube floated the Dry Fork to it's mouth on that fine Ozark river, the upper Meramec. I shivered at that thought and backed away. The large signs informed me that this water was part of the Guadalupe--Blanco River Authority, and, although it is *extremely* hazardous to do so, it is for our use—enjoy safe boating! I'm thinking that this is somewhat a mixed message.

This is similar to the Rio Grande/*Rio Bravo* in that prior to damming and channelization, the Guadalupe River too, would have been meandering and flooding. I now stood close to a stagnant oxbow, a cutoff, with no real flow except for possibly when water is discharged from upstream dams.

Then I imagined 176 years ago, with many more people gathered with a stream of shimmering water between two distinct groups: inordinately beautifully dressed Mexican soldiers on one side, poised to enforce the rules, while on the other were somewhat grubby-looking, rough clothed men hovering around the famous cannon, some bearing muskets or swords, refusing to cooperate. They probably weren't waving buzzing mosquitoes away like myself—the pesky insects weren't out yet in early March. However, the colonists were likely sweating like me—they were under tension, I was under the Sun.

Camping here for the night was possible—I had plenty of supplies and it is a most historic site—but two other factors had to be considered: the Sun was several palms up in the sky, and, darn it,

Louisiana was still at least another couple of days hard ride (Hadn't it been hard enough already?) away. Once resolved to get along, I pedaled back to 97, which, predictably enough, was uphill and against the wind!

A combination Shell gas station and restaurant at the junction of 97 with US 183 was a welcome stop. Yes, I had plenty of emergency food, but the temptation of a meal prepared by someone other than myself was too strong. Parking in the shade, I peered through the window but saw no one dining. It's Sunday, they must've closed this section down. Walking around to the main entrance, I learned that the restaurant was not open but there are plenty available just up the road, in Gonzales. I did purchase a Heath Bar—after all, I didn't want to feel guilty about using the bathroom and replenishing my water buffaloes with fresh, clean, icy-cold water from their dispensers.

Pedaling now was delightful, upon a truly flat, wide road with ample shoulder and a tailwind, too. The countryside was largely agricultural, although I crossed a swampy, even green, park-like area before turning off onto a road that led into suburbia. The temptation to stop at a Dairy Queen and an HEB was strong, but I needed to put in distance—I *had* to get to 90A. After coming to an intersection with Spur 146, I turned North, almost certain it would take me there.

What I didn't know was that this was a historic street, and inevitably made multiple stops. Not only did I admire the private, ornate mansions to my right, (Can I discretely hide myself tonight in those bushes or behind that fence?) but two significant structures on my left.

First was the Eggleston House, carefully preserved *au naturel* in an attractive, manicured setting behind a wrought iron fence. The bronze plaque revealed fascinating details such as it's being one of the first structures built in Gonzales after the town had been razed during the Runaway Scrape. It's initial construction/subsequent renovation came from the hardwoods lining the banks of the Guadalupe River; and, although no contemporary construction parallels it, this two-room, dog-run home was considered a mid-19th century frontier model.

Moving two blocks North, I was flabbergasted by the second structure, a well-kept truss bridge spanning Kerr Creek. It had to be one of the most beautiful spans I've ever seen, and most strongly reminded me of the Mine Creek bridge I crossed many years ago in Western Missouri. The biggest difference, other than location, was that the Mine Creek bridge was infinitely more deteriorated, still used by vehicular traffic, while this span before me was restricted to pedestrian-use only.

The bronze plaques clearly identified it as the Oak Forest Bridge and used to span the Guadalupe River for access between the county seat (Gonzales) with more remote communities (Oak Forest and Monthalia) in 1914. Parking, I luxuriously strolled across it, examining every aspect of it's construction, literally counting rivets, bolts, and planks in the wooden deck. I felt a profound joy with this preservation knowing that the foresightedness of Gonzales (both city and county), Gonzales Historical Commission, Texas DOT, and the Federal Highway Administration attracts young, old, adventurers—and bicyclists like me.

In between these wonderful sites was a memorial, but the Sun had set, limiting the light for me to easily read the markers. My bike lights work exceptionally well to make me visible in darkness, but not necessarily to read by. Which is just as well, because, unfortunately, this exquisite area was a little too pristine for me to overnight in, even discretely. I pedaled on, anxious to get to 90A before total darkness.

A short distance later, I breathed a sigh of relief when Spur 146 T-intersected 90A. Even more relieving (pun intended) was an Exxon Station, which, while not a Subway, Whataburger, or HEB, would satisfy my minimal requirements. Surprisingly, it was named "Lexington" (Another same-named site in Massachusetts is considered where the American Revolution began-coincidence?), as was the adjacent motel. Torn between spending on a room—I'd have to stay on the ground floor to accommodate my Doublevision—and risking the authorities requesting me to relocate from a "free" site, I chose the latter. I had had extremely good luck so far, especially last night in Floresville, so maybe my luck'll continue?

Overnight Sixteen: US 90A/spur 146

I was indeed lucky—again—and was undisturbed, but I didn't overstay my "free" site. Breakfast at the Exxon Station was filling (another pun), but I needed to get underway, having only put away 69 miles/ 110kms yesterday. There was no wind (yet) and knew that I *could* make it to Houston today! Then while tweeting, I was surprised to hear my Nokia cell beeping an incoming message.

It was Son Erik; I immediately returned his call. He was curious about my location and route. During our conversation, he doubted that, based upon my pace since departure on 11JUN, I'd be able to cover the 130 miles/206kms in one day, especially if headwinds came up. Additionally, since he and his fianceé, Ankita, were leaving for the holidays, beginning 01JUL and thought that I should focus on going to Houston instead of Louisiana where I could have a respite in his apartment. He also suggested the convenience of such a plan if I wanted to visit with Katy in Austin over the 4th of July.

"I know you've been pushing pretty hard," Erik added, "and it won't hurt for you to rest up before going West."

"Good points, to be sure," I replied. "and I'm already heading more in your direction than along the coast." I looked at my map and added, "I could go from here to Eagle Lake, then take ten ninety-three into Houston. If all goes well and I show up tonight, it'll be easy for me to go onto Louisiana, cross the Sabine, then immediately turn around and head West—I'll make it to Austin in plenty of time."

"The key word is 'if'," Erik said, "according to your daily average, you won't be here tonight. *IF* you make it tonight, fine; but I'll plan on you tomorrow night. See you then."

The terrain became a series of low rolling hills, but at least 90A was a superb bicycling route with broad shoulders, although the bridges, just like US90, were narrower. After crossing one of those skinny bridges, I stopped at a historic 1936 centennial gray granite headstone, inscribed with details about a nearby San Houston Oak tree, where General Houston had made temporary headquarters while fleeing the Mexican army in the Runaway Scrape. I sorely wanted to pedal the ⅛ mile/.2km gravel road, but it was not a fine paved road like the one to the first shot of the Texas Revolution, and, even though there was little wind, I'd be returning into it, which had increasing velocity as the day got longer. I pushed on.

Fortunately, traffic was light, and by mid-morning I was in Shiner. At the intersection of 90A with state route 95, I saw my salvation: Snowflake Donuts. Now, I can live for a while on donuts and pastry, but what made the difference here were colaches and other more substantial food. I kind of made myself at home, ordering and eating several nutritious breakfast sandwiches—besides the namesake and chocolate milk infused coffee. Or was that drink the other way around?

Not only was I revived by the great food and drink, but carrying on conversation with numerous other patrons also elevated my feelings. I needed it all, too, because when I pedaled out of town, the headwinds had increased significantly—almost as if on cue. Not yet entirely withered, I pushed on.

When 77A from the South merged with 90A, I stopped for a moment to analyze the intersection. I'm not sure why, because I wasn't innervated to the point of not being cognizant. However, a half-hour later, I passed Janak's Country Market. Then I caught a whiff of beef jerky, and realized that my supply was nil. Besides, I might even find some postcards or other easily portable knick-knacks.

Returning to this bright store, the scent carried me right to the front counter where I was waylaid by an assortment of dips and sauces of local origin, along with crackers to sample them. Oh, definitely a purchase was going to be made, but the question was, which one?

Or two? I stayed a bit longer than anticipated—such a decision is not easily made without a thorough tasting—and ended up buying two sauces, one cheese, and a box of biscuits to go.

This was truly a country market, a cavernous building with a high back wall mural of the lush surrounding area with a stream flowing through it. I noted that a white-tail deer and an eagle were prominent features in the landscape, and that gorgeous bird was alighting upon the branches of a tree. Was that the same tree which, no longer living, now preserved inside Janak's? I went up the open stairwell to a balcony where these most amazing quilts abounded. I couldn't stay there—the accumulation of scents spiraling up from below drove me back to the samples—would I buy more?

As I began to remount for departure, a woman had stopped just short of parking on top of me and my Doublevision. I quickly pulled the Doublevision to the side to make room for her car. After she parked, I continued my service by opening her car door, escorting her to Janak's, and opening that door for her.

"There are a lot of Janak's around here—all family, you know," she said, "but this is the nicest because of your gentlemanliness. Thank you."

The compliment was all I needed and happily returned to the road, exultant. Pedaling into Halletsville proper, my mouth dropped open. I'd forgotten to buy any jerky, my original reason for stopping at Janaks! Then I saw the Jalisco restaurant, and figured just as well, I'll have lunch, albeit a little late.

After taking my usual full parking slot in front, I stepped to the building side and discretely changed from my smelly biking UBS tee into my slightly less smelly non-biking UBS tee before entering the restaurant. The aroma was overwhelming, the service impeccable—Rudy made sure of that. Despite other mouth-watering temptations, I had to have the wild Quail. Back home, my friend Robert is an expert auto tech/business owner of McCrae Car Care, but his passion is also as an avid hunter who had long regaled me with stories about flushing coveys of quail which later became the tastiest meals. Now was my chance to enjoy the delicacy; besides this being a special treat, here it was at such a low price and so close to the source. I do try to support local businesses as well as supporting the local environmentalists using one of the best remedies for overpopulation. The biggest benefit, the same as all of my previous mid-day stops, was to be out of the headwinds, heat, AND to replenish my water buffaloes with fresh, clean, icy-cold water from their pitchers.

The headwind *may* have diminished somewhat as I pushed on, silently counting off the distance in Spanish. Within an hour, I stopped under the shade tree at Red's Bar, Sublime. Time for another break! Going inside, I nearly swooned as the cold refrigerated air swept over me, turning my muscles into quivering ripples. It felt so good! Also good was the rush from the caffeine and sugar of Mountain Dew and ice creams. Best of all, Christian, the owner, gave me water; "This's the best around, from a thousand feet down."

"Exactly what I need to keep my engine from overheating," I told him. "Left out of El Paso a week-and-a-half ago, I'll be stopping in Houston either later today or tomorrow to see my son. He told me that if I take ten ninety-three out of Eagle Lake, it'll put me in real close to him."

From the dark recesses of this cool tavern came a surprise, in the form of barely audible growl.

"If yourn' goin' Eagle Lake, be careful. Lot's of darkies there."

"Yeah," piped in another higher-pitched slur, "don't even stop there. You'se too white. Gonna' getch'ur throat sliced up good."

Then, as if telling each other secrets, I could hear the four mumbling to each other their own personal problems with people different than themselves. Actually, I was relieved to no longer be the topic for being saved from sure death by these narrow-minded bigots. Their wrong-headed thinking is a certain recipe for disaster and death.

"Don't pay them no mind," Christian said, "that's just likker talkin'. Your still got a hunnert miles to go. If you can make it, Eagle Lake's got a real nice park, but if not, there's some good campin' around the Colorado River, an' with no rain, it's sure t'be a dry road t'the bank there, or you might try the rest area."

Thanking him, I pushed back onto that wonderfully wide shoulder of 90A. I enjoyed the solace of this pedaling. I could hear birds twittering in trees, and even see a few flitting about the sky despite the heat. Ahead of me, it appeared that the roadway had suffered major damage, but as I drew alongside the area, it was the remains of a tire.

A *lot* of that tire re-cap was strewn all over 90A, but I didn't see any 17-wheeler around. This disintegration must have occurred quite recently as the hazardous stuff was still close to the center line—the first time I've ever seen a shoulder or bike lane so usable *because* of debris not yet having dispersed to it.

I stopped after passing it, parked, and walked back to pick up all the scrap, depositing it into neat piles beside the roadway. I did this not necessarily because it was a magnanimous act on my part, but because it was also an act of self-preservation. Should any motor vehicle moving on 90A at high speed (or any speed, for that matter), the operator would swerve to avoid colliding with the scrap. Such a maneuver would inevitably mean steering where there are no tire pieces—the shoulder. What if I, or some other hapless person, should happen to be on the shoulder at that particular moment?

It's all simple physics: impact between two masses will reposition energy from the greater mass to the lesser mass. In other words, a bicycle has a fraction of the mass of a motor vehicle, yet it will take all of the impact energy, often destroying the bike while barely scratching the car or truck. That also means the operator of the bicycle could suffer serious and significant injury.

I know from experience, having been in three low-speed collisions with motor vehicles. The first two occurred during the early '80s in ColumbiaMO, the third two years ago in El PasoTX. Had any of those collision been at a higher speed, I probably wouldn't be capable of writing these words—for obvious reasons.

The headwind and heat were unmerciful, but I pushed on, grateful for these long Summer days of excellent visibility, when I spent nearly equal time sheltered from those two debilitating effects as pedaling. My next opportunity for a respite came when my body wanted more energy, and, not without surprise, I had just entered the tidy community of Sheridan.

Much to my delight, a brand-new restaurant, the Korner Kitchen, was having it's grand opening today, and I was the very first customer to arrive on a bicycle. Everything was spic-and-span clean, bright, and most inviting—you can bet I changed into my less-stinky UBS tee for this, as well as rolling on more deodorant. Inside, the huge dining area opened up to knotty pine walls were adorned with antlers, (more visible evidence of efficient population control by hunters), slowly rotating fans hanging from the high ceiling, and solid furniture ready to accommodate all eaters, from the youngest to the oldest. Sitting next to one of the large windows, I could see my Doublevision and, across 90A, kids clambering to the top of a giant slide. For the moment, I was happy, relaxed, and soon-to-be, well-fed.

All good things come to an end, and within an hour, I was back out on 90A, Eastbound, more cognizant than ever of my time. I pedaled by Splashway Water Park and Red's Drive-In, thinking that perhaps I worked my short stay here wrong; maybe I should have gotten wet first then find out if this Red is related to the Red in Sublime...!

But, no, no, I *had* to get going because Houston needed to be closer. Once out of Sheridan, the traffic lessened immediately and I was usually the only vehicle on the road. Even going by Rock Island and school zones for the Rice Consolidated School District, where the roadway actually widened for turning traffic, I was able to maintain a reasonably high* speed, which was not high enough to have to slow down. That's one positive aspect of Sunday—no school, no buses, no students, no traffic. *10-15mph/16-24kph is high speed for me when fully loaded

My first stop came in Altair, where East-West US90A crossed North-South route 71, which had both a flashing red light and an enormous stop sign. Despite my making good time—the headwinds had diminished markedly and the road was quite flat, relatively straight, and even had a slight decline as I pedaled toward the Colorado River—the stop, albeit brief, was an enjoyable break from the cycling, that constant smooth motion. It was that, the repetitive motion, ironically, which had torn the meniscus in my left knee several years ago and forced me to seek the exceptionally fine services of orthopedic surgeon Dr. Luis Urrea back home to eliminate the pain. Interestingly, the only time I ever feel the loss of that sliver of cartilage is when I'm *not* pedaling. Not a biggie as this is the only alternative activity I really care about anyway.

However, I had a much more pressing concern: the Sun was setting, and I hadn't even gotten to the Colorado River yet. I stopped across from rice drying elevators to put on my lights, then continued, now pedaling with an increased amount of anxiety. Crossing the railroad tracks posed no difficulty, what, with no other vehicles on the road, I veered far left and made a precise 90° angle over the tracks without reducing speed. When I finally arrived at the Colorado River, relief flooded through me and I began to look for the places that Christian had told me about.

The bridge itself was no different from most of the previous bridges—a narrow, 2-laned, no shoulder affair, but, since no other vehicles were present, I easily pedaled across. I couldn't see too much of any kind of camping possibilities on the bank; heck, I couldn't see much of anything other than that twilight-lit train trestle and track on my left.

I pushed on, knowing that the picnic area would be perfect. It might have been dark by the time I arrived there, but it didn't keep me from seeing that it was not only closed, it was so securely closed that concrete barriers had been placed across the entrance so no one, including an innocuous bicyclist such as myself, would be tempted to use the area. Disillusioned, I had to consider my actions.

Should I go onto Eagle Lake, which can't be too far, or head back to the bridge, which I know is close and can likely find something around there?

I chose the latter, uncomfortable with the possibility of intruding in an area known to be inhabited by snakes. Besides being morbidly terrified by the reptiles, which should be ludicrous because much of my childhood was on the Upper Meramec River in Missouri and had had innumerable encounters with the serpents. Regardless, what really bothered me is that while I can't see them in the dark, even with a weakening bike light, they can easily sense my presence. They can be, literally, cold-blooded, nocturnal killers, and, despite my great size, I could be a good long-term meal. In the back of my mind, I hoped that my odoriferous self and clothing would dissuade any critter from checking me out, although a vulture could like the smell.

While pedaling back, my headlamp shined upon the reflector of a guard rail. I stopped, parked beside it and quickly decided that there was sufficient shoulder between that rail and the adjacent swamp for me to camp. Yes, there I'd be safe from motor traffic and, provided I don't roll over too far, not a likely candidate for any snake or other varmit, venomous or not. I quickly backed the Doublevision into place, pulled out my pad, water bottle, toothkit, OFF, and made camp.

I took off my Avocet biking sandals and moved about the Z-rest, positioning things so as to not knock them into either the road or the water. Glad to have resolved my overnighting issue; tomorrow, Houston for sure....

Ooouuuucccccchhhhh!

Arghhhhh!

Bitten!

My worst fears realized!

The fangs had pierced my left foot, and now blood was pouring onto the pad.

Forget trying to catch and ID the snake, I needed to stem the bleeding, and applied direct pressure with my hands. One thing about my blood, it is abundantly full of platelets—I *am* a regular UBS donor—and the flow quickly stopped with a little help. Unable to see much, I wrapped a sock around my foot, then pulled another sock over it to keep it in place.

Having stabilized the injury, I began my search. What I found was a broken glass bottle, still lodged into the thin Z-rest, waiting for my other foot or another piece of flesh. I carefully removed the glass and cleared away anything else that might be a problem. Relieved that I didn't need immediate medical treatment, my next concern was about my last tetanus booster.

Another aspect of my being a regular donor is that I am universal; my blood type is O +. Not only is it good for humans, but mosquitoes also fancy it and my recent gusher was a perfect training ground for the young as well as a feast for the more experienced insects. I sprayed the rest of my OFF on my body and around me, creating an invisible noseeum screen which the buzzing masses could not penetrate. In fact, their rapidly beating wing beats quickly lulled me into deep sleep.

Overnight Seventeen: US 90A berm

Confident as I was about the guard rail keeping me safe from a fatal squashing by motor traffic, it didn't stop the rumbling of those big 80,000 pound/36,287kgs rigs passing so close. Indeed, not only would bursts of air, pushed out by each axled wheel, blow into my face, but so also did little bits of roadway and other particulates. That being said, I am grateful to the truckers, those professional over-the-road haulers who begin their workday early in the morning.

That, too, was time to begin my bikeday. I could see the slightest amount of gray sky in the East and knew, barring any additional problems with my foot, I'd be at my son's apartment in Houston today.

I was a little bit slow—my foot was throbbing some and I dreaded the possibility of complications—but I was soon up and pedaling. I passed that rotten picnic area, and knew it would have probably been the best place possible for me to overnight—had I been able to get my Doublevision over the barricade. I pushed on, sucking down more (warm) water than I can remember since leaving El Paso on 11JUN.

I was in Eagle Lake before Sunrise, and the first visible establishments were Taco Tony's and Brookshire Brothers foodstore, where I could have also gotten gasoline. But I needed a different kind of fuel, but it was too early for them to be open, as it was for Subway, a short distance later.

Looking down at my foot, I could finally see bloody sock encapsulating it. Interestingly, the sock was also a burial ground, peppered with mosquitoes who had given their final full measure for a taste of my (or anybody, for that matter) delicious bodily fluid. In a very bizarre and morbid mental twist, I swear they looked like young military personnel who just finished boot camp. What I also saw was no red streaks or signs of infection other than a steady pain, part of which was due to my pushing the pedal with the field dressing last night.

Cycling into town proper, it was still too early for Subway, definitely too early for Dairy Queen.

Then my eyes saw a motorist pulling into the parking just beyond an abandoned gas station, where a plain sort of building was marked as The Cattleman's Restaurant. Perfect! I parked the Doublevision in the rising Sun between a parking curb and the building—hang being able to watch it or give heed to any of yesterday's dire warnings—and hobbled inside.

I passed through the atrium into the dining room, hearing a few tables full of casually-dressed men carrying on greetings of the day. All sounds immediately stopped when I stumped in, selecting a table an isolated table close to an outlet for my cell phone recharger. Seeing one man with a VietVet cap on, I saluted, saying, "Go Navy! As you were! Carry on!"

The crowd of men laughed, and the climate returned to the classic jabber of informal meetings, where real decisions are made.

Waitress Crystal gave me the opportunity for an easy decision, asking me if I wanted cream and sugar with my coffee.

"No mamm', just hot and black and a menu," I replied, "and, if possible, could you ask the cook for a piece of raw bacon. I'll be happy to pay for it, but it's the perfect remedy for my foot."

A trace of alarm went across her eyes upon seeing my foot, but assured me that it was "no trouble and no charge, either."

Definitely my kind of place to start the day.

After refueling my body with plenty of coffee and a "Cattleman's Breakfast", I made the inevitable rounds, telling this group of businessmen all about my bicycling, my injury, and my good fortune to be here with them here in this wonderful community as well as being in Texas.

They agreed with my assessment, but they had to get on with the rest of their day—not continue to eat and pedal away. Wishing me well, they departed while Crystal brought me two strips of raw bacon and a basin of warm water. I returned to the serious business of foot repair, removing the crusty socks and giving the wound a thorough washing. Except for my toenails being in need of a clipping, my foot felt almost as good as new after smoothly stacking the bacon on the punctures, wrapping it with napkins, and putting a bit of ductape on to hold it in place. In Boy Scout tradition, I turned the socks inside out before putting them back on.

Once again, bacon has proved the perfect remedy when bike touring.

The first time this method worked so wonderful was 08JUL1983, on the third day of my circum-Missouri odyssey. I was pedaling my Stumpjumper on route 10 toward Richmond when I stopped to enjoy a squirt of warm water from my bottle and consider a photo. Standing over the top tube, the front wheel twisted and the tire caught the nail of my big toe in a startling avulsion. Naturally, it was painful, but I was more concerned about infection and, gross as it might seem, I urinated on it. Knowing that was only a temporary solution and meat fat would be far better for that exposed tender subdermal layer of living cells. At the local Village Inn Cafe, I obtained a strip of raw bacon in addition to a cooked BLT. Henrietta Park was just as good as anyplace to stop riding, and there I wrapped the bacon around my toe, elevating my foot for the night. By the next morning, I was pleased to see no streaks or scars and, with exhilaration, pedaled route H in the Missouri River bottoms toward Kansas City.

My extremely satisfying morning was topped with an interview by reporter Alicia from the Eagle Lake Headlight. While reciting the virtues of bicycling and the specifics of my own Trans-Texas odyssey thus far, I could see she was intrigued. Once I had finished my own exhaustive tale, she professionally told me about Eagle Lake being the goose hunting capital of the World and invited me to cycle by the lake, cryptically saying, "As a teacher, I think you'll appreciate the sweet history of sugar cane there, then go downtown for a better understanding of what built Eagle Lake. You mentioned liking historical markers; we have'em and an exciting depot, too."

"Eagle Lake," she said proudly, "is a thriving, safe town and I've come back to raise my family here. It's a great place to live!"

Following her directions, I pedaled toward the lake, but was unable to get much beyond a swimming pool area, and turned East. Even though it was later than I liked—mid-morning—any earlier departure would have been premature. Frustrated that I couldn't follow Alicia's lead and explore the sugar cane boom (which should return as a biofuel source for the USA, much like Brazil), I chose to get going—I'll surely make Houston today. Leaving now had a good omen—I was quite able to lightly push with my now-recovering foot. I was surprised at the large amount of motor traffic at this busy crossroads of 90A, FM 102, FM3013, and FM1093—my road into Houston—especially since yesterday had had many fewer vehicles.

Easily crossing railroad tracks, I turned North on FM3013 and crossed two more sets before finally pedaling on the Houston road, FM1093. Erik had told me that it becomes the major artery Westheimer, and that once there, I could call him for further directions to his apartment. My elation went untempered—not only is Houston achievable today, but this narrow two-lane road was exceptionally flat, straight with few curves, and little motor traffic. Surrounded by slightly lower agricultural lands bordered by windbreak trees, there was a higher, built-up parallel roadbed for trains , as if when the ricefields (and roadway) are flooded, the surest transportation was on tracks. I took the right lane for myself.

Entering Wallis, I was absolutely pleased to find another Snowflake Donut shop, having already been biased toward it in Shiner. Oh, so nice! To be out of those headwinds, enjoy the last of those delectable colaches, and re-energize in the cool a/c. Recharged, I continued pushing on, crossing the tracks and noting that this was another historic community.

One plaque on the Wallis State Bank noted settlement in the 1830s, but the real stimulus came when railroad tracks were laid through here in 1880. Virtually everywhere I've pedaled since 11JUN, the rise or fall of communities was often dependent upon whether or not a railroad connections were established and maintained. Equally often, the community would take it's name from the railstop, frequently named after a prominent mover-and shaker. Here, that person was J.E. Wallis, an executive with the Gulf, Colorado, & Santa Fe Railroad who was apparently instrumental in getting a railspur here; the station was called Wallis. Such economic development was enough to create a need for an institution that could address the financial need for credit, hence the Wallis State Bank, which has since thrived and spread throughout the local area.

Crossing the Brazos River was even better than yesterday's crossing of the Colorado, which in itself was quite decent because of the lack of motor traffic, although the rest area was a failure and I injured myself. (Thank you, Crystal and the Cattleman's in Eagle Lake for my recovery.) I was quite pleased to be on FM1093; it was proving to be a fantastic way to enter a major metropolitan area. This road had all the superior qualities that every roadway should have: broad, clean, and debris-free shoulder, excellent lane lines, and, now, with an ATLM, I had much more peace of mind with the rare motor vehicle passing me.

I was plenty ready, though, for another stop when the road made a gradual curve to the right into a long straightaway. Seeing Ropers County Store and Cafe, I parked in the shade and went inside. I knew my scent might arouse refusal, but I was exhausted and undoubtedly looked it, too. Then I saw exactly what I needed: a 132 ounce(3.9 liters) jumbo mug, ready for that sugar and caffeine boost of Mountain Dew and endless ice from the dispenser.

That electrolyte was all I needed. I retired to an out of the way seat, promptly spilling it when it slipped between the fingers of my trembling hands as I lifted the cup to my mouth. The owner quickly pulled out a mop, which proved infinitely more effective than the hundred napkins I began laying on it. He allowed me to top-off the drink one more time, and I was sure to not have another accident.

Refreshed, the next community I came to was Simonton, but it was much too soon for me to stop again. But I had to stop; this fine route soon T-intersected into another road, with an extra-large stop sigh governing East-bound traffic. I followed the obvious main road, beside the clearly-marked FM1093, turning first toward Orchard on a zig, then next toward Fulshear on a zag.

The signs of increasing proximity to my destination were becoming obvious. 1093 had become three laned, the center lane for double left-turns. At least the fine shoulder still existed, though it diminished while atop a bridge crossing an oxbow. It was pleasing to see a long wooden trestle, now on my left, was being maintained even though I hadn't seen a train anytime today. My excitement was on the upswing—I was going to see my son later today! I kept pushing into the increasing headwind and temperatures. At least the road was as flat as the hot side of a clothes iron.

At Fulshear City Hall, I stopped again, this time for a historical marker, which noted the namesake, Churchill Fulshear as being one of the "Old 300" settlers—those who made homesteads in this Mexican state of *Coahuila y Tejas* under the Father of Texas, Stephen F. Austin, *prior to* the Texas Revolution. This area had been part of a land grant to Churchill, and it was through his actions that the railroad laid track here in 1890, formally marking Fulshear for growth as a trade center. Prior to incorporation in 1977, it had been a general law community, governed by the constitution, commission, and common sense.

At the traffic light intersection where FM359 Northbound separates from FM1093 Eastbound/ 359 Southbound, I kept my heading on 1093—the route into Houston. I hadn't gone very far before deciding it was time for another break; but where?

Seeing a shady spot on a grassy ditch, I turned right onto Bois D'Arc Road to stop and catch my breath. As soon as I sat down, a shiny black SUV with dark-tinted windows slowly passed in front of me as if stuck in slow motion. A shiver passed through my body, feeling an intense examination by whomever it's occupants might be. Was this the same vehicle that had stopped three nights ago when I camped in front of the Mr. W fireworks factory?

Even though it did not stop, I felt uncomfortable enough to get out of there, and resumed pedaling. Getting close to the intersection with 1093, another SUV quickly came around the corner from the depths of Bois D'Arc Road. In my rear view, I could see it rushing up on me then quickly lunging to the left and passing me before cutting back, brake lights screaming red.

This time I saw the personalized license plate—it was a hunter. Morbidly, I smiled at the thought of this person's momento wall; there, amongst the display of gameheads and tusks of Oryx, Gazelle, Wildebeast, Whitetail, and similarly projected out, was the 20-inch Maxxis wheel, nose & handlebars of a Toyota-white Doublevision tandem recumbent. What a taxidermy challenge I would be!

Fortunately, that hazardous motor vehicle made a left turn onto 1093 and I easily made my right turn. Other than that, I was so impressed with all other traffic, it giving me a wide berth, even at the beginning of the Westpark tollway. In other words, I had the entire right-lane (of three lanes) to myself as there was no shoulder. Some motorists even gave me the thumb's up when passing, and one must have been a diver—she gave me the universal diver's signal of "OK?" to which I replied "OK!"

Feeling pretty good but in need of another break, I pulled into the backside of Richmond Walgreens for shade. Maybe fatigue was creeping in, but I didn't lock the Doublevision and casually strolled into the store. Like HEB, this was another ready source of cash when I used my VISA debit card. It is also a source of quick energy, usually a Toblerone or Ghirardelli intense dark chocolate such as Sea Salt Soiree, Twilight Delight, Midnight Reverie, or, well, *any* of the Ghirardelli products. The tasty, high cacao bars are usually a bit more pricey, but the heart-healthy value of them is worth it. I also took advantage of a half-price sale for Arnold Palmer half-iced tea, half-lemonade drink. Returning outside, I laid down beside the Doublevision, resting and reinvigorating myself with the electrolyte.

Back on the road, I felt empowered, a true equal to all other vehicles, (even though I knew I wasn't) and had little difficulty when 1093/Westheimer cut North beneath the tollway. Pedaling this pleasurable road was exquisite, but all good things come to an end. Not because all of a sudden motorists became hostile—anything but that—but because instant recall inspired me to turn right onto Richmond Avenue.

Last year, I had helped Erik relocate from Austin to Houston and he had chosen an apartment complex that had frontage on this road. Heck, there was no need for me to pedal any farther than necessary—I had already come this far, why make it any longer?

The road characteristics immediately changed, from the broad, congested, divided 3-lane 1093/Westheimer to a much-less congested divided 2-lane Richmond Avenue with sufficient width for me to comfortably pedal. It was very bike-friendly because of—and this is most important—the exceptionally courteous motorists. This was even true at the busy State Highway 6 crossing and underneath Beltway 8, Sam Houston Tollway; but, then when I use my bicycle on the road, I expect to be respected and treated the same as any other vehicle on the road—just follow the rules of the road!

One thing was a problem though: Richmond was constructed of concrete, with expansion joints allowed for the segments to move in response to the temperature. Unfortunately, some of the slabs have settled and those joints have become virtual cliffs. The Doublevision would shake from front wheel to rear wheel and everything in between, including me. Wearing padded gloves and having underseat handlebars helped eliminate most of the shock, though my body and head would bobble comically. Fortunately, I was able to steer around the larger potholes, some of which were substantial.

I felt as if back home, pedaling North Yarbrough between Pebble Hills and Montana. Although the surfaces are quite different—this is concrete, Yarbrough is asphalt—both had those demonic ridges that threatened to upset me and my load with every time I crossed over. Aggravatingly, the protrusions were most pronounced exactly where I was pedaling, on the far right-hand side, while the more massive motor traffic was continually compacting the surface elsewhere. The easy solution would be to move left, take a lane, but that would be foolish, greatly increasing the chances for a collision. Bicycles are such a less-massive object than a motor vehicle that any contact between them virtually guarantees problems for the 2-wheeler. Bicycle safety is NO accident!

My instant recall was muddled; all of these apartment complexes looked so familiar! So there was only one that would do, and, thinking

I had found his complex, began piping my well-used whistle as loudly as possible.

This is no ordinary whistle, but a sturdy black plastic police whistle that was part of a bulk purchase from REI some thirty years ago. This is the very same that had recalled my children from their foray into Great Slave LakeNWT or in the Blue MountainsNSW or Clear LakeIA or my lost family in *Venezia* or Little Hueco TanksTX or as the tail-bicyclist on a Mike's Bikes tour in Amsterdam or with a frozen pea inside it while pedaling in Winter or a multitude of other locations throughout our travels over the years. It is the same one that has always been strung around my neck on a leather thong, which had been replaced with a shoelace and now a bootlace, which, from it's bellow-ready

After 900 miles (1440kms) East, time to go West!
(www.juanitohayburg.com)

position between my lips, kept me safe with a loud aural alert to any and all traffic on the road when pedaling. And now it once again served as a clarion call to Erik, while repeatedly emptying my lungs—which caused only very slight dizziness.

Then I recognized his apartment complex immediately—the Woodtrail. I had to wait at the electric gate entrance for a motor vehicle to either enter or exit so that I could quickly wheel in, thus avoiding getting trapped by the steadily advancing gate. I pedaled to the quad he called home and jubilantly met him waiting for me.

"I heard you loud and clear," Erik told me, as we hugged each other. "and so did everybody else. Let me help you get that upstairs—it'll fit on the back porch."

"First," I said, "let me lighten it as much as possible, pull off all the gear but not the Kirtland panniers.

They're pretty much permanently attached now."

Then, almost as if in a trance, I started rambling: "Used'em for years—toured Eastern and Western Europe in nineteen eighty-one, cross-country to beautiful BC in eighty-two, perimeter of Missouri in eighty-three. They used to have real effective 3M Scotchlite reflective beads, which came in quite handy the time your Uncle Nils and I were pedaling out of the mountains of Northern Greece after finding the paved road into Bulgraia was non-existant beyond Exochi Pass. I was steadily braking while descending, which heated up the rim and when I went over a bump where the road had sunk over a culvert, the rear wheel potato chipped. Your Uncle Nils was pretty far ahead and came back by foot searching for me, yelling my name, but nearly ran into me in the darkness. After finding me standing on that wheel, we decided to not attempt going farther that night, that we'd camp close-by. He needed to walk back to get his bike, then I got worried about him, so I unclipped a front Kirtland for it's reflective ability to increase my visibility. 'course, no motorcar dared be on that road at night, so I never knew if it was a good idea or not. I nearly ran into *him* in the darkness, and we agreed to not get so separated when traveling, especially when we got into Eastern Europe. It was a good plan—it took us half the next day before we arrived at Lefkonis. It never fails to amaze me that we didn't have more problems then."

"Yeah, well, uhm, you always seemed to have a good idea about where to go when we traveled with you," Erik commented. "You take the front end, I'll take the rear, and we'll get it up the stairs. I've opened up the front door and the patio door; let's put it out there, by the gloves you asked me to bring."

I was too weak to disagree; we moved it up the narrow stairwell, which was good as I braced myself several times on the rail. The 13-foot (4 meter) long tandem was almost a bit much for small apartment, but we finally got it onto the porch without scraping and scratching. There was surprisingly little room left once all of the gear was spread out beside it, including my new Nashbar crochet gloves. I was extremely satisfied, though, because it was secure—very few people will attempt to steal my Doublevision from that lofty perch!

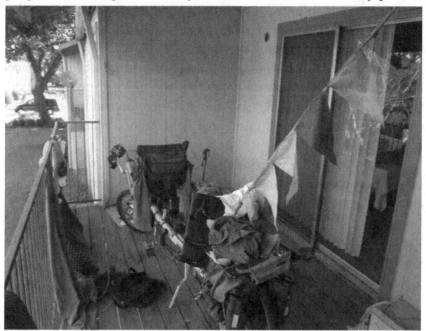

Doublevision on back porch (www.juanitohayburg.com)

"Your shirt really reeks, ought to burn it—after gettin' a hazardous waste permit, " Erik razzed me. "No way do I want to run it through my washer. And you look exhausted. Just take it easy for now—I've got to go back to my office for a moment, then make us something to eat when I return."

I had been sucking on my water bottles but that wasn't enough; I needed immersion. I went to the swim pool and plunged in, hang my filthy smelling shirt or grimy body. It was perfect. I found a water fill valve and contorted my body around it; feeling that massaging jet of fluid was heavenly.

The Sun still had several hours before setting, but I was relaxed and ready to stay in this water until my skin had wrinkled! While being one with the cool water, I watched a couple of young children across from me, playing on the pool steps as their mother sat beside them. They were so carefree—and so was I—it was such a relief to hydrate and, dare I confess, to not be pedaling into a headwind.

Closing my eyes, I may have gone to sleep or entered a suspended state of peace or some other dimension. I was uncertain as to how long this condition lasted, but knew it had been a good long while. The children and their mother had gone, the shadows were long with the Sun was now skimming the horizon.

"You looked too comfortable when I returned," I heard a voice breaking into my ephemeral condition, and cracked my eyes open to see Erik. He continued, "so I didn't bother you and instead made chicken tetrazzini. Come on up and have a good meal before you zonk out for the night."

I began the process of regaining this-world status, slowly moving out of the water, retrieving my eyeglasses and a towel from a chair, and walking at a snail's pace to his apartment. This was the first night I was going to be inside since leaving El Paso—17 days ago. The first night that I would actually have to put a blanket on because of the air conditioning. The first night I actually...

OVERNIGHT EIGHTEEN: HOUSTON

"I'm off to work now," I heard Erik through the mist of drowsiness. He was carrying his lighter-than-air Giant road bike past me. "The key to my Prius is on the table, if you need to use it for any reason. I'll be back by six. Call me if you have any problems or questions."

This carpeted floor was amazingly comfortable, certainly better than what I known for the previous 2½ weeks, and fell back asleep.

Sometime later, I aroused, picked myself up off the floor, stretching like a dog, the guttural sound escaping my yawning mouth. Collecting my thoughts, I assessed my situation. I limped only slightly as my foot had recuperated incredibly fast—Crystal's meat fat poultice and the swim pool immersion yesterday had cured me. I knew I had to buy more MREs for my return trip and, conveniently enough, a motor vehicle was at my disposal. I was also hungry and finished off the cranberry juice, along with the cherries atop of a bowl of cereal.

Taking advantage of Erik's Prius and following his excellent directions, I motored to the Command Post, 11650 South Sam Houston Parkway. It was quite easy motoring—in Erik's car, enabled with the EZ toll pass—and after I had assured him that despite outward appearances, my abilities to operate it were superb. He demonstrated the exact kind of generous behavior that we had raised in him.

I bought a case of these MREs, which had proved essential to my staying alive while pedaling in West Texas. Handling that heavy full box, I knew I'd take only a portion of them with me on the Doublevision—I was already pushing enough weight.

Returning to his apartment, I saw a stalled car at the corner of Richmond and Tanglewood, and pulled into the Four Star Food Mart parking lot. Piping loudly on my whistle, I alerted other motorists to a disabled vehicle while scrambling over to help push it.

Any roadway—congested or not—which has an impediment to the smooth flow of traffic is a dangerous one. That includes me on my Doublevision; while I'm not stopped, I am a slow moving vehicle, a hazard in itself. Remarkably, these motorists (except for the Fulshear hunter) demonstrated the same courtesy and respect now as I'd received while cycling yesterday in this fine city.

I always feel good when assisting other roadusers, remembering how well I've been helped: Mr. Robert Smith-Yañez, after being rear-ended 29MAR2009 by a hit-and-run motorist; and, while coping with a constant flats and headwind, Ms. Barbara Brown of AnthonyNM on 21NOV2010. They both returned me and my broken bicycle home. Neither Robert nor Barbara would accept payment for their service, even as gas money, but I pledged to help others as they helped me. I firmly believe in what goes around, comes around—and I practice it.

Feeling elated, my next stop was at Big Lots, 9597 Westheimer, where I bought replacement Cranberry Juice and toe nail clippers. The cashier saw to it that I was checked through quickly and efficiently. Seeing my VISA card, personalized with me upon my Doublevision, also gave me some pointers about pedaling in Houston. I recognized her complaint, one of the most common: "I almost hit one last night 'cause I couldn't see'em. And they're always runnin' red lights!"

I might have enjoyed pedaling to both Command Post and Big Lots, but having Erik's car to drive sure did make it easier. Besides, I wasn't entirely sure that I was fully recovered from my arduous 949 miles/1519kms pedal of the previous 17 days. This was proved when I got back to his apartment, returning to a deep sleep.

"Well, I though we might go downtown to this restaurant," I heard Erik saying. "You'd probably like seeing Houston at night—it's completely different from day."

"That would be interesting," I agreed. "As long as I don't have to dress up too much."

"There is a dress code," he said, "but you're gonna' have to clean up—there is a 'smell code'! You'll have to borrow one of my shirts, but I don't know about the other stuff."

"No worries, mate," I said with a laugh, "I stuffed a pair of slacks and a decent shirt Mike Badley gave me into one of my panniers and if you'll loan me a pair of black socks, I'll be fine."

"Good; we'll go as soon as I shower. Do you want me to save the water for you?" he asked.

"Absolutely!" I responded. "It doesn't make any difference whether you're in the desert like El Paso or in a wet place like Houston, fresh water is a vital resource *always* to be conserved."

"Yeah, I know, you've been drilling that into me and Katy's heads forever," he stated. "You want to borrow some deodorant, too?"

"Nope, I brought some of that, too. I know I stink when pedaling, so the least I can do is put it on before going into eateries," I told him. "Also, I'll be leaving the toe nail clippers here—too much weight for me to carry back to El Paso." The Gillette Clear Gel deodorant, my favorite, was packed in one of the zipper pockets in my rear Kirtland Tourpak pannier, was not so easy to apply. It had liquefied inside it's container, so my fingers became the applicator of the viscous solution. It still did the same job, just messier to put it where it works best.

Erik was right—Houston at night is dramatically different from it's day version. There was no huge number of motor vehicles lined up in the stop-and-go procession, but a polite scattering moving about the streets, all obeying the rules. Erik found parking and we strolled into the Grove Restaurant on the Discovery Green.

We sat at in a dimly lit area, looking out at lush greenery. I noticed an open stairwell, but Erik was ready with "We're dressed well enough to get in, but up there is pretty much for alcohol consumption and I know you don't drink. But if you're real interested in seeing better..."

Regardless of which floor we were on, the service was superb, our meals delicious, and the highlight for me should have been looking around the area. Despite its immense attractiveness, I was starting to fade...

OVERNIGHT NINETEEN: HOUSTON

Waking early the next morning, I felt immensely better, very well rested and actually ready to pedal. Good thing, too, because Erik was gone, and had taken his car. Going out to the porch, I gave my Doublevision a thorough going over while lubing the chain with White Lightning clean ride.

Perhaps most amazing was the front wheel (not that the rear wheel isn't equally amazing) and its ability to withstand massive abuse. It was during the inspection of this stupendous wheel when I came to an unbelievable sight. The head of a Phillips screw was perfectly flush with the Maxxis Hookworm tire surface as if it belonged there, and should I look on the side opposite, I'd see a corresponding washer and nut. Remarkably, the tire was not flat; it didn't even have low pressure. I reflected for a moment, unable to think of where over the previous 949miles/ 1519kms the tire might've picked it up, much less to have driven it so perfectly into the tire. Reasoning that another 949 miles/1519kms returning probably wouldn't make any difference, I decided to remove it.

But would it go flat? If it did, I could take another day for repairs at the Daniel Boone Cycle shop, 5318 Crawford, and if needed, even overnight at the adjacent International Hostel, before pedaling West. I unscrewed it, slowly backing it out, listening intently for the tell-tale hiss of a tube loosing air.

Looks like skilled carpentry!   *So far, so good! (www.*
(www.juanitohayburg.com)   *juanitohayburg.com)*

Amazing! (www.juanitohayburg.com)

Nada. Nothing. No sound, no loss of tube pressure, only a small hole in the tire.

It seemed incredibly long, a half-inch/1.3cm with a sharp point associated with all wood screws. There must be a reason why the tire didn't immediately go flat; an explanation is warranted. Maybe it was my almost 40 years cycling experience, but there are other factors, too.

A bicycle wheel, good or bad, consists of several parts, primarily a flexible pneumatic tire mounted upon a rigid rim, usually made of an alloy, which is held equidistant from a heavier duty alloy hub by an array of 24 to 48 stainless steel spokes, in a 3- or 4-cross pattern. Generally, the more spokes, the stronger the wheel but it weighs more.

For example, 35 years ago, I had owned a Puegeot tandem constructed of Reynolds 531, which had Super Champion 27-inch wheels, each with 48-Swiss DT spokes in an extremely tight 4-cross pattern. Very strong indeed. I also pedaled a prototype Specialized Stumpjumper for 12 years which had Araya 26-inch wheels, 36-spoke, 3-cross pattern. It, too, was unbelievably strong. There were a few occasions in which I built my own wheels, lacing 36 spokes in a 4-cross pattern, then truing and dishing it correctly. All of these wheels held up quite well, even after the abuse of ledge drop offs, spoke loss by abrupt extraction, or incompetent wheelsmithing.

The latter refers to me. It became quite obvious that I had neither the patience nor the temperament for such precision work. More than once did I have the wheel perfectly trued when I gave one of the spoke nuts a quarter-turn too much and it potato chipped. It was worth far more to me to buy a new, perfectly true and strong wheel from Tandems Limited, BirminghamAL.

Having received a perfect rigid part of the wheel, the rest of it is in my domain and I have developed as system that generally guarantees a flat-free tour. My goal is *trouble free touring with no flats*, which means no problems while cycling. Without a doubt, I have demonstrated that there is no guarantee of it, including a flat. That's why it's a goal.

Regarding the tires, over the years I have learned that it is better to spend a little bit extra money for a reputable one which is the first line of defense against flats. I almost always use a 20-inch Maxxis Hookworm, 110psi/7.6bar tire, which has the toughness and durability to stop *most* penetrations by a foreign object. Beneath that, is a Stop Flats tire liner—not only is Crazy Cat Cyclery the shop of great wrenches, but also where I can buy high-quality parts like this liner. Next is one of my previously- used thorn-proof tubes, slit along the inside seam with the valve stem removed so that, lastly, a slimed schrader-valve BikeNashbar BMX innertube can be put inside it. All of this is mounted in an extremely high-quality Rhyno Lite rim attached to a stout Phil Wood quick-release hub via 36, 4-cross Swiss spokes, straight gauge 14. This is a nearly indestructible combination, perfect for me and my strenuous touring.

I only wish I could say the same for all of the components, as evidenced by this biketour.

I also detected that the chainrings I had labored over a week ago had a slight wobble—again. Then there was the broken lever for my rear Magura HS33 hydraulic rim brake. I was comforted by the fact that I was in Houston, a major port for the USA. Surely I'd be able to find both another lever *and* fix whatever was causing the wobble. My only discomfort was because it might take a pretty penny. My ever-thinning VISA card may be extremely handy.

Opening Erik's iPad, I had little trouble finding numerous bike shops and proceeded to call each one. By early afternoon, I was distressed that not a single shop had any Magura products, much less an HS33. What's more, I was doubly frustrated since I could not accurately describe the chainring wobble, thus not receive any possible remedy. There is, as always, one sure way for me to exorcise the unhappiness and that is with exercise.

In a surprising display of brute strength, I picked up and carried my Doublevision from the porch, through the small apartment, down the stairwell to the parking lot. Of course, it helped immensely that much of the weight had been left on the porch, and gravity was working in my favor. After again waiting for a motor vehicle to trip the automatic gate opener to quickly wheel through, I pedaled out of the apartment complex onto Elmside Drive.

Going North on this pleasant drive took me to a very familiar road, FM1093, aka Westheimer. It wasn't entirely the same—there were a whole heck of a lot more motor vehicles and much commercial development. What was the same, I'm pleased to report, was the superior respect and courtesy (except for the Fulshears hunter) I'd received two days ago pedaling into Houston. Houstonians know how to share the roadways.

It was great that the Houston motorists were making me feel as much a member of the traffic as they were, but the ultimate factors of integration for me were the receptive businesses. First and foremost was breakfast at my turn-around point, Subway, 7507 Westheimer, with much appreciated attention from Subman Julian. I went inside at (07:00) to smell fresh Seattle's Best coffee brewing and see the glistening containers of various sandwich elements, from which he expertly prepared my sub. As always, avocado is my most favorite add-on, but this morning I wasted no time preparing my half-and-half electrolyte: chocolate milk and coffee in a large cup! My solid consumption was a toasted flatbread-egg & steak combo followed by a chaser of another half-and-half.

Adequately refueled, I pedaled across the parking lot to Performance Bike shop, 7549 Westheimer, where I bought the last two camelbacks, clearing the shelf. Wrenches Desmond and Andy gave me their professional opinion about my chainring wobble: "... the Independent Pedaling System (IPS) is shot, but if you've made it this far, you'll probably go equally as far before it falls off..." I had concluded the same and pedaled across FM1093 to Academy Sports, 7600 Westheimer.

I wasn't certain of any specific purchase, but might find something useful with all my camping. After locking the Doublevision to itself through the rear wheel and frame, I entered to find Stephanie more than ready to help me. This saleswoman virtually read my mind, and, based upon my biketour description, accurately directed me to a counter of high SPF lotions. Then I saw Quench gum, which makes a huge difference when pushing hard. Alas, no picture postcards were available for purchase, but she did direct me to the Barnes and Noble bookstore, 7626 Westheimer, in this same shopping square as a possible source.

I was ecstatic to find a card which gave a few stats about the Port of Houston—perfect for my turn around notice. What made this purchase of a couple dozen so good was not only Alicia's willingness to ring it up, but she also found a preferred customer discount for me. I owe thanks to B&N registering it's steady clientèle, one of whom is Ellen and her regular purchases through the years.

Supremely satisfied, I pedaled back to Erik's apartment in an easy box around pattern: South on Fondren then West on Richmond to Elmside. Buoyed by success, a lightened Doublevision and a secure handrail, I managed to get that long two-wheeler back into the space it had occupied several hours before. This was to be another day of taking it easy, all very necessary for my full and complete recovery. I pragmatically accepted the problems with my Doublevision: at least the most important front hydraulic brake worked well, and had already repaired the chainring wobble once—if another was needed, I could do that, too. The incongruity between the 8-speed derailleur and 9-speed shifter was minor although the gear cable was still not lined up as well as I'd like. I could fix that, too. In fact, the only thing that could stop me from pedaling 800 miles/1287kms West would be if the frame broke in two!

That thought dredged up a long-ago memory of a West German, Horst, who had been pedaling around the World for a few years and was now cycling through North America. I remember it was around the 4th of July, 1973, because he was with us in celebration at the Cabin. When he departed from our home on Salem Avenue in RollaMO, the welds on his steel-framed bicycle separated at the junction of the bottom bracket/down tube/seat tube.

I grimaced at the memory of his greatest loss, which were the notes he kept during his bicycle odyssey—they were last seen on the flatbed of my 1959 Chevy Apache ¾-ton, 17.5-inch wheeled truck on I-270, where we had stopped while delivering him and his broken bike to the Beaumont Scout Ranch.

In this moment of regression, I felt his pain because I had had a similar loss of vital documentation twice in my life. The first time was and inadvertent case of simply *not* keeping them in my hands when departing from a blood donation at Red Cross in ColumbusOH, 1985. The second was the notes had fallen out of my *bolsa* in the trunk of a *taxisto* in Ibague, 1986, when Ellen and I were crossing the border from Ecuador to Colombia.

In the former, I was extremely gratified that one of the technicians at the Red Cross donation center had recognized the value of my notes and held onto them, which she gave to me when we returned two months later to donate again. In the latter, alas, no such luck with the *taxisto*—there were numerous look-alike vehicles in a queue, and, once I found the right one, my notes were nowhere to be seen. I was crushed by the loss, but life goes on, with or without documentation.

I was confident neither loss would happen with the Doublevision; it was a cro-moly monotube with few welded parts. The forward nose had been remanufactured under warranty, and my seat, demolished

201

when rear-ended by a hit-and-run motorist 29MAR2009, had been completely rebuilt out of my old Stumpjumper cro-moly frame. The only thing that could break would be where the two paired monotubes (one for the front wheel, steering, captain's chair; the other for the rear wheel, rack, stoker's chair) were joined together. Although the 'tubes can be separated, I never have and it is as strong as the day I bought it, eleven years ago.

I spent the rest of the day relaxing, writing postcards, being wilted in the swim pool, and planning the route back, this time either being on I-10 or staying North of it. Most pleasing, though, was answering my cell phone.

"You could have been killed back at Mr. W Fireworks stand," my good friend Mike told me. "I've read had ruthless those drug dealers are and I'll bet Meth was being manufactured there. You were in between them and their product."

I chuckled, saying, "But it's also possible they were DEA agents just using it as a meeting site. It was a bit scary, but I was really too tired to do more than sleep. I'll never know because proper introductions were never made."

"And you could've died at Eagle Lake if it hadn't been for the Cattleman's Restaurant," he said. "I wasn't able to get the interview article from the Headlamp because you have to subscribe first before reading anything they publish. I want to see it, but it's just not worth it."

"I understand, Mike," I told him. "I'll check it out when I get back. Say, I leave tomorrow and I'll see you within three weeks—I have three workshops starting on the eighteenth."

"I'm amazed you were able to move the tandem in and out of the back porch like you did" Erik said to me later. "But let me help you get it down tomorrow—I don't want any wall damage."

OVERNIGHT TWENTY: HOUSTON

"Anything else before I lock up?" asked Erik as I began strapping gear onto my Doublevision.

"Nope," I replied confidently, "everything I need is here. You're off to DC now?"

"Yep, but I need to pick up Ankita first, then to the Hobby," he said. "We're supposed to be there two hours before departure 'cause there's supposed to be a lot of travelers catching morning flights. You have a good pedal back home, and don't have any problems. I won't be able to rescue you now!"

I finished packing my Doublevision and pedaled away, following the route we had mapped out on his iPad last night: West on Richmond to North on Briarpark with some winding through suburbia to Briar Forest; then West to Eldridge Road, North to the I-10 frontage road for a long Western pedal to Sealy to Columbus and up 71 to Austin. Easy.

And it was easy, all flat pedaling and the most critical part was the other vehicle operators: Houstonians (Fulshear is not Houston!) really do know how to share the road! Of course, part of what made the difference was that Briar Forest had a worn lane-line on the right hand side and was posted as a bike lane. It reminded me of the bike lane on South McCombs Street back home—narrow, obviously added after first construction of the road. I do *not* like bikelanes—unless it has real application, which this one does. It is a superb bike lane signs, great green bike route signs and yellow diamond bicycle stenciled signs spaced along the berm. Excellent!

I could tell that the three day respite had taken a toll on my conditioning, and was flagging. Then my situation improved immensely upon crossing Kirkwood: Walgreens! Time for my first break

FANTASTIC! (www.juanitohayburg.com)

of the day, and I would toast my success (thus far) with a chocolate milk/coffee combo. And why not a little cash, too?! It was perfect—all those previous days of headwind were now the tailwind I expected, although the heat was creeping above 100°F (38°C) in high humidity.

Refreshed, I pushed on. Then I began to feel peckish, and turned into Five Guys Burgers and Fries for a more filling meal. They weren't open yet! Just knowing that I was making good time gave me a jolt of energy and I happily pedaled another block to turn right on the divided Eldridge Parkway.

This road has two narrow lanes for each North-South direction, and I had lost the slim bike lane, though a yellow diamond bike stencil sign could still be seen. But I had not lost the respect of the marvelous Houstonian motorists! I absolutely had to take the right-hand lane, as legally allowed in the operator's handbook, and despite my being a slow-moving vehicle, the other vehicle operators gave me the same courtesy as always. I was thrilled, and made it a point to give each and every motorist a friendly wave.

It wasn't long before I came to the Enclave Parkway, the significance being that the long-running sidewalk became a divided sidepath. But a quick analysis of the cut-curb access told me that my vehicle was just a little bit too wide to safely get pass the traffic light, center post, and the "NO MOTOR VEHICLES" signpost.

Somewhat disappointed, I pedaled on, coming to a bridge posted "Buffalo Bayou" and cycled across, then pulling off onto a driveway apron on the North side. This is great! As a former Texas History teacher, this body of water figures prominently in the making of the Lone Star State. Even with my sometimes clear-eyed view of the murky past that this heavily manicured contemporary area didn't show the back then, only the present. In an effort to preserve what historically was a meander and continues today to be a floodplain, I could see that excessive commercial development was wisely restricted. A much more democratic and efficient paved path and bridge for non-motorized vehicles, safely removed from the road and bridge for motorized vehicles, had been constructed.

If I had only been able to merge onto it without hazard of knocking my flag off...!

A strong urge nearly convinced me to easily pedal that path but something went against my grain. I'd be cycling opposite to my route; did I really want to go into the headwind *again* and lose the good timing I made already this morning?

No.

I wanted to get to Austin, I wanted to see daughter Katy.

I resumed pedaling North on Eldrige, passing underneath I-10, then taking the far-right lane of the frontage road going West. Traffic was not heavy, and, as before, the motorists (except for the Fulshear hunter!) was extremely respectful of me and my vehicle.

The day had started cloudy before becoming brilliantly Sunny, but a cloud was still over my mind. I was troubled; I had reached my turn-around date before reaching my turn-around point of Louisiana, just another 100 miles (160kms) or so. My thoughts were almost as oppressive as the increasingly sweltering heat. I spotted a post office, and pedaled there to mail postcards, relieving some of this massive load on my Doublevision. But I had to rest, drink more water, eat, and stopped in the shade close to the junction of South Creek Drive and

Barker Spring Road. Taking off my helmet, new gloves, and Shimano sandals, I lay back, closing my eyes.

After a very short while, I bolted upright. *Of course! I have the answer!* With Erik here in Houston, I had a base from which to pedal. I *had* to return; *then* I could pedal through the delightfully preserved Buffalo Bayou as well as cross into Louisiana. And I'd definitely go through Beaumont, too, hopefully overnighting in Diane's (mother of Don, Katy's boyfriend) home. Yes, that is a good plan. No, it is a *great* plan!

Newly re-invigorated, I went back to pedaling West on that fine concrete frontage road, which varied in width between three and seven lanes. I knew Houston was behind me when I saw the I-10 sign indicating that the next five exits were for the grand town of Katy. My stomach was starting to growl, which I also knew to be a sign of needed nourishment. Unfortunately, there was a lot more open space or commercial space, including hospitals, before I came into several potential luncheon stops.

I was tempted to stop at the HEB, but pushed on through the busy Fry Road intersection. The closest eatery was the 59 Diner, and backed my Doublevision into a parking slot easily seen from inside. The blast of a/c was much appreciated, but my stomach was infinitely more interested in a waffle, coffee, a classic vanilla shake with maraschino cherry, onion rings, hash browns, and, for lunch— since it was that time anyway—a buffalo burger.

What was really nice, besides the cool air, was how friendly the staff were; they were always ready to serve me, and I especially like that they refilled my water buffaloes for me! They knew the way to this bicyclist was through his stomach and fresh-water supply. Another thing that super impressed me was the Hunt's tomato ketchup had been made without high fructose corn syrup. Considering my current food intake, this was an incredibly insignificant victory for my heart.

Even through I basked in this comfort zone, I wanted to be in Austin tomorrow night and that meant getting underway. The heat and humidity had only spiraled upward during my refueling stop, so I was grateful for the much deserved tailwind.

It wasn't long before I passed another hospital, and was faced with the decision of continuing to take a lane while pedaling the frontage road, or peel off onto US90. Ah, yes, I remembered it well. That was the wonderful road which I had pedaled such a great distance from Van Horn to Anderson Loop, and had been, a route of immense highs and lows, acceleration and deceleration, (in every sense of the phrases) for me.

I couldn't resist the pull of a less-congested road, one that narrowed to an undivided 4-lane route with a decent shoulder. Maybe it was the old grain tower that attracted me, or the railroad tracks, or even the water tower. The truth is that US90 had been such a superior bicycle route that, with the exception of bridges, I *wanted* to return to a semi-secure path for my vehicle, delineated from the other much more massive and faster vehicles by a solid white lane line. While nothing guarantees safety on the road, I felt a small measure of comfort knowing that most vehicle operators will recognize the solid white line as if it was a curb or drop-off and will avoid crossing it.

And so I cycled West into town and was not disappointed. This was the original Katy, not the tony suburbia I had pedaled through on FM 1093 a few days ago. US90 was one of the premier routes crossing Texas before interstate construction; surely I would see glimpses of that marvelous past, that time when all towns were located within an hour of each other with gas pumps and auto courts and cafes serving delicious home-made meals of locally produced food. Those were the times of when a 'good day out' in a motor vehicle meant going as much as 100 miles/60 kms without a flat tire or radiator boil over—usually the limit of the car's capability and speed.

Nowadays, that is *bicycle* distance, though not necessarily for me—I frequently seemed to encounter a mechanical problem or dreaded headwind which retarded my progress.

I turned North on Avenue B and rumbled over the tracks toward the water tower. I had a nice visit in a park and enjoyed a brief rest in the lovely shade, although my Doublevision had to stay on the street! Across 2nd street, Ohana Shaved Ice wasn't exactly the old-timey diner I was thinking of, but the icy snowballs with flavored sugar water poured on it would just have to do.

Leaving Katy, traffic lessened and US90 became a 2-lane, broad shouldered, superb route. It amused me passing Igloo road and factory, which looks like a massive version of my own Igloo 124-quart cooler, by noting the irony that igloo, associated with ice, snow, cold could possibly survive in this suffocating heat...!

In Brookshire, US90 West lost the fine shoulder, but traffic was still light. After a few traffic lights, I impulsively turned North on Otto Street, crossed the tracks and soon came to isolated Bostick Park. Leaving my Doublevision parked on the gravel shoulder, I entered the small grounds, seeking out the shade over two picnic tables where I enjoyed snacks and hot water. No surprise to me to find that the drinking fountain dispensed even hotter water! A headstone told me of the perseverance of an individual to create this likable space, but I soon liked getting underway—onto Austin!

I pedaled West on 1st Street a couple of blocks to FM362, which merged into FM359, then turned South to US90, where I once again was pushing West on US90. Feeling pretty relaxed, it was easy for me to stop and read the historical marker about Kellner Townsite before continuing. Probably it was inevitable, I read about the combination of fertile land producing crops such as nuts, animal stock, and fossil fuel (natural gas) with effective transportation (railroad) of the year (1893) that led to the founding of Brookshire. Interestingly, this was a constant refrain I'd seen throughout my odyssey, and, indeed, virtually anywhere my travels around the World have taken me.

The excellent shoulder had diminished markedly, but other traffic was diminished as well, and I was making good time. My excitement grew when I passed a road sign noting only 12 miles/19kms to Sealy, and only 36 miles/57kms to Columbus. This is great! I pedaled straight ahead while other (motorized) traffic could veer left and take the ramp onto I-10 West. It might have been blazing mid-afternoon hot, but I felt confidently cool with visions of being with Katy tomorrow night.

Any fatigue creeping in was banished at the next sign, which indicated San Antonio was only 159 miles/254kms away. Not that I had any intention of passing through there now, but the distance already covered did inspire me to think about how much I accomplished and how little remained. I passed another exit ramp for I-10, then an underpass for Peach Ridge Road.

Nope! I only need to keep pedaling West!

A near-claustrophobic feeling started to come over me when I saw that both I-10, on my left, and the railroad tracks, on my right, were rising above US90. But I calmed down upon seeing I-10 was clogged with motor vehicles, each progressively getting slower. I thought it strange that none of them were scrambling down the exit ramp to bypass the crawl and crowd me on this super nice road, but, hey, no complaints on my part. Probably a collision somewhere ahead forcing them to a stop-and-go status, and they can't quite figure out that US90 is now the faster way West. Oh, well, their loss, my gain, I chortled to myself.

Then I saw a left turn sign; this divine US90 West was making a sharp turn underneath I-10!

What?

I stopped abruptly at a guard rail and construction cones to observe this situation. I couldn't believe my eyes; both Erik and I had checked this route on his iPad last night, and it looked fine! Did the iPad lie? Did Google Earth lie?

There must be another way, but the only crossings for the Brazos River here was either interstate or railroad via bridges and trestle, respectively. Could I struggle across on the trestle? Not only is that exceedingly illegal, it was a dangerous and stupid thought. Additionally, access to the tracks was all but impossible. Could I join the slow moving motor vehicles on I-10 to make the crossing? Not necessarily illegal, doing so was only mildly dangerous and stupid, but access meant backtracking the wrong way on a one-way road as well as on the ramp.

With no other choice, I pedaled under the bridges and marvelous frontage road US90 West became marvelous frontage road US90 East, passing Siedel Road, which spurred off parallel to Brazos as a gravel road. That might yield a river crossing but no way did I want to go South. I wanted to go West. What's more, I was now vexed with a *headwind!* Pushing hard on the pedals, I was no longer relaxed nor delighting in the slow I-10 motor traffic.

This Eastbound road was just as empty as the Westbound road had been, and I doggedly push past a truck weigh station, Peach Ridge Road underpass, and the entrance ramp from I-10 East when it T-intersected with Donigan Road. This was one of the few times in my adult life as a bicyclist, I was fixated on backtracking as quickly as possible and ran the stop sign, turning left to cross over the I-10 East and West.

Much to my chagrin it appeared that the motorists got the last laugh—their vehicles were buzzing along at high rates of speed—as opposed to my vehicle grinding along at a low rate! My aggravation boiled over in the headwind and heat when I saw a road sign letting me know that Houston was now 38 miles/61kms away, exactly where I did not want to go.

I soon turned North on FM 359, once again crossing the tracks and stopped where FM362 diverged. I waved at a couple on an upright tandem as they sped by—he, as captain, concentrated on the road, she, as stoker, returned the greeting with a smile. The greened-up area between the roads had a sign, "Brookshire welcomes cyclists". That was a warming reception, although I didn't need any more warmth.

In fact, I was wanting to be chilled and stopped at the Food & Fuel Depot for icy water and some directional advice. I was a bit surprised to find that few people seemed interested in me and my unusual bicycle, although motorcyclist Mike gave me attention. It was from him that I learned the reason for why so little attention was give me and my Doublevision.

Brookshire is a significant joint in the MS150, a bicycle tour that raises funds for MS in which *15,000* people ride their bikes for two days. During this sanctioned event, police hold all other traffic at bay while the bikes are wheeling by. I shuddered to think about that—I remember only too well the 400 who rode in a memorial for Commissioner Pat O'Rourke on El Paso's West side, and the ensuing abuse by the mob. Doubtless that Commissioner O'Rourke, who had been killed while solo cycling, would roll over in his casket had he known the travesty occurring on Mesa Street in his honor. I can only imagine forty times such a mob and the attendant abuse;

now I understood why people swirled around me, not smiling, even avoiding me.

"But it's not so bad right now," Motorcycle Mike told me. "You're only one, an' you're bein' real courteous. Three fifty-nine's a great road if you keep on goin' up it, an' fourteen fifty-eight at Pattison will take you across th' Brazos into San Felipe, where there's a coupla' nice parks."

Thanking him, I pushed on into the lowering Sun. At the junction of FM1458 and FM359 in Pattison, I stood on the white stop line debating my direction. From behind me, this immense throbbing motorcycle driven by a leather-jacketed Hell's Angel-type guy in dark sunglasses went around me and roared straight through the stop sign, on FM1458. Watching him speed down the hill, his ratted hair—I guess it could have been a her—I knew that a collision between the two of us would likely do him/her as much damage to both our vehicles and selves as opposed to the injury from collision with a 4-wheeler. Regardless, his singular act of ignoring the stop sign (Of course, you realize that when *I* pedaled through the stop sign a few hours ago, that was OK because, well, I'm innocuous, frustrated, tired, etc....!) convinced me that I did not want to go *anywhere* that might be remotely close to him/her, so I turned North.

True to Mike's words, 359 was a great bicycling road, with a broad shoulder. So what if I didn't make it to Sealy or Columbus tonight? This was superb pedaling, and, once I accepted the fact that I won't meet Katy as planned, this was great.

What was not great was my progress. I was steadily weakening, finding it a near struggle to keep pushing one foot in front of the other. I needed a break. The air conditioned C & D Grocery at Harbison Drive provided me such an opportunity. I replenished my electrolytes with Mountain Dew, rested, then pedaled on feeling recharged. The greatness had returned.

359 was so nice, in fact, that when passing a road sign which put Monaville 9 miles/14kms and Hempstead 21 miles/34kms further, I felt it could easily be accomplished before complete darkness. Then I encountered the rolling hills and it was plainly evident that I was out of the coastal plains and into the blackland prairies. I balanced for a split second at the stop sign intersection with FM529 before

continuing on 359. A moderately strong Easterly could push me West on 529, but it wasn't worth it to me; that road was narrow without the fabulous shoulder I was now pedaling.

At the Monaville junction with FM 1887, I vainly looked for the Historical Marker, but was unwilling to go that far off my path, especially since the cross route was of such dubious cycling quality—no shoulder. Besides, the road had flattened out with long straight stretches and I only had 12 more miles (19kms) to go before Hempstead and a hot meal.

The Sun was beginning to set when I saw a pair of simple crosses silently marking road deaths on the West side of 359. It was a sobering reminder to me that regardless of how much visibility I had or how incredibly good this road is for bicycling, there is always risk of injury or death. It can even be self-imposed, like what happened to me in 1982.

Back then, brother Nils and I had been biketouring during the Summer months from Missouri to the Pacific Northwest, and had gone our separate ways at Prince Rupert by ferryboats—he to Alaska, me to Port Hardy, Vancouver Island. On my second day pedaling South on route 19, I had come to an old wooden bridge and stopped to investigate it for structural soundness. No way did I want to inadvertently plunge into the frigid creek water below simply because of my failure to ensure a safe crossing. Interestingly, the wooden slats were sheathed with roll roofing, but I was able to pedal across without problem.

Later that day, I was whipping down a hill at 25mph/40kph and recognized this bridge ahead as a twin of the one crossed earlier. I also saw a motorhome coming around the corner toward me just as I began to cross the bridge. Next thing I knew, the motorhome was stopped beside me, the operator asking me if I was alright. I was dazed and staggering around when I slowly realized what had happened.

This bridge *looked* like the previous one, but it was not. The sheathing was missing, and the bare wooden slats ran *with* the road. Midway across the bridge, the front tire of my Mercian had sucked down and stopped while everything else kept going at the high velocity.

My Mercian was flipped over, my right shoulder was in pain, and I had been laying on the deck. The force that had slammed my body onto the slats knocked me out for 11 seconds, approximately the amount of time the motorhome would have taken to go from the corner where I had seen it to beside me. I figured this out because the next person to show up was a Mountie, and I counted the seconds it took for him to go from the corner to beside me. He politely declined to help me pop my arm back into it's socket, but did deliver me and my bicycle to the Campbell River General Hospital.

Never before, and hopefully never again, has wearing a helmet made such a difference. If my Skid-lid had not been on when I did this header, I am certain I would be dead. My right clavicle had been broken, my chest was thoroughly blackened, and my Mercian would have been in fine working order except the front tire, still in good shape, was now next to the bottom bracket. The tremendous impact of such a sudden stop had forced the tire back, causing both the top tube and the down tube to buckle at the double-butted joints. I've never had any use for double-butted tubes since.

Double-butted tubing: too fragile for me!
(www.juanitohayburg.com)

213

Excellent photo of me on Stumpjumper pulling Trailabike (now in the possession of Brother Carl) with Katy & Erik on it.(www. juanitohayburg.com)

Those tubes may make for a lighter machine, but way too fragile for me and my bicycling style. Brad, chief wrench at Walt's Bike Shop, ColumbiaMO, 1982, identified my *modus birota* and sold me a prototype Stumpjumper. What a magnificent heavy duty machine! It survived 12 punishing years under me, likely being the first all-terrain bike in *Medellín*, if not all of *Colómbia,* when Ellen and I taught at The Columbus School, 1986-7. (Ellen had the second all-terrain bike there, brought by my mother when she came down for a visit in December.) I was never involved in a collision while on the Stumpjumper, but I did wear it out and now it's tubing lives on as the Captain's chair on my Doublevision.

My stumpjumper continues to serve! (www.juanitohayburg.com)

My desire for stout components was further strengthened by the fact that the Shadow 9-speed derailleur was too easily mangled into worthlessness, but it's replacement, a beefy Alivio 8-speed, has held enormously well.

Light weight equals light duty, but heavy problems. I'll take light problems and heavy duty anytime.

Those crosses were screaming to me that I had to stop for the night. I neither wanted nor needed a third cross to be erected in my honor.

There wasn't really any decent camping around, except across the road was a gravel apron that had possibilities. Attempting to appear as nonchalant as possible, I ate a quick meal, then surreptitiously put out my Z-rest, finding that magic spot between rolling into the ditch and protruding to much into the drive. It turned out to be quite safe as I tucked in below a billboard and doused around me with OFF. The pump spray is a marvelous applicator. I was exceedingly grateful that an obviously bright light for the advertisement towering above did not come on—a good omen.

Overnight Twenty-one: FM
359/under billboard

Not only was it safe, I actually slept at least 20 or 30 winks, and rose at first light. After another quick meal, I was underway with light beginning to fill the sky. I thought I was early, but it appeared the real early birds were golfers wanting the perfect tee-off; many motorcars, much more than the few last night were zooming in from both directions on 359, converging upon one location: the Fox Creek Golf Club. I was tempted to stop in myself, not to strike a little white ball (I'd more likely cut up the turf with multiple divots) but maybe for a coffee or a more reasonable breakfast?

Can't do that; I'd already eaten and was making good time despite a suffocating early morning (actually, anytime out East) humidity. At least there was no wind and the temperature was not excessively high. All-in-all, Farm-to-Market 359 was excellent pedaling, with an exceptional shoulder.

359 became a bit more sinewy as I cycled by the Waller County Fairgrounds, through Pine Island, and across the railroad tracks. Here, I had to make a choice: go straight on new roadway, or to my left on Business 290? It really wasn't much of a choice—I was hungry and that means business!

This would've been my route anyway; I know by-passes when I see'em, and I wanted to go into town. Besides, the broad, 5-lane avenue was a pleasurable down-hilly ride in little traffic. What really made it for me, of course, was seeing Subway, 350 Austin Street East (Highway 290), arriving there to open up the restaurant. Really, there is nothing better than Seattle's Best Coffee in my cup, cut in half with chocolate milk. Even though I'd already been awake and pedaling for a couple of hours, this is the best way to start my cycling day.

I knew it was humid and hot out, but the buildup of condensation on the Subway window was the best indicator. Cold and dry inside, hot and wet outside. Besides the delicious breakfast, coffee, and a/c, I was also allowed to recharge my cell phone. It sure didn't hurt to be a paying customer—not only did I have a necessary meal, but my continued tweeting was assured.

Following Business 290, I pedaled under the fly-over and soon rejoined the by-pass on the Northwestern edge of Hempstead. My safety awareness was on high alert when a ramp merged on my right, but once on US290 Westbound, I found this to be by far one of the very best roads I've ever pedaled—anywhere. It is of interstate quality, broad shouldered, and, in my opinion had an outstanding ATLM on the right lane line, which dynamically increased safety as an effective alert between fast-moving and slow-moving vehicles.

The headwind and moderately rolling terrain was negligible as I pushed on, but the humidity and heat was beginning to have a debilitating effect. However, my spirits were lifted when I recognized that the stretch of 290 over which I was moving was built on mammoth amounts of fill, that I had entered the floodplain of the Brazos River. The bridge and trees delineated the current river, though much bridgeworks were also over dry land. This is an obvious basin which could fill with water during a flood, taking up all of the space around the two highly elevated roadbeds of 290 East and West.

I got a rough idea of how much water that could be when I saw a motor vehicle on the Eastbound 290 pulled onto it's shoulder, obviously in need of assistance. This was my chance for another good deed. Nearly opposite it, I parked my Doublevision on the Westbound shoulder, and, carefully avoiding traffic, I darted across the road and down the steep embankment, through brown thigh-high grass crinkling under my feet. Climbing up the next embankment, I again darted across the Eastbound 290, just as wary of the traffic as before.

Meeting up with the occupants at their disabled vehicle, I learned that they were on their way to a wedding, and they learned about me.

Our costumes couldn't have been more different; all of them were attired in their Sunday best, while I looked like a limp UBS rag in Shimano biking sandals wearing a strange looking helmet. The man-in-charge, father of a gaily dressed young daughter, husband of an distraught wife, son of a monolingual (Spanish) parent, expressed his gratitude to me for stopping and what he needed was a tire tool. I do carry such instruments, but they work best on bicycle tires—not the lug nuts on his car. I told him that if nothing else, there is an auto shop I had seen while pedaling out of Hempstead, a town not too far back.

He appreciated my stopping regardless that there was little I could do. In the hour since their car had the flat, *no one* had even slowed down, much less pulled over to offer assistance. In the back of my mind, I considered pedaling back to Hempstead to buy him a lug wrench, something that would surely give me an even later arrival in Austin, but I had an inspiration. Maybe, I suggested, we might have better success if we worked as a group. And, sure enough, when all of us gave a flagging of desperation a car did pull over. My job was done; I bid them *adiós* and returned to my Doublevision.

Being able to help them in a small way boosted my esteem, but exhilaration took over when I *finally* crossed over the Brazos River, that impediment my Westward progress and had caused a 24-hour delay arriving into Austin. I pedaled around the bend to see a rough-hewn granite abutment standing out from the North cut. Upon it was a bright blue sign with white lettering announcing that I was in the "Birthplace of Texas" beside equally 3-dimensional black lettering noting that I was now entering Washington County. I was already familiar with this claim, not only because I was a Texas history teacher, but also due to having visited Washington-on-the-Brazos and camping in the area with my family in the early 1990s. What a thrill a thrill to now be passing through on my Trans-Texas Bicycle Odyssey!

Over the next couple of hours, the rolling hills, mild headwind, and increasingly oppressive heat put a damper on my thrill. Wishing I had stopped at the Chappel Hill Sausage Company earlier, I hungrily eyed the billboard advertising a Shell Station with clean restrooms. Not that a bathroom isn't important, but the most significant part of the sign was that Burger King was part of the station, too. It brought back a week-old memory of the gas station-Burger King combo on Anderson Loop which had made it possible for me to get as far as Floresville. Maybe if I recharge enough at this one, I could make Austin tonight? Another billboard advertised Chappel Hill Bakery, and the random thought passed through my mind that maybe I would still have the opportunity to taste some Chappel Hill Sausage? And yet another billboard only exacerbated my hunger, this time for Brenham.

Ascending another hill, my salivary glands went into overdrive when I spied the Shell station-Burger King combo and pulled in. As enervated as I was, I couldn't pass up the landscaped "Welcome to Historic Chappell Hill" at the intersection of 290 and FM1155 (Main Street). Wheeling through the parking lot to it, the markers revealed that the namesake was Robert Chappell, an early settler of the area, which was an initial focus of education.

As interesting as that was, I needed to eat. However, instead of returning to the Burger King, I spied the towering sign of Chappell Hill cafe and was torn between the two. I ultimately decided upon the cafe, basing my choice upon knowing exactly what BK offered and taking a chance on what CH might offer.

It was a chance well-taken; the Chappell Hill bakery-deli had a wide ranging menu meant to satisfy any palate. Of course, my palate could only be satisfied by quantity, and in this case, the high quality helped. From main entrees of BBQ meats (Chappell Hill sausage at last!) to pies, kolaches, and other sweet treats, I enjoyed a repast in the chilled a/c. It was wonderful and refreshing.

My Doublevision drew attention, and I never hesitated to promote it, my ongoing odyssey, and distributing personal cards, always asking to be followed on Twitter and friended on Facebook. Everybody I encountered were friendly and interested in me. Regardless that many considered my biketour a bit weird and certainly extreme in this weather, I loved being the focal point of conversation. But, I had to get along—my goal was to be with daughter Katy in Austin over the 4th of July holiday!

Approaching Brenham, the road construction signs forecast some challenging pedaling ahead. Indeed, those orange barrels were starting to the narrow the roadway when I saw Business 290 (Market Street) and was pleased to pedal right on an original route through town. Despite the lack of a shoulder, this 4-lane road was quite decent because it was exceptionally free of debris and traffic was light. No bypass needed for me.

At the Stone Street intersection, I deviated to a traffic berm on the left to read a prominent historical marker which gave the namesake for this county seat when it was established in 1844: Dr. Richard Fox Brenham, surgeon in the Republic of Texas Army. He was a member of the Mier Expedition to claim Mexican territory, but was captured. He was killed during an escape attempt at Salado, Mexico, while the prisoners were force-marched to Mexico City.

Continuing West, Main Street/290 Business decreased to a three-lane, double-left road which was still had light traffic. I passed several good eateries—Sonic, Churches, Dairy Queen, and the most difficult, Mobius Coffee House, where the in"scent"ive was the strongest. I was tempted to stop at the Brenham Heritage Museum, but time was of the essence and the only stop, other than for red lights and stop signs, was to be at the Blue Bell World Headquarters.

Following US290 West, I turned left on Main Street and stopped in front of the courthouse. The best shade—the *only* shade—that was afforded on the sidewalk and in the parking slot reserved for county officials only under a skinny Oak tree. I parked my body in that same shade, simultaneously slumping and slurping down warm water out of my Camelback.

Weakly rejuvenated, I read the historical markers close-by, taking note that Brenham has a solid past as a member of the Confederate States of America, and, being the junction of several rail lines, was a key element in supplying the area's forces. I also learned that this fine courthouse had been constructed of white limestone in 1940 in an "Art Moderne" style incorporating aluminum and distinctive Eagle statuary. It was rather impressive and imposing, for it "...STANDS AS A SYMBOL OF WASHINGTON COUNTY GOVERNMENT." I was actually reminded a little bit of the Nazi-style construction during that same time period in historic footage I'd seen; instead of Eagles, the swastika was the symbol of choice. That casual thought wasn't too disturbing because all I wanted was to do was cool off, with ice-cold water and a/c—something not possible with an inside visit due to it being closed. It was both a Saturday *and* the 4th of July holiday.

There were a few people around, venturing into other shops and, much to my surprise, sipping on cups of *very cold, icy* drinks. My exhausted condition spoke louder as they kindly directed me toward Alamo Street shops. Unfortunately, beautiful historic downtown Brenham is a series of one-way streets, with Alamo going the wrong way and had to pass it while pedaling downhill. Finally able to turn right on two-way Commerce, I planned to approach Alamo Street from the backside.

Much to my delight, what I found instead was the Funky Art Café & Catering, a very casual establishment and was fully welcomed by Jaycee. It was mutual; I especially welcomed that wonderful air-conditioning! Jaycee took excellent care of me, plying me with ice water and her own specially recommended Italian soda, which is a superb electrolyte. She, and her colleagues, were intrigued by my travels, but I was disappointed to hear that Blue Bell headquarters was actually going to be a backpedal for me. Besides, like the courthouse, it was closed to tours today. My send-off inside was gratifyingly *cold*, but, alas, the send-off outside was a stultifying *hot*.

I returned to Main/US290, and continued pedaling West on that fine shoulder, slowly pushing some 400 pounds/181kgs of me and machine. Jaycee had recharged my water buffaloes with fresh, *cold* water, which I enjoyed very much and was able to keep pushing for another hour. I felt a small surge of energy when I passed a blue sign notifying Westbound traffic of a picnic area in 1 mile/1.6km—I *knew* it meant shade and respite from the glowing Sun.

The rest area met my expectations as I parked the Doublevision in the shade and walked downhill to bedrock, where a shadow-protected pool of stagnant water had not evaporated. I poked my finger into the water, finding it slightly warmer than what I was drinking. Not that I would ever drink from this pool of water, but the thought of wetting my body did cross my mind.

After snacks and water, I resumed pedaling West. It was actually becoming pleasant; I think the extreme mid-day heat had lapsed into the cooler temps (if only a few degrees, but still cooler) of late-day, and another road sign advised me that Carmine was now only 7 miles/11kms away, Giddings 23 miles/37 kms. Checking my map, the distance was too great to pedal to Austin by tonight—maybe Giddings? I increased my cadences, glad that road construction was halted for the day.

Ahead, I saw an idling car parked on the shoulder and when I stopped, Dillon and Jason, two young men were inside enjoying cool a/c. Obviously they weren't out of fuel, but their vehicle did have a flat tire and they had neither tire tools nor even a spare tire. Dillon had already contacted his family, and rescue was on its way.

I started to get underway myself when, within a few minutes, I saw an Eastbound car across the grassy berm cruise slowly to a stop.

Well, I'd better check this out, too. I parked and crossed over to meet an elderly Anglo woman who told me her plight. "I'm out of gas. There is a station just below the hill, but I couldn't stop because there were three black fellas around the pumps..."

I was surprised to hear this—she didn't seem the kind of person who might be prejudiced, but then images of Missouri, Kansas, and San DiegoCA where I had experienced similar ignorant manifestations flashed through my mind, in addition to a few days ago in Sublime. I understood what she was saying, and knew how to handle this crisis. I quickly volunteered to help her out; "I'll pedal to that station, buy a gas can, and return with enough fuel for you to at least make it as far as the Citgo station I had passed a few miles back. Scout's honor!" She gave me a ten dollar bill to cover costs, and I was soon pedaling down the hill.

However, there was no gas station there, only an exit/entrance for the Texas 125 Spur. So I pedaled on another half-mile/0.8 km before arriving at the station, where there must have been 30 African Americans filling the lot along with their artisanally painted and expertly maintained cars. That woman should have not been afraid; this was a car club meeting.

All eyes were on me when I stopped and parked in the shade, which is to be expected since my own vehicle, though not nearly as sleek or stunning as their's, was unusual. I found one car exquisitely detailed, with the owner's daughter proudly occupying the front passenger seat. I complimented not only him, but all of them at being able to have such fantastic machines, so superbly clean and neat and which far exceed my own two-wheeler.

"Nah, man," said the girl's father, "you doin' alright, travelin' like that."

"If I wasn't loaded down," I replied, "I'd give your lovely daughter a ride. But, strange as it might seem, I need is to get some fuel to take to someone who ran out of it back on ninety. This is my good deed for the day!"

"You go right ahead, man," he said, "an' good luck on your travels!"

Turns out the station was closed, so no luck in buying a small gas can. However, I did have a former Gatorade 64 ounce/1.9 liters plastic container of red liquid, composed of the Parade Cherry Drink powder purchased way back in Bracketville mixed with water from Houston. I took a sip of the Sun-scorched liquid, then quickly spit the nasty stuff out, and dumped the rest. If that jug had survived this long, maybe it'll hold gasoline as long as it takes for me to return? I filled it with a half-gallon/1.9 liters of fuel and strenuously pedaled back uphill to the stranded woman.

Instead of seeing her car, I saw an industrial-strength, Chevy pickup truck. Then, as I got closer, I was much surprised to see a man standing outside her car, pouring fuel into the tank from a bright red 5-gallon/18.9 liters plastic gas can. Someone else must've also come to her rescue during my absence!

The woman was completely amazed to see me, but with mock indignation, I told her that I "had given my Scout's Honor, even if I didn't complete the entire trail to Eagle."

As soon as the other Good Samaritan emptied his gas can, I poured in the pittance I had bought. Then we engaged in conversation—both of us curious about the other: me, in my Skid-lid on my Doublevision; he, in a kilt.

Like the car club situation at the gas station, I began with a compliment about his kilt. He, Linn, was initially taken aback at my familiarity with this article of clothing.

"Yeah," Linn said, "I always have to send my wife out first when I'm wearin' this 'cause most people think it's a skirt, get scared.

Y'see, we're headin' to the highland games in Houston, and I saw her standin' there." In a whisper he continued, "I guessed she was out of gas 'cause there musta' been forty blacks around the station you went to, and she's awfully white. I was right." Back in his commanding volume, "She said you went after the gas, but wasn't sure you'd be able to get any. So we drove down the road, bought this can full, and, as you saw, put it in her tank."

"You already know the mission I was on for her," I told him, "and I had just finished stopping for another couple of guys who needed another spare tire when I saw her coast to a stop. I try to help everybody on the road, especially when bicycling. It's good karma that way—I've been helped multiple times by motorists, and what goes around comes around." Then I gave a more detailed explanation of my oft-repeated Trans-Texas Bicycle Odyssey.

Our separation was imminent when the woman expressed her gratitude by forcing a twenty dollar bill into my hand. Reluctantly, I accepted it, and waving good bye to all, I pedaled the crossover to the shoulder of US90 West and went back downhill. This time, though, I peeled right onto the spur, up and over the hill into the historic community of Burton. During all this emergency action, I had built up an aching hunger and, with the newly acquired cash wealth, figured there might be an eatery in town.

With little traffic on this narrow road, so I easily took the right lane. When it T-intersected with Main Street, I turned right, going down a slight hill into a small town, dying because US290 had bypassed it. Like Brenham, there were numerous historic plaques erected on equally historic buildings, but my focus was on replenishing my body. It looked grim and I might have to eat the emergency rations I always carry—even if it was as grungey as the drink I had dumped earlier.

I turned left on FM390 toward what looked like downtown, passing the Burton Cafe. The sounds of an accordion were emanating from within, so I wheeled around, parked my Doublevision on the East side, beside a window, and quickly changed into my now-most appropriate American Flag UBS T-shirt, as well as adding lots of highly viscous deodorant. Going through the door, I left the hot and humid central Texas town, and entered a cold Bavarian Alpine village, complete with in-character live polka music & singing. And with the last name of "Eyberg", I was instantly welcomed.

I polished off the glass of water before me, and attempted to analyze the proffered menu for something of interest. It was *all* interesting, causing my mouth to gush saliva and my brain to cease effective functioning. I had to ask for a recommendation, on special or not, that could fill my empty stomach.

"Our *Rouladen* would do you well," said co-owner Lucy, "and we have lots of other deserts that will finish you off. You aren't going to leave hungry."

I also enjoyed the live entertainment of Gene and Gorg, who transported me along with everyone else in this small bypassed Texan town eatery back to the old country. For an hour while supping, I remembered pedaling with brother Nils in West Germany, Switzerland, Lichtenstein, and the fringe of Austria. Lucy was right and wrong—I left physically sated, but was hungry for a return, not only to the old country, but also back here. What a filling (in every sense of the word) experience, and I left several dollars in the donations jar for the musicians.

I initially thought of continuing West on FM390, believing it would connect to 290, but wasn't sure. Maybe someone back at the cafe could give me better directions? Then I was distracted by the historical plaques and, faced with my urge to get a move-on, ended up returning to 290—the same way I had entered this fine burg. A future return just to read those plaques as well as feasting is imminent, if nothing else.

Feeling quite fine, I was moving along without hindrance in the setting Sun. Most interesting to me was another rough-hewn granite abutment projecting out on the Eastbound berm marking the Western edge of Washington County, a near duplicate of the Eastern entrance I had passed earlier today after crossing the Brazos River. Before I knew it, I was in Carmine and at the only place that appeared to be open, the Conoco Gas Station-store. Good thing I had arrived when I did to get last minute chocolate and bathroom use because it was closing.

I felt good, turned on my lights, and maneuvered through the parking lot for the quick 20-mile/ 32km jaunt to Giddings on this extremely bike-friendly route. Unlike the superb shoulder, the lot was a bit rougher, covered with loose gravel debris. This gravel meant little to motor vehicle tires, but to much smaller bicycle tires, they were monstrous sized ball-bearings with only one purpose: reduce friction. And so it was when attempting to make a right-hand turn, I obeyed gravity.

Unable to react as quickly as before, I went down. Completely down.

Shaking my head as I crawled out from under the bike, I righted and inspected it. No damage done, but I interpreted the incident that Giddings was *not* going to be my campsite tonight. Instead, I wheeled to the back of the store, put out my Z-rest, brushed and flossed, thoroughly sprayed the area and myself with OFF, and, while reflecting on this remarkable day, fell fast asleep.

OVERNIGHT TWENTY-TWO: CARMINE

I jerked awake at the sound of motor vehicle pass close-by, that slippery gravel crunching inanimate obeisance to the car tires, as opposed to the revolution routinely given to my Doublevision tires. The Sun was already a finger above the horizon and this was the first time camping that I had ever slept in. In amazement and shock, I quickly re-stowed my overnight gear and began pedaling West. Even in daylight, that ball-bearing gravel *still* tried to upend me.

It was 20 miles/32kms of blissful pedaling West on the US290 debris-free shoulder to Giddings, though I was a bit distressed to not find a food source in the community of Ledbetter. It *is* Sunday *and* the 3rd of July on a holiday weekend; it's foolish of me to think much will be open today.

But my thinking was soon corrected when I entered the thriving city of Giddings and immediately saw that the first eatery on my route was a Subway, 2490 E. Austin (aka US 290). *Saved again! I will not starve to death!*

I backed the Doublevision into a slot in front, went inside with my wallet, cell phone, and recharger. Surrounded by the smells of nutritious victuals that would satisfy my ravenous hunger. I was fully awake, but the Seattle's Best Coffee, combined with chocolate milk re-energized me as only caffeine and sugar can when biketouring. The other nutrients of a breakfast sandwish and yoghurt helped my body, too, by renewing my muscular strength.

As always, I didn't hesitate to introduce myself to the manager, Julie, giving her my personal card and elaborating on the specifics of me and my Doublevision. Likewise, she told me about herself and her other paid employment, as a PEIMS officer for the Giddings ISD. I knew we had something in common more than just a superb restaurant manager and a hungry patron.

Her snippet of information revealed what a small world it truly is.

"You PEIMS folks are so critical to the district's success," I told her. "Ernie, who is your counterpart in my district, makes all the difference when it comes to decoding the funding web. Thank you!"

The yogurt was kept at the correct temperature behind glass in a refrigerator. Unfortunately, I could neither pull nor push in the handle and the treat remained out of my grasp. Julie, with an exasperated sigh, came over and easily gave the handle a sideways push with her pinky, reached in for the yogurt cup and handed it to me.

"Isn't it ironic," I said with a laugh in a feeble effort to cover up my own incompetence, "that even if you're not at central office, you're still helping us teachers."

Without a trace of a smile, she deadpanned, "If you only knew..."

Other customers began arriving, and none said I was actually annoying them; all were interested in my odyssey. When a heavy duty Chevrolet delivery truck, labeled "Two Men and a Truck—movers who care" parked outside,", a pair of husky guys got out of the cab and entered, ready for lunch. They were delivering goods to Houston, and, in jest, I asked if they could take an exceptionally long bicycle to El Paso.

"No," replied the driver, Johnny, "not that we wouldn't want to help you, but that's a bit out of our zone."

"Thanks for the non-offer," I told them with a smile, "but I'm more than halfway through my Trans-Texas Bicycle Odyssey and I'll finish it quick if I have this tailwind all the way back."

"More power to ya', BikerJohn," said Johnny.

"Yeah, but we gotta' get goin' now," urged the other mover. "Good luck to ya'."

I got going too, and pedaled through this busy city. All was fine for a half-hour, when on it's Western edge, the shoulder disappeared. It became a 4-lane US290 with a double-left turn center and *no shoulder.* All of a sudden, 290 went from the best cycle route to the absolute worst. Why? What could have caused this calamity?

My calm, luxuriant pedal instantly transformed me into a terror-stricken cyclist fixated on watching the motor vehicles in my rear view rushing upon me. I was tense, ready for the inevitable impact.

Then, shock!

All of the cars came to a nearly simultaneously virtual halt in both lanes. Then, with the utmost care, the motorists politely merged with each other in the "fast" lane, give me the rightmost lane. Some even exchanged friendly waves with me or the "OK" sign.

These road users knew and practiced the rules of the road. The tailwind alleviated some of the challenge, but the heat was taking its toll upon my body. I don't care if an 8-speed derailleur was jury rigged with my 9-speed shifter, I was ever-so-grateful for the gears, especially the low ones.

My first opportunity for a break from that wholly inadequate 290 came at Paige, when it became a divided highway. I pulled into the parking lot of The Old Frontier Bar and Grill for two reasons: 1) it was time to eat again, and 2) to tweet my recent extreme dissatisfaction with 290. In the former, tragically, the establishment was closed and wanting a new owner; in the latter, I most successfully contacted Twitter with the poorly constructed roadway info, and was even comfortable doing so laying down in the shade of the porch overhang. An added benefit was a short nap.

Returning to cycling, the new high-quality road didn't last; on the Western edge of Paige, 290 went from being divided back into a narrow 4-lane affair with little shoulder.

Parking in the shade of a Valero station in McDade, I slowly wandered the aisles looking for just the right snacks. At the checkout, I conversed briefly with the cashier, encouraging her to continue attending community college, even if only part time.

Much to my surprise, two other customers. Lisa and her son Luke, presented me with a loaf of bread, a quart of milk, and a can of chili.

"Bicycling all the way from El Paso to your son in Houston, and now to your daughter in Austin before going back to El Paso can't be easy," said Lisa. "At least let us buy you this."

Overwhelmed by their generosity, I grinned wildly, saying, "I'm very grateful but there is no way I can carry the extra weight, especially of the can."

They looked crestfallen; then I added, "However, I'll be happy to accept the milk, bread, and Heath bar!"

Another man behind them swelled the discussion with: "I was glad that the drivers are being real courteous an' polite around you, an' it's a good thing you're not bikin' at night—some people really tie it on an' go drivin' real dangerously. You were talkin' about how two ninety changed after Giddin's. My uncle was workin' on it an' they ran out of money. Since you're headin' to Austin, you'll find it real good after Elgin, an' you're real lucky it's Sunday 'cause there won't be any operatin' machines at the interchange with one eighty-three. Now, there's a real problem for you any other time."

"Well, heck, thanks for all that good info," I said. "I'll give my daughter a call when I get close. Thanks again."

"You're welcome. Just be careful out there; remember, no matter how nice the drivers are out there, there's always one fool who's gonna' try to scare ya'."

Almost immediately, 290 did go back to its miserable bicycling condition of no shoulder. Fortunately, motorists continued their exemplary road sharing.

As promised, 290 improved considerably at Elgin. However, I was once again beat and needed to seek refreshment and stopped at the Exxon-Country Store. Being that it was decidedly past noon, the building easily provided shade, but the ominous aspect of that was darkness within a few hours. However, I couldn't leave immediately—I had an absorbing conversation with Adam about Austin Community College, and I absolutely *had* to re-fuel with a syrupy, iced-slush that gave me the necessary cold electrolyte of caffeine and sugar!

I could see a water tower and...is...that...the...UT tower?

Pulling off onto uncompleted Shadow Glen amenity center drive in Manor, I called Katy.

"OK, Dad," she said, "I know where you are. Call me back when you get to one eighty-three and I'll give you specific directions."

"Right. Talk to you then. Love you, bye"

"Love you, too. Bye for now."

Pedaling out of Manor, 290 upgraded to a very bicycle friendly divided highway with ample shoulder although the ATLM was worn down. Very enjoyable. I gave little heed to signs informing vehicle operators about upcoming toll roads 45/130—routes neither intended for nor to be used by my vehicle or any other such HPV. Besides, my goal was Austin, not Waco nor San Antonio. After pedaling through the trumpet interchange, I could see a water tower and...is that the UT Tower?

Crossing Tuscany Road, warning signs ["BEGIN WORK ZONE", "TRAFFIC FINE DOUBLE when workers are present", "ROAD WORK AHEAD", "WORK ZONE speed reduced to 50"] of impending highway building began to appear advising me of a forthcoming US 183 cloverleaf. When I saw the orange construction barrels, I knew it was the interchange. It was also, as it just so happened, the ideal location for a McDonald's restaurant—and my first experience with a delightful frozen Strawberry Lemonade.

"Hi, Katy," I said while slurping down the crushed ice drink, "I'm real close to one eighty-three. How do I get to you?"

"It'll be a bit complicated, Dad," she returned, "but not so bad if you follow these directions." After booting up her laptop, she instructed: "First, get off two ninety as soon as you cross one eighty-three and onto the frontage road. You'll go for a mile or two when it intersects Cameron Road. Take a left and follow it to East fifty-first street, and turn right to get across eye-thirty-five. You'll cross the railroad tracks, go to Duval and turn left. From there, go all the way to thirty-first, turn right and go to the Speedway Food Mart. Call me again when you get there and I'll take you to my apartment."

After a moment so I could absorb all this, she resumed: "*Mira,* I know you've biked here a lot, and I don't want you to be insulted but it's complicated getting to my apartment. Just this once, do it my way. OK, Dad?"

"Sure. I'm too tired to do otherwise. I'll call you again soon."

With the Sun setting—one of the two most dangerous times to be cycling (Sunrise is the other; the danger comes if traveling *into* the Sun and being blinded)—I pedaled on super-smooth, exceptionally clean, newly laid roadway unmarred by tracks or debris. Magnificent. It was so good that I didn't know why the thought entered my mind that I should get onto the sidewalk. I was about to do exactly that when I suddenly jerked the handlebars left, swerving out into the lane. There was a phenomenally huge curb that, had I not swerved, would have certainly put both me and my Doublevision in a horizontal position, probably with significant injury to both, too.

I soon came to another sharp edge, but this time loose asphalt had been packed along it to form a rough ramp. *Aha!* That explains why no other vehicles are in this lane, the construction barrels, and the squeaky clean newness. I was pedaling the subroad, yet to receive the topcoat.

Elated that I had narrowly avoided a serious fall, I stopped and dismounted, breathing a sigh of relief. I turned on all my lights, and was filled with a sense of unbeatable safety. My two forward lights are white, one flashing and one Harbor Freight spot. My six rear are red, consisting of five flashing Hokey Spokes, and one Harbor Freight spot. My Pedalights are always on whenever I am pedaling.

I was particularly proud of this visibility arrangement, especially the front headlamp. It was the combination of an auto headlamp shell that I had found to which I had epoxied a NR 4-cell white LED unit into an enlarged orifice, and mounted it on strap iron to the front of my Doublevision. The Hokey Spokes were originally mounted on the spokes, but after seeing the broad signal given by each one, I repositioned them. I knew they would give me a much larger rear end, thus more visible and ultimately, much safer. If safety is not first, then possible injury or even death is first.

I pushed off, pedaling with great satisfaction on the 290 overpass. Looking over the side onto US183 below, I saw a mess of cones, lights, and signs strategically directing motor vehicles crawling along as if the queen had commanded her ants to get in line. Regardless of that order, I felt relief at not having to cope with it, though figured it'll happen soon, when I leave 290 to take Cameron Road.

Which came awfully quickly, and I pedaled the ramp down to the frontage road, continuing until I came to a traffic light at Berkman Drive. Red means **STOP!** (All too often have I seen bike riders slowing then running this most crucial of all traffic control devices in the presence of other vehicles.) Despite the long length and mass of my Doublevision, I knew it would not likely be able to trip the signal. On *very rare* occasions, I myself have run a red but only, and I emphasize this, *only* after coming to a complete and full stop.

However, even if one other (motor) vehicle was close, I'd wait for that car or truck to trip the signal, as was the case now. When the light turned green, I looked left-right-left several times and safely pedaled through.

Almost as quickly, I arrived at the Cameron Road intersection and, ensuring that the few other vehicles were obeying the rules too, looked both ways multiple times again and pedaled through the green, piping my whistle as loudly as possible. This narrow 4-lane arterial would have been extremely hazardous had it been more congested and had I been less visible.

I appreciated the precise directions Katy had given me because 51st Street bridge over I-35 was amazing. It was broad, with 5 lanes and has a well-marked bike route on it. This street in itself was signed bike route 30, part of a much more extensive bike route system throughout this fine city. There were even sharrows ("share the road") with bicycle stencils painted on the roadway, a safety enhancement I'd last seen in ColumbiaMO, another leader among bicycle-friendly communities.

Crossing the tracks to Duval Street (bike route 49), I turned left and entered familiar territory. Once before, when visiting the capital of Texas, my children, and attending a VAC conference, I had brought my Doublevision. I had pedaled around quite a bit, including Mount Bonnell as well as to my overnight stops at the practical international hostel on Lakeshore Boulevard, the Rodeway Inn on 30th and I-35 frontage road South, and the Travelodge.

Besides pedaling recognizable terrain, I knew this area was primarily dominated by the University of Texas, with one of the largest enrollments in the nation, if not the state. That means a heck of a lot of young adults, mostly pursuing a better life but temporarily impoverished while paying for school. It is also strongly indicative that they will use less-expensive transportation, often a bicycle. I saw many, many people (not necessarily just students) riding bikes, and most were following the rules of the road. I was especially appreciative of those who pedaled with both the required front white light and the *recommended*, but not yet required, rear red light. Unfortunately, there was a sizable number of individuals lacking one or both lights, which suggests they might not be students because they were lacking the intelligence cognizant road users have.

Safely using the road—one of the most universal human-constructed features found upon Planet Earth—is really a highly complex act of intelligence, combining visual cues, written instructions, sharing, physical prowess, and common sense, garnered only with time and experience. Whenever a bicycle is used upon the road, it becomes a vehicle upon the road, subject to all of the same responsibilities as any other vehicle upon the road, as well as having a right to use the road.

That said, a bicycle (aka pedacycle aka human powered vehicle aka push bike) is *not* like other vehicles because of the obvious difference in the energy source: bikes have a human engine, (motor) vehicles have a mechanical engine. There are other obvious differences, primarily in mass and exposure. The mass of a bicycle is a fraction of that of a motor vehicle, even a motorcycle. Simple physics dictates that objects of larger mass will have significantly more impact on objects of less mass in the event of collision. Tangent to that, a person astride a bicycle is far more exposed than a person operating a motor vehicle, thus should the two vehicles ever collide, the former could suffer great injury, even death, while the latter will likely not have any problem, except for possible mental remorse or aggravation.

Stopping in front of the Speedway Food Mart, I saw the headlight of a bicyclist coming toward me down University Avenue, and heard "Dad!"

It was Katy.

In utter contradistinction, moving toward me, was a foolish young woman cruising down Speedway who nearly collided with me.

"WATCH OUT! WHERE ARE YOUR LIGHTS?" I yelled at the co-ed bike rider.

Thoroughly aggravated with this hazardous individual, I added, *"If you don't know how to use the road legally, stay off it!"*

"Sorry," was her fading reply as she, quite literally, disappeared into the darkness.

"Wow, Dad," said Katy, "you sure gave her a hard time."

"Better that than a dead time," I replied. "She's not the only one around here who refuses to follow the rules of the road. I can't believe there are so many individuals attending college who are presumably 'smart' and learning how to work in a World that necessitates a modicum of cooperation, yet don't even practice the most universal tool of sharing the road! There is little that scares me more than a road user who operates their vehicle illegally."

"C'mon, Dad," she said, "they aren't *all* that smart. Most are around my age, just a couple of years out of high school, and none of them were probably as lucky as me to have a hard-core biking father who demanded following the rules. And aren't you being a little bit hypocritical?"

"Well...," I hesitated. "sometimes I run a red light, but *only* after stopping, if no other vehicles are around, and if I can't trip it. I do remember riding without lights when I was in high school and would have gotten seriously injured by a car if I hadn't jumped off the bike. In fact, I seem to recall that the car ran a stop sign—which is one of my greatest fears: someone on the road not following the rules."

"What about the stop signs?" she persisted.

"Always stop," I said. "Even though my nano-stop makes it look like I don't."

We pedaled to her apartment on 28th Street, I pulled my Doublevision through the gate, locked it up on the far side of a small swim pool, and checked the odometer of my Beta-1 cyclecomputer while she put her upright inside.

"It isn't too big, but it has great air conditioning..." she began to explain when I cut her off.

"As long as you are able to keep your grades up, and I'm going to jump into that pool, if you don't mind."

"Oh no, not at all," she said. "Be sure you don't lock the door until your in for the night. Make yourself at home—you can sleep on the futon or the floor. I'll bet you like the floor, although it's not carpeted like Erik's."

"It's fine, Katy," I told her, "the floor is no problem—I've got a Z-rest. Thank you so much for being here."

"You're the one I should thank," she said. "I'm glad you're here, Dad, but right now I need to study for a test later this week."

Laying down, I thought for a few moments about the 78.76 miles (127kms) pedaled today—another remarkable day.

OVERNIGHT TWENTY-THREE: AUSTIN

"Sorry about my scratchy throat," Katy exclaimed, "but Happy Fourth of July, Dad!"

Rubbing my eyes, I parroted it back.

"You look terrible, but if you're able, maybe we can pedal over to see the house I'm renting with four other girls next semester," Katy proposed. "I'll show you where Don lives, and we can get lunch over there, too."

"You should talk, you look like you've not slept at all, and your voice is really hoarse," I replied. "Of course I'm able. That pool was super nice, and the a/c is just as good as you said. The reason I look the way I do is I started reading that 'America' book by Jon Stewart last night. Quite interesting satire."

"Good," she said, "you can read it more because I need to finish up some studying before we go."

I delved back into it when music outside started to grow. Katy poked her head around the corner to tell me, "This is West Campus where there are lots of parties, especially today. But it won't get too loud in here."

Going outside for a dip, the decibels were already high enough to cause vibrations in the pool water. It reminded me of my youth, when loudness trumped quality music, and G-L-O-R-I-A is firmly implanted in my brain. I also distinctly remember the throbbing beat and jarring sounds being used as a cover for other adolescents— none of my friends—and their fall into illicit drug use, as well to hide discussions about the latest in paraphernalia when my family lived in WichitaKS and on Mercer IslandWA. I can still see youths staggering, falling, vomiting, passing out, the flashing red lights of police vehicles and the cops busting up these pot parties. I narrowly escaped the late '60s and early '70s intact, and within a decade, when the Marias had in-ported SouthamptonUK, it was Beatles' music which had drawn me (and a multitude of others) to the University ballroom at night. In my humble opinion, *that* was worth listening to, even to the point of deafness.

Anyway, it sounded like times have not changed that much—there was a drunken clot of students milling, swaying, stumbling, vomiting, and passing out, blocking the street while speakers blared a mix of patriotic tunes, rap, and other indistinguishable melodies. Except this time, no police were present, neither by motorcar, nor bicycle, nor foot.

#1 Daughter!(www.juanitohayburg.com)

With already extreme temperatures ascending and carrying large amounts of water, Katy and I slowly pedaled to her new neighborhood, Hyde Park, where we saw her beau's apartment, her future rental, and finally to the corner of Duval and 43rd Street. I recognized the buildings from last night's pedaling, but now we stopped for lunch. Parking our bikes in the shade between two fine eateries, I definitely locked her upright to my Doublevision. I wasn't too worried about my bike, but it would be ridiculously easy for her's to be spirited off.

Yours truly kept alive by great eateries, Dulce Vita & Quacks, 43rd & Duval (www.juanitohayburg.com)

The first restaurant, Dolce Vita Gelato and Espresso was our source for organic sandwiches and coffee, all of it delicious. We walked across the slight way to the next restaurant, Quack's, for fabulous desert. Being the old man, I also happened to be paying— good thing my VISA cards hadn't worn out. The food was excellent, but what I enjoyed most was the cool air inside both establishments. Judging from the large number of other patrons, that was likely the universal agreement. In fact, I didn't really feel like biking on, the midday heat—outside—was oppressive.

We returned to her apartment by mid-afternoon, and I avoided more punishing heat with another dip in that wonderful pool. Maybe I'm getting *real* old, because the discordant sound waves drove me inside pretty quickly.

"Dad, are you sure you're OK?" asked rough-voiced Katy when she was getting a drink out of the fridge. "I mean, you were going really slow a lot of the time, and..."

"Katy," I interrupted her, "I was going so slow because I have only one brake, and pipe my whistle more than ever because I'm absolutely paranoid about getting hit, even by another bicycle—that silly girl last night was a little too close for me."

Being inside was OK—I read more 'America' while she studied.

Later, Katy said with a raspy voice, "Dad, if we go out for Mediterranean food, I can show you the best way to leave tomorrow."

"Sounds delicious, but you'll have to let me buy some Ricola drops and tea for your throat."

"Ricola?" she asked. "Aren't those the kind you were given when we visited the Gafafer-Lüthis in Switzerland?"

"You've got a good memory, Katy," I said, surprised. "Besides the superb bread she baked, Christine was also a specialist for Ricola and she gave me a package of the drops. Too bad we couldn't stay longer with them. Bloody Italian trains!"

"Give it up, Dad," she said. "Milano wasn't such a terrible place to overnight."

I continued to scowl while walking from her apartment, the area was still crowded with shaking students and pulsating music. At the "drag", also known as Guadalupe Street, we turned South and I spotted a drugstore.

"I remember forty-fifth when you were in the dorm, Katy," I said, my attitude somewhat improved. "Let's stop in here; they might also have some postcards."

"You don't have to do this," Katy croaked.

"I know, but I *am* your father," I said passionately, "and this alternative sure beats going to a doctor. If what I get you doesn't work, you can also gargle some salt water."

All three items—Ricola, tea, UT postcards—were available, and I gave the cashier a ten-dollar bill. Looking at Katy, many dollars and change were plopped into my open hand, which surprised me.

"What is all this?" I questioned him.

"I apologize, Sir," said Aldrick, "but I only have ones in my drawer and you gave me a twenty."

"I thought I gave you a ten," I said credulously. "Your honesty is absolutely amazing. Are you planning a career beyond CVS?"

"Oh, to be sure. I'll be a mathematician when I graduate next year," he said.

Looking at his name tag, I complimented him: "What an appropriate profession for you, Aldrick. I know you'll do well with numbers, and your honesty will take you far. There are really good jobs out there for someone of your caliber. Congratulations, and thanks again!"

Katy popped one of the lozenges into her mouth as we walked back to the Kismet Cafe for vastly superior Middle Eastern food anywhere, short of being *in situ*. For Katy, a simple gyro and a cup of hot water for one of her tea bags, and me, well, I had to have the Lamb Mashawi platter. Of course, I might not be the most discriminating when it comes to chow.

"Dad, thanks for the tea and drops. My throat feels better already. I'm sacking out now—classes start early. Thank you for coming here," Katy told me later.

"Thanks for putting me up," I replied. "It's too bad I was a day late getting here, but..."

"No worries!" she said with a sparkle. "See you in the morning!"

OVERNIGHT TWENTY-FOUR: AUSTIN

We both stopped pedaling at 28th and Nueces, where Katy pointed down the latter and said, "Dad, this is one way and probably a lot easier than trying to take the drag."

Hugging each other, we were a bit misty-eyed as we said our good-byes. I watched her slim frame diminish as she pedaled toward campus, looked at my pale thighs, well-greased with a thick layer of Sunblock.

I saw another building of great interest to me: Whataburger. Unfortunately, I wasn't particularly hungry and my water buffaloes had just been filled with refrigerated water. Still...I needed to get going.

It was about another 600 miles (966kms) back to El Paso, and I smiled at an irony that flashed through my mind.

My hometown is ranked as one of the safest cities, yet it is adjacent to *Ciudad Juarez*, one of the most dangerous cities. As much I love that Mexican city, I hadn't gone across the border since Spring Break 2007, Erik's graduating year from Eastwood High School, when *la familia* Eyberg visited the great World-class Mexico City after the short 3-hour flight there aboard *Aero Mexicano*.

Then, when Katy graduated two years later, I asked my mother and cousin, who were attending her graduation ceremony, specifically to bring their passports, Ellen emphatically declared we were *not* going to *Juarez*. I assured her, "Of course not; we are going to the much safer *Palomas*!" (About an hour West of El Paso, adjacent to

ColumbusNM which is the last place the lower 48 were invaded by a foreign militia, under Pancho Villa for its claim to fame.) *En route*, I made it a particular point of visiting one of the most significant sites in modern World history, Boundary Marker number 1. This is where the Western border between the USA and the USM had been calculated from following the Treaty of Guadalupe Hidalgo(1848) and the Gadsen Purchase(1853), where one can stand in both countries simultaneously without need for a passport. Adjacent to this point, one can enjoy wooded *Parque Madero* by rough access along the levee or *Anapra Calle*, where *Mejícanos* swim in the *Río Bravo,* cavort and dive off American Dam and the water measuring station.

Contrast that to immediately North, which is nothing more than a Border Patrol turn-around point. We had motored in by even rougher access from the McNutt Road, stopping in this most disrespected area. Once there, we enjoyed for bi-national pix, saddened by the disgusting lack of even minimal upkeep on the USA side.

And that sums up one of the most deplorable yet historically significant sites for the past I've seen. How tragic.

As Katy had said, Nueces Street was an easier cycle route—until I reached 24th, where it disappeared into an alley. Even that was OK albeit hazardous, but at 23rd, I pedaled West a half-block to resume pedaling Nueces. From there, I kept my bearings on El Paso, cycling to Martin Luther King Junior Drive, where I moved East to Congress Avenue. Faint tugs upon my heart gave me an impulse to visit the state capitol, Bat Bridge, or even the International Hostel, all sites of previous pedals. This was a very nice route—even sharrows, which look like chevrons and indicate to "share the road", had been stenciled onto the roadway.

Easily descending, I had been lulled into a sense of complacency when, unpredictably, a motorist in a Ford pick-up abruptly ended my daydream. He crossed the solid double-yellows, steering straight toward me. I stubbornly maintained my place, as any vehicle would do, although making plans to jump if he didn't alter his course. Distraction while operating a vehicle by the user is absolutely *verboten* despite it occurring with 100% of all operators, if only for a fraction of time. However, he was not distracted; his eyes showed a maniacal madness, as he would not tolerate anybody usurping his suzerainty of the road, *especially* a bicyclist. Had he reached the breaking point of having to cope with insouciant college kids on their bikes? And here I was, audaciously moving down Congress as if I owned the lane.

Which, of course, I did. In fact, I was totally compliant with the law.

This was a deadly game of 'chicken' and if neither of us relented, I was guaranteed to lose, regardless of my being right.

All of a sudden, his eyes changed and the hood of hate in them lifted—thank goodness he realized his error at the last moment. He pulled hard right on his steering wheel, swerving back into his lane and beyond.

Blinking back a vision of certain death, I was breathing hard.

After having pedaled across Texas and now on my way back home, I had had amazingly good fortune; only a low-speed near-physical contact with the intimidating Fulshears hunter, and now this.

I remembered what brother Nils had told me about some bike riders where he lived, St. LouisMO. He has seen where riders who would intentionally buddy-up in pairs, triplets, or more, and deliberately take over half the roadway, refusing to allow a motorist to pass when the opportunity arose.

Of course, I, too, have seen such hostile on-road behavior and know it can irritate other vehicle operators to the point where she/he might just recklessly try to teach the 2-wheelers a lesson. Maybe that Ford truck operator was in that state of mind, ready to front-end me; I was the one to cause him to snap. Thank goodness he snapped back to reality!

All the same, I needed to get a safer street, and quickly turned right on one-way 6th Street.

My recovery from the not-quite-fatal collision was almost as fast as the incident itself, and my mood swung back to buoyant because it was still the beginning of the day *and* I was finally on the last segment of my biketour.

West. I was going West!

At Guadalupe Street, I saw a post office. Perfect! I wouldn't have to carry the postcards written yesterday anymore. I pulled in, parked beside the building, and took the half-dozen inside. The line was short, something unusual after a 3-day weekend, but that didn't stop me from letting everybody know about me, my get-up, and my quest. Like most all people I've met along the way, they were very kind and considerate and probably thinking that my mental processes were a bit off.

I swear my Doublevision was lighter now that those few ounces were mailed. Well, it might also be that gravity was pulling me down Guadalupe and my sole front Magura was retarding exactly as designed, in spite of the double-duty.

Turning West again, I took the far-right lane of Cesar Chavez Street and immediately after crossing Shoal Creek, I went up the substation cut-curb onto the amazingly exquisite, separate Lance Armstrong Bikeway. This broad alternative-transportation route specifically for bicycles was dual-laned; the rules of the road apply here as well and I stayed to the right.

The well-engineered route is named for 7-time Tour de France winner, Lance Armstrong, who lives in the area. Other than pedaling this fine route, my only other connection to Mr. Armstrong is from 2004, when I had viewed him slowly pedaling the Champs-Elysées, then standing on the podium with *his* children, being hailed for another win. I and *my* children were aboard a Stena Line ferryboat between Stranraer and Belfast Port, where I sat in the television room with numerous other fathers, all of us watching the cycling champion receive his laurels.

Just like then, I was now going West, my preferred direction of travel for the next two weeks or so. Passing beneath a Union Pacific trestle, I soon came to a choice in my direction: continue straight ahead, passing beneath another bridge to Lamar Boulevard; or turn North, which would give me access to the bridge itself. (This overpass is the Pfluger Pedestrian Bridge crossing Lady Bird Lake/Colorado River.) I chose the latter, because my goal was to rejoin US 290 West on the South edge of Austin. Before discovering this fine pedestrian crossing, I had thought Lamar Boulevard (route 343) would be my connector to 290—the only road needed to get back home.

I proudly walked my Doublevision South on this fine, crowded bridge, stopping infrequently for outstanding views of the Austin skyline, Lady Bird Lake, the UP trestle, and the Lamar bridge. One large area was occupied by a wedding party, posing for excellent pix. (Although there are undoubtedly multiple sites, the most notable place I've pedaled to that is such a fine picture-point is Mount Bonnell.) Lovely as this new overpass is, I could not dawdle—I needed to stay focused and *must* continue heading West.

Pedaling uphill on Lamar, I was impressed to see a yellow warning diamond with a wheelchair stencil on it, only to become distressed at the next information sign that the bike lane was ending. Fortunately, the lane line had returned by the time I was losing focus—hunger was pushing me to consider several eateries. Feeling faint and wanting the best brunch, I made a right turn into the parking lot of a strip mall, taking a slot for my Doublevision in front of the Moonlight Bakery, 2300 S. Lamar.

Owners Norma & Derrick made me feel extremely welcome; I took my Skid-Lid off and settled into my temporary home. My arrival at this fine establishment was a propitious moment; the *kolaches* were hot, as was the coffee which easily mixed with cold chocolate milks.

It was a opportune moment for me to discuss future prospects with the young cashier, whom I strongly encouraged to continue her education through ACC and look at www.careercrusing.com for additional guidance. More important was the information I gathered from *le Cordon Bleu* externist Andrea. What I learned from her will help me when I am discussing culinary careers with my students, especially since they hold that institution as a pinnacle of education.

Sitting there in the cooled air of Moonlight Bakery, a steady stream of regulars filtered in and out, each knowing everybody else. It became obvious to me that Austin is really a collection of small, distinct locales, much like the Hyde Park Katy and I had pedaled yesterday, each unique and nearly self-supporting. I tried to join this "in-crowd", always giving my personal card, cajoling, and readily sharing my tale. Likewise, everyone was kind to me, especially the youngsters. Kenny, Hill Autoworks owner and triathlete, entered to post flyers concerning an upcoming event, was able to give me specific details about how to navigate the complexities of going West on 290 through the forthcoming interchanges of Capital of Texas Highway (360) and MoPac (1).

Kenny had given me knowledge, which added to the power and energy I used to get underway.

Unfortunately, I didn't effectively use that knowledge and turned left into the Lamar Oaks shopping center. I wandered through the parking lot but soon became aware that it was not a short cut. Why hadn't I taken more careful note of what Kenny told me?

No matter, I returned to Lamar Boulevard upon my vehicle and entered the first interchange. I was exceptionally pleased to find a decent, albeit debris ridden, shoulder and pedaled West. Motor vehicles were whipping by me, small pebbles occasionally spewing from underneath their tires and small drafts of wind lightly buffeting me, but I was undisturbed. My tension level was heightened when the interstate-quality roadway became elevated, and, quite unlike the elevated 290 I had pedaled across 183, I was not too comfortable. Even with the reasonably broad shoulder, there was little room for error, either from me or from the other vehicle operators.

My quick glances over the side gave me with a good feeling, pleased to be avoiding the congested stop-and-go traffic below. It seemed for a moment that perhaps I really should be down there, attempting to negotiate my way through the chaos, but *I* saw no signs, nor police, nor any other indicator prohibiting my actions. So I continued to push on, now through the MoPac interchange. Once across, I breathed with relief when I was finally able to peel right into the Conoco-Phillips station-store. It was time for a break after an hour of sweaty, heady roadwork, and the cool a/c inside was most appreciated. Along with vital Mountain Dew electrolyte, I also bought a fresh gallon of drinking water to refill the re-iced water buffaloes. I was making *excellent* progress, and expected to be in Johnson City before dark.

That optimistic assessment was soon tempered by the reality of afternoon temperatures and one last particularly challenging section to pedal. From the Conoco-Phillips station-store West, US290 and Texas 71 were combined into a narrow 5-lane route with little shoulder and *much* (motor) vehicular traffic. I pushed on, stopping for the red signal at William Cannon Drive, and, when it became green, carefully looking left-right-left before proceeding.

I saw a picnic table with shelter, and became ebullient. I easily veered to my right, with the shade needed now more than ever. Although the ice cubes had thawed, the water was not yet heated and felt so wonderful as the cool ribbon flowed down my parched throat.

Unfortunately, the traffic was increasing, which meant I had to keep moving before it got any more congested. My heart jumped a bit when I passed the sign indicating that the two routes were diverging, 71 peeling to the right, 290 remaining straight. I knew this was my last major hurdle before open road—all I had to do was successfully make that dangerous crossing. Fully confident and not too worried because, after all, I had navigated the far more difficult interchanges earlier today *and* 183-290 seventy-two hours ago.

An HEB, also as ridiculously easy to get to as the picnic shelter had been, could have been a stop, but my goal was to get as far as possible today which meant no more stopping (unless for a red light). The interchange seemed relatively easy—a T-intersection with no flyovers and only a single lane of 71 to cross with a signal light. It was a brilliant red when I stopped, but, shades of Pattison, a truck on my left barreled through, ignoring the stop light. I blinked. Was I going to witness a massive collision, a twisting pile of metal, plastic, glass and human flesh?

Fortunately, no. But it served as a good reminder to *always* bicycle defensively.

As soon as I crossed the intersection and after a merge lane, 290 opened up into the kind of superior route I hadn't pedaled since before Giddings. It became a divided road, with ample shoulder and, as an unexpected bonus, the road sign indicated 13 miles/21kms to Dripping Springs, 38 miles/ 61kms to Junction, and 73 miles/117kms to Fredericksburg. Consumed with delight, and I pushed harder. But not much harder, because, despite all the positives, it was hitting 101°F/39°C) with a suffocating humidity of 87%.

Then 290 changed, back into a narrow 4- and 5-lane road, made even more hazardous when the shoulder width varied, sometimes

John Eyberg

reduced by the presence of steel barriers. I often had to take a lane—moving slower to grind up the long inclines followed by a quick coast down.

At the intersection of 8600 290 West with Circle Drive and Southview Road, I saw the best respite on my right: a Texaco station, and, most importantly, the shaded patio of Señor Buddy's, the accompanying store/dance hall/eatery. I wheeled into the shade, which, like getting into the box culverts on 90, knocked off 15-20°F/7-10°C degrees. Thankfully, wind was not an issue.

After resting my body, I arose and met the owner, Jorge Garcia. After introducing myself, giving him my personal card, and detailing my actions, he graciously invited me to stay as long as needed to recuperated from the chaos of Austin traffic. He also asked me to attend the grand opening celebration on Labor Day Weekend, but I had to decline—El Paso is a little too far away.

Inside his brand new establishment, I paid for fajitas at a separate counter that was set at windows in view of the pumps, then sat at another counter where I watched, and smelled, the delicious food being grilled. I stoked up on coffee, chocolate milk, as well as putting fresh ice and water into my buffaloes. Since this was still a recent addition to the motoring landscape, only a few patrons were present—all of whom I made myself known to. Even without my Skid-lid on, I surely looked a bedraggled rag doll, and probably smelled pretty bad, too. I felt alright upon departure, circling through the parking lot and around the pumps a couple of times, piping my whistle and waving *adiós*.

Pushing on, I soon crossed into Hays County and 290 became almost as good as pre-Giddings, but no ATLM. Seeing a familiar red oval ahead, it was time for another break and since I'd already eaten my main dish at Señor Buddy's, dessert was needed. And what better place than Dairy Queen? My dessert was a big banana split: fruit and sugar. While slowly eating it inside and enjoying the a/c, I considered my friend Doctor Mike.

I stared at the map for a long time and saw that his town of Wimberley was at least 15 miles/ 24kms South one way. It was only the 5th of July, but how much longer would this increase my return time? That was the first factor. I know myself well enough

248

that I intensely dislike backtracking, so going to his home would add no less than 32 miles/51kms, although I would rejoin 290 closer to Junction City. That long detour was the second factor. The third factor: terrain—I was definitely in Hill Country. And the final factor was time of day: late afternoon.

Just like altering my original goal of the Sabine River/LA, I was fearful that I'd run out of time. That is, I *had* to be back in El Paso within two weeks, which should be plenty of time, but—my confidence notwithstanding—what if my Doublevision had similar mechanical problems as when going East? I knew the stoker crankset was not good. What if I was truly isolated when a breakdown occurred? My anxiety was becoming larger, and I ultimately chose to not visit him.

I circled around the DQ, waving goodbye to the few people there I had befriended and continued West on 290. I hadn't gone very far when I saw a road sign, with the arrows pointing South to Wimberley and San Marcos. If I was going to visit him, this would be my last chance. No. Too many factors against the Southern detour. Once past the intersection, my anxiety level reduced significantly.

Then it went up.

All too soon, 290 took up the post-Giddings problem of narrowness and little shoulder, except now the traffic didn't seem as forgiving. Going East, it was the draft of big tractor-trailer units I felt; now, I could feel much smaller motor vehicles zooming past me. After one particularly close pass, a car stopped in a gravel pull-out ahead of me.

A bronzed, muscular man leaped out of the Toyota-white Beemer and waved me over.

"Man, what you're doin' is fantastic but that car came really close to you!" he said in a concerned voice. "You need to get off this road. Do you wanta' place to stay the night?"

This was the same kind of invitation that Connie and Ed had given me a fortnight ago, when it was too early to stop, but now it was late and I was starting to look for campsites. I thought, "Heck, why not?" and replied, "Yes! Where?"

"Great! I'm about seven miles away, by Perdenales Falls State Park," he said.

"Yes, yes, I'm familiar with it," I acknowledged. "My family and I camped there many years ago."

"Good! Just down from here is farm-to-market road thirty-two thirty-two. Turn right an' go all the way to where it dead-ends into another road. Turn left, an' your real close to where I live."

"If you miss seein' the thirty-two thirty-two sign," he added, "there's an official Perdenales Falls State Park sign on the road. too. Anyway, it's part of a short-cut into Johnson City, an' you'll skip this dangerous two ninety."

I nodded my head in agreement.

"Oh, once you get up there, I have a big scary tan dog that'll be waitin' to greet you. But don't be scared—he's a worthless guard," he said with a chuckle.

"Hey, my name is 'John' or 'Juanito' or 'BikerJohn'," I started to introduce myself, "and I'll be there in about an hour. Thanks!"

"Yeah, my name is Pablo," he said, "an' I'm the one who should thank *you*. See you later!" He throttled up, gravel kicking out from under his tires.

I throttled up, nearly slipping over on the gravel.

Coasting downhill, I saw both the Perdenales Falls sign and road marker 3232.

Completely confident of myself, I turned North, pedaling up steeper hills but then coasting faster down them. It *was* familiar. Not that I could accurately remember when I had camped out here so many years ago, but this was an Ozarks-style road—that was the familiarity. In my many Missouri biketours, I had pedaled virtually the same kinds of roads, a narrow 2-lane cement route that closely followed the contours of a barely-scraped Earth, always uphill followed by a downhill with a scrawny bridge across a creekbed.

This was true Texas Hill Country, known as the Balcones Escarpment, a zone of transition from between the lowlands of the coastal plains and uplands the Edwards Plateau. I had pedaled the Southern edge of this unique geography on US 90 when going East on my last week, and now I was cutting through it going West. From past studies and expeditions, I knew this was the reason why water, as it drained toward the Gulf of Mexico, would rise at springs or other outlets to combine from streams into large rivers.

Like the Ozarks, this is karst topography, which is not unlike a sponge full of voids and cavities physically represented by caves, sinkholes, springs, underground rivers and reservoirs. It had been created over hundreds of millions of years by rainwater (H_2O) that was made slightly acidic while passing through the air, in which trace carbon dioxide (CO_2) joined those drops to make carbonic acid (H_2CO_3). These drops would fall upon the ground, percolating ever-so-slowly through the soil and rocks. A weak acid raindrop would dissolve an equally minute amount of limestone. This simple erosive act would be repeated constantly for the geologic blink of an eye, which cumulatively created spaces, small and mammoth, that were often filled with fresh water, both deep and at the surface.

Unrestrained water obeys gravity (not only in this part of Texas, but everywhere), flowing downhill, usually passing to man-man-made structures such as reservoirs behind dams, water towers/tanks, irrigation systems and the like, all to keep us humans alive.

Without it, we die.

So every effort is taken to obtain and control water, such as the pipelines sprouting in Connie and Ed's field on Anderson Loop, or the Kay Bailey Hutchinson Desalination Plant back home. Most the time we borrow this most essential of fluids, we in developed nations take it for granted and subject it to some of the most horrific processes imaginable, rendering it unfit for consumption by Humans and most living things. The irony is, we then expend huge resources cleaning that water making it consumable—again.

The Sun was setting when I turned on Ranch Road 2766, where a huge tan-colored lab dog, leaking copious fluid from the mouth, lumbered out to me. Good thing Pablo had clued me that he was a friendly dog, or I would have been terrified by this cross between a Great Dane, Lab, and a small horse. The mutant horse-dog led me down a semi-rough corduroy gravel road, soon stopping on what could have been the cement pad for a small house, and backed my Doublevision onto it's kickstand. From there, a paving stone path led me to the front door of a modern 2-story home as the colossal canine almost aggressively nudged me along the way. Opening the door a crack so as to not allowed that 4-legged creature access, he adroitly pushed the door wide open and bounded in.

The scent of sauté steak drenched in herbs and mushrooms overtook me, and I salivated much like the dog—fluid began dripping from the corners of my mouth. I nearly collapsed as that fragrance overpowered me!

"Didn't I tell you right about the road?" Pablo asked from around the hallway.

"Ooohhh, yes," I agreed. "It was wonderful, and I was really glad not having any other vehicles trying to share that narrow road with me."

Rather indelicately I asked, "Is that, by any chance, a meal for *us*?"

"It sure is! Come on in, get it while it's hot! Let's go out on the deck to eat and watch the colors," he replied.

"You don't have to say that twice!" and I was soon sitting beside a hot tub, attempting to not swallow the plateful at once.

It was time to re-introduce ourselves again, to get a more in-depth view of each other. I was glad to disclose first, boldly proclaiming the who, what, where, when, and why of myself. The how was blatantly obvious. I concluded with, "You were right, the road here is *much* safer than two ninety because there were no other vehicles on it. And your putting me up for the night, well, it is great. This'll make my return to El Paso easier. Thank you, Pablo."

"Juanito, this is fate. I grew up in El Paso an' my parents still live there. I love what you're doin', an' I'd be surfin' if not tied down!"

"Oh?" I inquired.

"Yeah, I've got major expenses—paying for this place, a building in downtown Austin with my partners, an' transportation. Drivin' everyday between here an' Austin is a killer—two-ninety is really bad."

"I know exactly what you're saying—I've been on two-ninety since Hempstead, and it is some of the best road I've ever pedaled *anywhere*—*until* just past Giddings, then it is atrocious most of the rest of the way, with some exceptions."

"You mean you biked through the Cannon-Seventy-one intersection? Man, I see a crash there all the time!"

"I almost witnessed one earlier today. I was stopped at seventy-one and this truck flew past me, right through the red. I don't blame you for not liking that road. But if the trade off is this beautiful spread out here, so quiet and peaceful—*and* you're an incredible cook. These are really great eats!" I mumbled while popping the last succulent spear of asparagus into my mouth. "You leave the dishes, I'll clean up, same thing I always do when my children make the meals—I clean up."

A bit more subdued, he spoke, "That's another reason for my bein' here instead of surfin'—my three year old daughter, who lives with my ex in South Austin."

"Well," I agreed, "family is the most important thing for anybody."

"You bet!" he enthusiastically replied, then in a more sober voice, he confessed, "I had another reason for inviting you here, Juanito: I'm lonely. My wife wenta' Caracas an' hasn't returned."

"Really?" my interest piqued.

"Yeah, she's a knock-out Venezuelan an' went to visit her family. Now they won't let her come back. They're keepin' her there, remade her Facebook page, deletin' anythin' about me, doin' everythin' for her but lettin' her come back to me."

"But you're married to her, right?"

"For almost four years now. I should've done it the way her family wanted, with a church an' all. Now they're sayin' that because we didn't do it that way, we aren't really married an' they won't let her leave. Oh, Juanito, I miss her; it really hurts an' I don't sleep well. This is terrible."

He was beside himself in pain from the self-contempt.

"Let me see if I understand this right: You've got a child from your first marriage, divorced, married a second time to a Venezuelan woman who returned home to visit her parents and now they won't let her leave?"

Pablo nodded his head yes, tears almost leaking out of his swollen eyes.

"I might not know all the specifics, but I'll bet it's a Catholic wedding they wanted and anything different isn't recognized. That's a tough one; when my wife and I married, we went to the mayor of Shelby, a small town close to where we lived in Ohio. He performed the civil ceremony for free as long as we donated to the Christmas

Tree Fund, and we had some friends, an elderly couple, Pearl and Limey, stand up for us. We didn't have any family at our wedding, but her parents, who are Catholic, accepted me anyway. My parents, who are Episcopalian, were just glad I found a woman who accepted *me!*"

"I hear you, Juanito, but this a way different. I'm a lot older than she is, but we've got a lot in common, surfin', healthy livin', an' especially bein' in love. We were accepted by both sets of our parents, too—until we got married. She loved it out here, bein' in the hot tub with me, Tan always at her side, away from the city, all the noise an'..." came Pablo's diminishing words. "Oh, only if I'd done it like her family wanted..."

I could see he was bleeding from his pores.

I could feel his pain, remembering the hurt I'd known when my ship would leave port and the women I loved...

Oh, who am I kidding?

That was decades ago and I was just the classic Sailor back then.

But now I am extremely happy with a few years beyond a quarter-century of wedded bliss, well beyond his four years. Heck, he's still in the honeymoon phase. However, upon reflection of my own life, I might be able to lighten his load.

"Pablo," I furthered clarified, "you've got some strikes against you: the May-December marriage and culture difference can be significant, but it sounds to me like you've done everything right except for including her family, and now they're trying to break you up for it?"

"You got that right. It's been a week an' my counselor is telling me to let it go. But I can't, I wracked with pain without her," he pleaded.

"So you haven't had any contact with her for a week?" I asked.

"Actually, nine days. It's been terrible, I don't know what to do."

"You said you're seeing a counselor; what does he say?"

"He's on the 'net, an' tellin' me to be strong, just let it go."

"So, you're legally married—here in the USA, anyway—and you're not communicating with your wife? And your internet counselor wants you to divorce? Do you think he wants you to be in the 'more than half of marriages' fail group?"

Looking down, he murmured, "Yeah."

"Well," I paused, thinking about one of the reasons for my long marriage, "my wife is a dynamo about communication. Can you contact your wife?"

Now looking at me, he whispered, "My counselor says to let her make the contact, that I need to wait it out. Oh, if I'd only told her to stay, not go back...."

I interrupted, "So you're telling me that your counselor is on the internet, that you've never met him in a bricks and sticks building? And you trust him?"

"I'm too busy runnin' my own 'bricks and sticks' construction to spend any time meetin' with him, and he has lots of awards on his site."

"Hmmm," was my thoughtful reply. "That's all?"

"Yeah."

"Well, I definitely not a certified or licensed counselor," I told him, "but I'm very real and I think the biggest problem you have is her family. Why don't you contact her?"

Pablo looked at me for the longest while, then reached for his cell phone and gingerly tapped multiple times on the screen, followed by an electric beep. Scarcely breathing, his attention was completely fixated on it as he waited.

All of a sudden, his face began glowing while he shouted, "She's there! She's wantsta' know if I'm at the airport! She wants me to come get her! But they've got her goin' to school! And tons of other boyfriends! Surfin'! She wants to go surfin' with me! That's how we met!"

Then he looked at me with the first joy I'd seen since meeting him, saying, "Juanito, I'm so glad you're here. You're the reason this is happenin'! Fate! It's fate that you're here! Thank you!"

Almost as quickly as he had taken on the countenance of a saved person, he became dark and troubled when he looked back at his phone.

"Now she wants to know when we're getting divorced!"

Looking back to me, "Why? Why would she be so glad to hear from me, then change just like that?"

"Well," I conjectured, "maybe there's someone sitting beside her coaching her just like I'm sitting beside you. Maybe a family member caught her texting you and now she has tell you what *they* are telling her to do."

"I don't know," he said. "Now she's sayin' it's late, an' she has early classes tomorrow, an' she needs sleep. We'll talk tomorrow."

"I won't disagree about it being late," I said through a yawn. "Tomorrow is already today."

"I don't know if I can make it through the night, Juanito," came his trembling comment. "My heart is racing, I feel desperate."

"Pablo, there's no way to sugar-coat this. It's going to be rough on you, no matter how legal or how much in love you are with her," I told him. "You've overcome nearly every roadblock possible except one—family. And that one alone can stop you, more than anything else."

"Yeah," came his glum reply.

Inspired with a new approach, I asked, "You know about all the pedaling I'm doing. I've had a lot of mechanical problems, but I've always been able to recover, whether getting more fresh water, patching a flat, or making repairs at a bike shop. I've come close to stopping my Trans-Texas Bicycle Odyssey, but I figured out a solution and kept going. That's because I'm a bicyclist. You're a surfer, right?"

Still downcast, he faintly replied, "Yeah."

"So what do you do when you fall off your board?" was my next question.

"Get back on it," came a stronger reply.

"So, now you've fallen off your board, what're you going to do?" I said, trying to lead him to his own solution.

"*I'm gonna' get back on the board, and keep on surfin'!*" was his robust answer. "Juanito, I'll make it through the night, through my life, because I'll keep on surfin'! Thanks!"

"OK," he continued, "you can sleep in a bed or on the couch..."

"If you won't be offended," I interrupted again, "I'll just sleep on the floor. It's what I've been doing since leaving El Paso on June eleven."

"Wherever you want, Juanito. Good night."

"See you in the morning, Pablo. Good night."

OVERNIGHT TWENTY-FIVE: *CASA DE PABLO A* HILL COUNTRY

Wishing for a cup of strong coffee, I went outside to pack my Doublevision, dominating the cement parking pad as Pablo's shorter car was parked to the far side of it. The Sun was just beginning to break the horizon—and with such little sleep, I knew today was going to be low mileage. Extended rest periods—naps—would be necessary.

"Whoomp!"

I nearly fell over when what felt like a length of water hose struck my thigh. Looking to my side, it was Tan, jumping up for a full-body slam of affection. This bloody dog might not be so good at guarding, but it could probably be great in *lucha libre*. I smiled, thinking that the 'dog-man' needed no mask.

I busied myself exploring the grounds with Tan, noting that this was definitely a transition zone—gone were the huge broadlleaf, deciduous trees in the more wet zone (although currently devastatingly dry) further East, replaced with stubbier Cedars and shorter shrubs the can subsist on a more arid diet. Having satisfied myself that this estate was more than adequate to sustain the few lives here, I returned and sat beside my Doublevision to write in my logbook—notes that would be essential for writing this manuscript.

With a steaming cups of tea and smoothies, Pablo joined me outside. Even with the Sun now partway up and the air rapidly heating, the hot and cold liquids re-invigorated me.

"Thanks, Pablo," I said gratefully, "this is perfect for me to get underway."

"No, Juanito," he replied, *"thank you.* I'm still torn up inside, but you've helped me at lot; your staying here was no mistake. Have a good rest of the trip. Let me know how it goes for you."

"Lo mismo, you let me know how it goes for you, too," I told him.

We parted with a solid handshake. He motored up the gravel lane, followed by me, pedaling carefully so that the gravel wouldn't dump me. Tan loped alongside me, although I had to warn him away—another affectionate bump from him would certainly put me down.

I hadn't gone very far on Ranch Road 2766 before my concern was not so much about getting knocked over by Tan, but by his panting. He apparently owns only a Winter coat, and in his eagerness to accompany me, was becoming obviously overheated. I stopped before a great descent, took a plastic bag from my pannier, and fashioned a basin between rocks, into which I poured fresh water from my water bottle. He lapped it up with gusto—once again, this fluid, no matter it's temperature, proves vital to all life.

I refilled the DIY bowl, growled as ugly a "**STAY!**" as I could and pedaled off. Tan raised his head, looking at me in disbelief. How could I, a new life-long friend, do this? The thought stayed with me as I quickly sped downhill, leaving Tan unable to catch up. I sort of hated myself for abandoning him, but was comforted with the knowledge that it would be impossible for him to stay with me. After all, Tan did belong to Pablo, who, while going through this crisis, needed him.

The cruise downhill was exhilarating, but the flipside is that there is always an upside, usually equally steep. I caught sight of the Johnson City water tower, perched at the highest point on a hill, then lost it while following this winding road. Then, when I came around another corner, it appeared again, a little closer and more distinct. This pattern continued for an hour when I saw other definite clues to my closeness: a lowered speed limit sign, then a US 281-290 junction marker, followed by a sign directing me left to Austin & San Antonio, right to Fredericksburg & Marble Falls, and finally a warning for the inevitable stop.

While stopped, I debated whether to turn left or right, but, really, there was no question: I was homebound and that meant WEST. To go that way, I had to turn right and continue pedaling on US290, Fredericksburg. But it was mid-morning, I was hot, exhausted, and remembered an excellent restaurant at the junction of 290/281.

The Hill Country Cupboard was just North, over the rise at the junction of routes 290 and 281. I knew I would be pedaling West from that intersection, but first *food* and *water*. After backing my Doublevision into a slot, I followed the scent into this fine eatery. The World famous chicken fried steak-and-egg meal was my key to rejuvenation, along with ample coffee to wash it down.

Well, that was part of the key; the rest of the key was the cold air, which, like the Subway in Hempstead, caused condensation to form on the window. How nice it would be to have condensation forming on me when I pedaled. I guess it does, except just the opposite; it is the sweat, which evaporates to keep my body cool. I was going to need that all-too-soon, but for now I had a pleasurable 2-hour stop of eating, drinking, and gabbing.

On the Western edge of Johnson City while speeding downhill, a glaring piece of metal reflected light at me, penetrating my Sunglasses, and I stopped across from it on Flat Creek bridge. Walking to this large organized mass of metal, it looked like a shiny exoskeleton for the mascot for UT-Austin that I had seen in the University co-op parking lot three nights ago.

Then another structure I had missed a few minutes before when going downhill caught my eye: a large, rusty-looking, bent coil-spring titled Cosmic Flows Eyfells. I pondered the work for a few moments before I concluded why it was almost invisible to a moving onlooker. It's colors nearly matched those of the surrounding dried out landscape!

Intrigued, I walked a few paces South on Flat Creek road and came upon another outdoor piece consisting of three mesh columns that bore a sign at the base:

Benini Galleries & Sculpture Ranch
Open 10 to 5 Fri. Sat. Sun 5.2 miles>>>
Other Days by Appointment 830-868-5244
Free admission

Several more steps South brought me in front of other whimsical structures: two three dimensional steel cubes, titled "The Blue Saint" (by Hamric), and really should have been plural. There were two nearly-duplicated sculptures, each mounted on poles of different height, a 'Senior' and a 'Junior' or a 'parent' and 'child', if you will. Another was a whimsical metallic depiction of a plant, the "Passion Flower" (by LaPaso), with orbs and petals mounted high.

This *is* interesting.

Returning to my Doublevision, I once again read the sign.

"Hah!" I thought, "I wouldn't pedal off the road for Dr. Mike and I for sure am not going out of my way now. I'll just admire the teasers for now."

Sweating profusely and desiring *cold* water to drink, I soon found myself coasting downhill into the small community of Hye, stopping in front of a most ornate, false-fronted building broadly titled "POST OFFICE". I could see that it was the community magnet, not unlike the Lake Springs Mercantile store that Dunky ran a half-century ago in Missouri, or it's modern-day equivalent in DrydenTX, the former a distant memory, the latter not a fortnight ago.

I was surprised to find it closed, despite being all lit up inside and on a Wednesday at that. I attempted to sop my brow with condensate wiped from the windows. A sign indicated that I could gain access through another door, but that, too, was locked. At least I could enjoy the shade of the broad porch, although distracted by an antique scale for weighing huge sacks of grain, bales of cotton, or even a bicyclist in pursuit of his boot camp 180 pounds/82kgsweight.

I was getting closer, about 200 pounds/90kgs, when the door behind me unlatched. The smiling woman motioned that entry was now possible. Entering, the cold air was incredibly refreshing, but I still went straight to the glass-fronted refrigerators. I rethought my need for cold water, opting instead for cold Mountain Dew and an ice cream treat, too. No picture postcards were available, disappointing me, but at least this was a brief respite from the heat.

Back on 290 and entering Gillispie County, I noticed a motor vehicle behind me. That is not unusual, but what made this car stand out was it didn't zoom by me. In fact, it seemed to slow down to a crawl; maybe there was engine trouble? I was ready to turn around and render aid when it began to speed up. The white sedan was nearly abreast me when I caught a glimpse of the driver. It looked like my MPO friend, Efrén Meza! No wonder the car was behaving the way it did—he is one of the most conscientious road users I know. Too bad not everybody operates their vehicle as well as he does. Regardless of whether it was actually him or not, I gave a friendly wav—my same action for almost all other vehicles out on the road.

I'll not alienate anybody out here.

It would do me no good to anger another road user, who might suddenly turn on me and their vehicle becomes a deadly weapon.

I passed a blue informational sign informing me of a rest area in one mile. Thank goodness! I needed to get off my Doublevision for another short break, and the Gillispie County Rest Area was probably one of the fanciest I'd seen yet. It was beautiful, with primary construction of limestone, including the apron in front of the main building. The Lone Star of Texas had been part of the landing design, which was quite decorative. But most importantly, a bathroom was available.

Departing, I couldn't hardly miss the brown informational sign about the Lyndon B. Johnson State and National Historical Park in a mile/1.6km, which, when I arrived at the intersection with State Park Road 52, was bordered by both state and national flags. I knew it reconnected with 290 further West, having explored this area by motorcar with my family years earlier, but no exploring now—I kept on pushing West.

During my bicycle odyssey, topography was a continually changing topic, beginning with long, slow hills of far-West Texas, slowly descending to the coastal flats, then onto rolling uplands, through a hilly escarpment onto a slightly hilly plateau. On both sides of the road, vineyards graced the fencelines—I'd seen many a winery signposted.

Peaches are also grown in straight rows, each tree strategically placed in relation to each other to ensure maximum production. This is a cash crop in this area, and I soon came to Burg's Corner, a regular stopping point when Ellen and I motor through. Even though I wasn't buying a peck, the welcome mat was still out for me—and I was sure to close the door behind me to keep the cool in.

Back on the road, I passed a roadsign advising me that the distance to Fredericksburg was 15 miles/24kms. The Sun was still quite high, and I was hoping to make Junction. I had to keep pedaling, and soon entered the community of Stonewall.

Just ahead of me, I saw a burn-off of dead grass alongside the ditch. Bizarrely, it was a similar scene of a decades-old process at #3 Hyer Valley Road, Lake SpringMO where my grandmother, Marjorie Bowles, carefully raked a row of burning grass along a broad front lawn. I, and my brothers, would help, each wielding a heavy rake—when we weren't chasing each other with it, threatening severe bodily injury.

I stopped pedaling and called to a man, stamping out the small blaze behind a fence, if he wanted help as some of the conflagration was closer to me.

"*No.* I've got it under control," was his response.

I shrugged and re-commenced pedaling.

At the corner, I saw another man wildly running along the ditch opposite me, also stepping on the flames.

I almost stopped again, thinking they'd be more effective if they used rakes, as I had done so many years ago in Lake Spring, instead of their shoes and how ineffective my own sandals would be, but, they are adults, they know what they are doing, and kept on pedaling. Far up ahead on the road, I saw flashing lights; must be getting exhausted again because the Sun was drying and frying my heat-addled brain. Time for another break.

The best, and only, store of choice was the Weinheimer & Son General Merchandise, opened since 1906, as the signs indicated, also informing me that I could find General Goods, Hardware, Grocery, Meats. The only thing I was really interested in was cold liquids— and getting out of that blazing Sun.

Parking my Doublevision on the shady Eastside in an unused drive-through, I entered this palace of coolness, purchased Twix and Heath candies, chocolate milk, and two gallons/7.6liters of bottled water. At the checkout, six bananas were parked at the end of the counter, each begging to be taken away by a famished bicyclist needing to replenish his potassium.

I responded, asking the cashier, "How much for your bananas?"

"Free," she replied, "they're overripe. Take'em if you want'em."

I didn't want to seem *too* greedy, so I picked up two, then thought that if they're free—I do need the energy,why not?—I doubled the number, leaving two. Pleased with my great bargains, I replenished my water buffaloes, consumed the bananas, and was back on the road.

The flashing bright lights were really close now and I could hear the siren wailing. I stopped on the shoulder while the emergency vehicle passed me and saw that it was the volunteer fire department, rushing to put out another fire somewhere.

All of a sudden, I nearly fell. My jaw dropped and eyes opened wide, my brain ridden with guilt. How could I have been so ignorant?

I remembered seeing burn ban signs almost everywhere in East Texas, including that fine modern-day Dunky-stop a minute before. With so little rainfall, the trees, grasses, and everything else normally green was anything but a verdant color.

I realized that I shouldn't have even asked about the grass fire a short while ago, that I should have immediately helped to stamp it out because it was a domestic wildfire, albeit minuscule, and that was what the volunteer fire truck was rushing for—to help extinguish it.

Turning around on broad 290—which I'd always been loathe to do, especially now on my homeward segment—then knew that I would likely just get in the way now that a crew of more able-bodied men were on the job for such a small fire. Again turning around, I accepted that I had been at the right time and place, yet not acted appropriately. It is a burden I continue to carry, another stone in my cranial load.

What an avalanche that'll be when *I* breakdown!

My mental torture was pushed aside when I passed another roadsign informing me that arrival in Fredericksburg was only *14* miles/*22* kms away. This delighted me, and I pushed my bike with renewed gusto. I could feel the newly-ingested potassium working its magic.

Working indeed.

By the time I reached Elgin-Behrends Road, peristalsis ambushed me, and not a bush in sight! I desperately looked about for some kind of privacy on this wide-open plain to no avail—except for maybe behind a small stone wall. Parking beside the decorative partition, I raced behind it, knowing that my plan for some kind of secrecy was for naught. My Doublevision generally attracts all eyes, and it didn't take much to see it's owner squatting a short distance away, keeping his head down—if I can't see you, you can't see me. Right? Right!

Seriously, when I returned to pedaling, my body acted most favorably, now that it was no longer carrying any quick-digestables inside. Mentally, I filed for future reference about timing, place, and appropriate actions: 4 over-ripe bananas, morning or night, but never mid-day; probably applies to all such fruits. I also noted, now that my emergency was over and was pedaling easy, trees, bushes, and all sorts of privacy barriers were in abundance. I groaned when passing a brown sign advising me of a historical marker in one mile, where often a discrete site is also located. Maybe this was the price of my earlier ignorance about the burn ban?

290 blossomed into a very respectable, well-shouldered, 5-lane bridge, including a center turn lane. Just as quickly, though, this lovely brief road clammed back into a narrow-shouldered 4-laner, having been altered strictly for the crossing of a very dry South Grape Creek. It was time for another break, this time at historical marker on the South side of 290.

This marker noted the plain building in front of me was typical of early 20th century schoolhouses, somewhat larger than the one-room affair typical of the previous century but was self-contained as possible. It made me think of the community center in Lake SpringMO, which had also been a small school if needed, and still sees limited use today. Alas, I was mistaken about increased privacy around *all* historical markers; fortunately, I had no need for it.

I passed the few buildings of Blumenthal, another community similar to Lake Spring—nothing appeared to be open, and no stop was needed. I still had ample fresh water, albeit warm, and continued to push on this less-than-satisfactory road. Before long, though, I absolutely had to stop at the chilling sight of another white painted ghost bike memorial. Dismounting, I read the inscribed plaque afixed to the center of a white cross, which itself was between my machine and fence:

265

Reinhold Buchdrucker
Born – Sept. 8, 1939
Died – Sept. 25, 1988
WE MISS YOU!1999

Mr. Buchdrucker only 49 years old—a full 5 years younger than myself.

I swallowed hard as memories of three other bicyclists killed in El Paso came to mind: County Judge Pat O'Rourke, Hueco Tanks Volunteer Heinz Duerkop, and Leviton Manufacturer Ruben Lemus. Mr. O'Rourke had been pedaling on the Pete Domenici Highway/ Artcraft Road at Sunrise (one of the two deadliest times to be on the road; the other is Sunset), killed by a motorist who claimed the Sun had blinded him. Mr. Duerkop was cycling South on George Dieter close to Montana, (the same route I used while a Cycling Merit Badge counselor for my son's scout troop) dying on the road after being rear-ended by a hit-and-run motorist. Mr. Lemus was pedaling to work when he was rear-ended and killed by a hit-and-run motorist.

Then there was my own two years ago. When I was pedaling East on Vista del Sol approaching Yarbrough, a hit-and-run motorist rear-ended me. Luck was with me as she/he was motoring at low speed; any higher and I'd be just as dead as the other three.

To be sure, there have been hundreds of collisions between motor vehicles and bicycles throughout the area, including more fatalities, but I could only think about how easy death can come upon a bicycle, how foolish some of us are when operating our push-bikes on the road. For all my huff and puff about bicycle safety, about the necessity of following the rules, we truly don't stand much of a chance after contact with another vehicle.

With grim determination, I pushed on, leaving an other-wise bucolic setting of a precisely ordered peach tree grove, marred only by the presence of a ghost bike. A gravel road separated it from the historic Shops at Rocky Hill. Among the many buildings, one matched the description of the historical marker I read at South Grape Creek: the schoolhouse. With no plaque to give detailed information, it's possible that this was not necessarily an original community, though the buildings seem to be genuine.

Then it came together for me; this whole area was uniquely blended and contained so much character that it would be disjointed should any single part be absent, specifically the ghost bike memorial. What a perfect arrangement and setting.

Passing a KOA, I briefly considered camping there for the night, but the Sun was still three palms high. More tempting was the adjacent Shell stage coach station—why continue to put up with warm water? But stopping again would drain me of another valuable resource: daylight. I pushed on, elated when another road sign let me know it was only 6 miles/10kms to Fredericksburg.

I did stop again, at my favorite place, an accessible picnic area which had a historical marker as well. This time, privacy was available, but, fortunately, my innards were pretty much empty and I had no need. However, I appreciated being able to get off my Doublevision and off 290 for a small snack-and-water, in addition to reading about The Pinta Trail.

This historic path ran in an oblique direction, originally used by Plains tribes, followed by later invasions of the Spanish, Mexicans, and other immigrant groups. It was the steady Westward expansion of the USA that likely lessened it's importance, especially when gold was discovered in California and '49ers swarmed there for new lives. However, the railroad was a final stake in the death of the Pinta Trail—doubtlessly those silver and gold spikes driven into a commemorative sleepers of transcontinental routes.

Rolling smoothly along, I needed to gear down at Schmidtzinsky Road for an incline, but the derailleur failed to respond to my command. I immediately knew what had happened. In fact, I had been anticipating the gear cable breaking ever since replacing it twenty-six days ago, at the Valero Station back in Horizon. Finally, I was going to fix the new cable correctly, routing it so that less strain would decrease the chance for failure. Up ahead, I saw the blue sign for a picnic area and knew it was the best place for me to make the repair—safely off the road.

Fixed in the highest gear of the middle range, I tightened my grasp on the underseat handlebars and pushed my feet into the pedals with my back pressing into the mesh of my seatback. This kind of leverage didn't make climbing uphill fun but it wasn't impossible, and infinitely better than trying to walk my Doublevision!

This picnic area was perfect for my task. I backed my machine up on to it's kickstand, pulled out my toolbag, and extracted the needed tools: Phillips, wire clippers, pliers, hex wrench, spare cables. The derailleur was already on the smallest cog; all I had to do was remove the broken cable. I shifted the Shimano index shifter all the way forward, unscrewed the cap, pulled the cable housing away, and pushed the cable back enough to grab the head. The broken cable came out remarkably easy, broken precisely where I had twisted the cable housing the wrong way in last month's repair.

That near-kink had become a weak point where constant shifting wore out each strand within the tightly-wound right-wrap cable until the strain became too much, causing what was left of it to snap.

At the derailleur, I loosened the hex bolt, unwrapped the cable, and pulled it out of the cable housing. It was a nice, shiny, stainless-steel, right-wrap stranded cable, utterly useless without a head on either end. I unwound a new nice, shiny, stainless, right-wrap stranded cable, utterly useful because the soldered round head would become the fulcrum inside the index shifter body which could pull the derailleur against it's strong spring to larger toothed cogs and lower gear settings.

I fed bare end through the cap-hole into the shifter, and, when it appeared on the other side, pulled the entire length, unhappy that it's 3500mm length meant that some of it laid on the dirty cement beside me. Cleaning it off while threading it into the first piece of housing, I carefully re-positioned it so that there was no significant bend to threaten the cable's integrity.

Pairing it to a lugged knob on the monotube, I fed it through another small hole, again pulling the long cable through, again draping it on the ground. Then I pushed it into a small housing liner for a straight run on the underside of the monotube, again, wiping the cable clean as it went in. Routing the cable through another lugged guide under the bottom bracket, I threaded it through more housing liner to another lugged guide. Pushing it through a hole in the kickstand that was only big enough for the cable, I eventually was able to thread it all the way to the derailleur, always wiping it clean.

At last! But when I pulled on the cable with the pliers, it didn't reach the hex nut.

Retracing the cable, I found that I had inadvertently wrapped it around the hydraulic brake line under the bracket.

There was only one thing I could do: pull the cable back to that point, unwrap it, then re-thread it. Instead of being frustrated or unhappy with myself, I merely repeated the process, except this time I was careful while passing it through.

Feeling both satisfaction and desirous to get going, I ignored the historical marker—first time ever—and quickly resumed pedaling West during the other most dangerous cycling time: Sunset. There really is no excuse for this when I could have waited five minutes and put on my lights, but rationalized that since the traffic was virtually non-existant...!

And, for the most part, it was as I passed the Hill Country University Center and formally entered Fredericksburg crossing the Barrons River. The small lane on that bridge disappeared along with the bridge itself, but the 290 soon expanded to five lanes, including a center turn. The motor vehicle congestion returned with a vengeance at the controlled intersection with Wal-Mart, but I was comfortable with my visibility—even more so with my whistle.

A sad memory while passing Gas Mart slowed my cadence for only a moment—it was the last place I'd refueled my beloved '93 4Runner before it died five miles South of Johnson City on US290-281 two years ago while transporting daughter Katy to UT. Then the light turned green and I sped up, ready to stop and eat.

Despite a large number of quality eateries, I targeted one: Subway. I knew it was in the center of town with excellent food, the ice-dispenser fit my water buffaloes perfectly, and I'd likely be able to recharge my phone there, too. So I pedaled on, eager to be stopping soon, ready to give my legs a well-deserved break.

Main Street (US290) is zoned to preserve the historical integrity of the limestone buildings and it's immigrant heritage, thoroughly enjoyable by me and a plethora of other tourists. But when the authentic structures gave way to an expanse of grass, I knew I had passed the Subway. Confused, I queried a pedestrian, who replied "Easy to miss, man. Go back two lights, to Washington Street."

Wheeling back two blocks, the code had been updated with ultra-friendly cut-curbs (*NEVER* should any urban or suburban road be built without them!) which greatly facilitated my rolling up in front of it.

The Subway blended in so well that had I not been re-directed, I would have missed it again.

This time, though, I had no trouble finding it, and parked alongside the bike rack. Subway was already a 5-star restaurant with me, and the rack adds to it's desirability. Going inside, I met Sub-masters Cam and Blair, who made me feel like an old friend.

"You look tired," he said. "Just make yourself comfortable as much as possible, although we close at nine."

"That's fine; would it be OK if I recharged my cell here, too?" I asked.

"Sure," he replied. "And take as much ice as you need."

I was slowly eating my steak sub (meat, cheese, & avocado doubled, of course) when a boy pointed at me.

"Pardon, but weren't you in Houston last week?" asked his father.

"Yes," I responded, and started to launch into the tale of my Trans-Texas Bicycle Odyssey when his other son exclaimed, "I told you it was the same guy!"

I smiled, asking, "So, where are you from?"

His father spoke again, "We're the Carr family from Beaumont, and we're on a short family excursion to Caverns of Sonora, Fort Lancaster, exploring World War Two here, and then back."

Giving him, his wife, and their two sons each a personal card, I said, "I'm John Eyberg aka Juanito Hayburg aka BikerJohn, and I left El Paso on the eleventh of June at two pm in hundred plus heat after recuperating from Project Celebration."

"A teacher?" commented his wife. "No wonder you have so much time off. We're home schooled, and this is our way of learning."

Nodding my head, I said, "I agree—travel is the best teacher; I've done the same with my two children. I firmly believe that 'you never know until you go', and what really helps is that they're in the same district I teach, so when they're off, I'm off and when I'm off, they're off. Works out great, plus I think it's the best district in the World."

Continuing, I added, "I would've gone through Beaumont but I reached my turn-around date of thirty June before my turn around point of Louisiana—just across the Sabine. Now I'm returning and need to be back in time for three inservices starting on the eighteenth. But I'll finish pedaling to Louisiana next year—maybe."

"Wow! Said their other wide-eyed son. "You're gonna' ride all that?"

"Oh, yes—and it's easier because the wind is now mostly behind me. My biggest problem is going West at Sunset. Motorists often can't see me because they are blinded by the setting Sun. But it's only real bad for ten or fifteen minutes, and I can pull over for that."

"Hey, BikerJohn," he said, "you can stay with us whenever you come to Beaumont. Right, Mom? Right, Dad?"

Laughing, they agreed.

Only slightly more serious, I addressed the boys, "You both need to be very grateful to your parents for giving you this opportunity. It's extremely difficult for one parent, much less both parents to be able to have this much quality time. Treasure and learn from all of it, even the bad times. As you get older, you'll have so many more demands upon your time which will take you away from your parents, and eventually you'll be on your own. I know. There were times when my wife couldn't travel with us, but we made do. Now that our children are on their own—our son is in Houston, convenient because it became my turn-around point anyway—and our daughter is in Austin, where I just spent the Fourth of July holiday—we hardly ever get to see them, much less travel with them."

Pausing, I continued, "I really envy the Carr Family; you are doing the right thing, being together. All of you are so polite and fantastic. If I ever make it to Beaumont, I'll try to make contact with you. Thank you so much for making the World a better place."

With hugs and handshakes, they left, and another group of merry individuals came in. I couldn't help but get drawn into their joy. They were celebrating another excellent softball game, and a Subway meal is one of the best. While Cam and Blair expertly prepared the sandwiches, I spoke with them.

"Congratulations! Coming here is a great way to celebrate!"

"Oh," said Mom-Coach, "win or lose, we'd be here anyway. We always feel like winners here."

"Yeah, this place is the best," said one girl in her slightly dirty uniform.

"I know it's the end of the day, but do you ever start your day here?" I asked.

"Hardly ever," said another girl. "Our games are always late, an' this is best finish."

"If I'm lucky, I'll be around a Subway early—they open at seven—and the breakfast sandwiches are just as good as the subs," I said. "Wouldn't that be something: start with Subway, win your game, finish with Subway..."

"Especially *this* Subway!" another girl jumped in with. "Aren't they great!" she said while gesturing toward Cam and Blair.

"And the subs they make are pretty good, too!" I said with a smile.

From behind the counter, Cam and Blair were busy putting together the subs but glowed upon hearing the compliments.

Unfortunately, nine o'clock came around too quickly, but my cell had recharged as had my body. My parting remark to Cam and Blair was, "YOU are the reason why I always come back to Subway, not just because my water buffalo fits the ice dispenser perfectly and the food is so deliciously nutritious. Every Subway I go to, it is always the personnel who make for a perfect meal. Thank you so much!"

Now to find a campsite. I initially thought about somehow squirming into the stoop of one of my most favorite shops here, *Fromage du Mond Fine Cheese,* but it was in no way possible. I had to get away from Main Street, still heavily populated by tourists and probably closely watched by the authorities. Slowly pedaling the back streets, I considered the grounds of the National Museum of the Pacific and the parking lot of the visitor information center, but figured that was a little too risky. Then, within a few blocks (my body was starting to shut down), well off the main drag, I amazingly found a vacant space—perfect for discrete, tucked away sleeping.

OVERNIGHT TWENTY-SIX:
FREDERICKSBURG

I awoke in my usual state of hunger, but knew morning victuals were closeby in this prosperous community. I didn't park my Doublevision as usual in a slot, instead using a portion of the generous sidewalk in front of the glass windows of the Fritz Family Mini-Mart and Diamond Gas station. This was an ideal way to start my day: coffee, breakfast and food-to-go, icewater, and lots of conversation. Manager Amanda was especially accommodating by allowing me to refill the bladders with fresh, clean water and ice. I was rather amazed at how well she handled keeping an eye on the pumps, the people, products, the cash register, and staying engaged at the same time. A true multi-tasker. Waiting in line, I passed out my personal card and shared tales of my bicycle odyssey with other patrons. Like every time, though, I needed to get underway, and bid all farewell.

Back outside while replacing newly-filled bladders, I struck up a conversation with a native, who cautioned me that I might encounter a different language.

"*Danke!*" I replied, to the surprised man.

"*Sprechen sie Deutsch?*" he asked.

Smiling, I told him that that was the extent of my German language, not having been in that fine country since 2004. I had to elaborate, and went into more detail about the long-sought visit to the German capital. He appeared sufficiently impressed, but was perhaps becoming annoyed with the additional excruciating points of my Navy days in Bremerhaven...

"Yah, yah, yah, goot," he said and abruptly closed the door of his truck, terminating any more conversation.

No matter; it was an outstanding morning, no wind and little vehicular traffic. Main Street Fredericksburg was 180° different from last night, when live music from different *bierhauses* bombarded the air. Now quiet except for the tweeting of birds and the rustling of cafes opening up, I was glad to have started my morning at the mini-mart—eating elsewhere in this authentic environment would have doubtlessly thinned out my plastic, reducing my weight minimally but burdening my brain with thoughts of future payment.

I felt honored to be pedaling on the Pearl Harbor Memorial Highway, and obvious tie-in to the National Musuem of the Pacific and Admiral Nimitz, the native son made good. So good, in fact, that he made Fleet Admiral—the only person to achieve the highest rank in WWII—and namesake for supercarrier CVN68. The homeport for that massive ship was NorfolkVA, and was deployed around the Med at about the same time as was my first ship, the *USNS Marias*. I don't accurately remember refueling it, though if we had, we would have only provided AVGAS for the aircraft—we carried no enriched uranium.

Fredericksburg may have initially started as a farming community, but now has two other strong economic pillars: *Deutschlander* heritage and the Pacific theater of World War Two. I wondered how this area coped during the war years, and suspect it had closer observation simply due to the fact that it's heritage was that of a combatant enemy, where sympathies might give way to collusion or even sabotage. However, nearly 70 years later, those pillars are the strong supports to a thriving community.

While going by a local newspaper headquarters, it occurred to me that possibly the Standard-Bearer might be interested in a story about a bicyclist who double-footedly pedaled across Texas through gale force winds and searing heat. I made a broad turn on 290 and returned to the immaculate limestone building, a latter-day construction to code, keeping in line with the historical setting. I parked my Doublevision in front, with an excellent view of the heavily loaded bike—an interesting security system. Theft was highly unlikely, requiring a thief to be skilled at pedaling a recumbent as well as coping with the physics of balance, gravity, and mass.

Inside, I enthusiastically spoke with Kathy about my biketour, but without a direct sponsor or cause (My self-described Irene's Pedal for breast cancer research and continual wearing of UBS Tees are not sufficient.) is simply not enough of a story. At least I tried. Returning to my Doublevision, I continued my journey West on 4-lane 290. It has an agreeably wide shoulder, but was being resurfaced disagreeably. Oil and gravel were being rolled on, which can make for an ugly cycle roadway, especially when new. A memory of a similar event many years ago while biketouring the perimeter of Missouri kept me away from that asphalt mix.

In 1983, I was headed toward the bootheel, and had been told of a shortcut across the Black River. It was late July and I recall it being just as hot then as now. The similarity continued: I was pedaling in sandals, shorts, T-shirt, and the same Skid-Lid. The difference was my machine—back then I was astride my extremely reliable Stumpjumper, purchased the year before from Frank, wrench *extraordinaire* at Walt's Bike Shop, ColumbiaMO.

The shortcut, County Road 214, was a newly graveled route; not only was my forward progress slightly retarded by the heat, but the thick furrows of fine rock also impeded smooth rolling of my 26 x 1.75inch (559mm x 38mm) tires. Despite my slow movement, a delicate rooster tail still followed my wheels. This road dust is common throughout the World on millions of miles of unpaved roads and is often suppressed by dowsing it with a coat of oil that could not be refined anymore. It not only keeps particulates from infiltrating into the air and causing severe pollution, but the weight of vehicular traffic compresses the granular film into a relatively smooth durable surface. Before then, though, it remains a gooey muck.

Back to my Black River shortcut; it was going fine until I met a slow moving tanker truck coming in the opposite direction. I and my Stumpjumper stood off to the side, well away from the road as it passed, and saw that it was spraying the near-universal answer to road dust. I returned to pedaling CR214, except this time my impediment was greatly magnified—a squishy oil-covered road that would flip up, covering the bottom third of my Stumpjumper and lower limbs with specks of the black stuff.

It was that aggravating experience 28 years ago which compelled me to take a lane. I *knew* to stay off that oily surface.

Eventually, this cheap road repair on 290 was discontinued and I returned to a decent shoulder. Ascending one incline, I was ready to take a break, conveniently close to the historic marker for the Philipp Hartmann Family Cemetery, and a well-barricaded graveyard beside it. The sign gave scant little shade from the Sun. Oh, well, preservation has it's price, and I pushed on.

Intermittent road construction continually built up my hopes for quick arrival at Harper, but within a few rotations of the wheels, the hopes were broken. I finally went downhill to the junction with RR783 and a small gas station-store. Resisting the temptation to stop there, I turned North into the Harper Community Park.

I sought the shade and considered a plunge into an equally well-shaded pool of water, but first had to find out why this woman was barricaded inside her truck with the windows rolled up, engine running, and dogs yapping soundlessly inside. Responding well to my visual communication, she rolled down the driver's side window. Giving her a personal card, we pleasantly conversed, each reflecting on the environment.

"It's mighty warm out there, BikerJohn," replied Linton the LabLady & Copper Bracelet Maker replying to my sweating self-proclamation of willingly subjecting myself to this torrid cycling. "And I wouldn't get into that still water because it could harbor Weil Disease."

"Oh?" I asked.

"Yeah. It kills by bleeding you to death," she replied with no equivocation about the gravity of such a problem. "I'd suggest going up to the Longhorn Cafe to cool off. Red's the new owner, and she'll take care of you. I'm sitting inside this air conditioned car, and with just the window rolled down, it's hot—you must be burning up.

Anyway, let's meet again online. Look for an email at your website from Linton the Lablady. OK? Now you go get cool!"

I couldn't have agreed more, but a historical marker and the Pioneer Memorial Museum were next in line for my attention. The marker stated that this park was a model for how a community can be enriched by the local citizenry, which surprised me, because 1946 is easily a century after Lone Star statehood. But I don't know the criteria for such a statement.

The Museum was closed, but the pavilion was plenty open. If I ever pedal through here again, I know exactly where to camp. My task now was to pedal back to 290 and up a slight hill to the Longhorn cafe. Going slightly beyond, I was able to more easily access the sidewalk, where I backed my Doublevision down to the front of the Longhorn. It needed to be in the shade, too, and the overhang was perfect.

In fact, it was a double overhang, as a broad banner strapped between the porch supports recommended going inside to meet the new owners. *Two* signs on the window about the burn ban and extreme wildfire danger caused me to grimace as a reminder of Stonewall yesterday. When I stepped through the front door, that memory was immediately supplanted by a blast of icy cold air—which sure did feel good. I slumped into a chair at the nearest table, removed my Skid-lid, Sunglasses, gloves, and Shimano sandals. Kenya strolled up, poured a large tumbler of iced tea, adding several extra cubes of ices. I looked at her gratefully, glurging "Thank you!"

"Got plenty more where it came from," she said. "Would you like the specialty of the house—chicken fried steak?"

"Absolutely! And I'll just write a few postcards while waiting," I told her.

I was wiping my mouth when Red, new owner of Longhorn Cafe, came around and we made small talk. The main topic concerned the heat and lack of moisture; I wondered how it affected the peach crop.

"Not in here," she said proudly. "I've got the best cobbler around!"

"Sounds like I ought to have a bite of it," I replied, then hopefully asked, "Could it come *á la mode?*" I was quite interested in the fresh dessert—and that it meant staying in that cold space a bit longer.

"You just stay right there," she said while putting up the "CLOSED" sign.

Kenya warmed it in the microwave, then plopped two large scoops of Blue Bell Homestyle Vanilla on top. During our brief discussion, I encouraged her to continue pursuing her degree in Criminal Justice, giving her Career Cruising information. Her last act before leaving was to refill my water buffaloes with fresh, cold water.

Pedaling West out of Harper, 290 was still 4-lane, but the shoulder had diminished considerably.

At the Kimble County line, the four lanes became two, but the shoulder broadened into what was essentially another lane, similar to Anderson Loop. Passing a roadsign, I learned two important distances: I-10 was 13 miles/21kms, Junction was 35 miles/56kms, then crossed the route 479 intersection. I stayed focused, and pushed straight on through. The next road sign showed that I had advanced only a mile/1.6 km. Somewhat disheartening, considering the apparent toll my body felt.

Palming the sky, I figured maybe 3 more hours of light, and would barely make it into Junction. My spirits didn't exactly leap. But up ahead was a truck, stopped and occupying the Eastbound shoulder. This would perk me up—another opportunity for me to help someone.

Stopping beside it, the window rolled down and I met Tony, who had pulled over to talk on his cell. We spoke for a bit, and he told me about the virtues of living in the small town of Harper, knowing everybody, being involved with the success of the community, and helping his son, who was doing extremely well because of the closeness. I concurred on all points, including that the only downside was his wife having to commute to Fredericksburg for paid employment at the Wal-Mart. My parting remark was about his wisdom in stopping to talk on the phone instead of continuing to motor along.

"Yep," he replied. "There may not be any traffic out here, but it don't take much to wander off the road into a field, fence, or worse."

Pedaling on, I went by my favorite blue sign and looked forward to stopping at the picnic area despite recently ingesting all that delicious food and cold freshwater from the Longhorn Cafe. It was late afternoon and the heat was still oppressive, so the anticipated shade would be much welcomed.

I was not disappointed; this picnic area had everything I could possibly want at that moment: *shade.* A single tree existed on the West edge of the cement pad, and an overflowing garbage can was placed on the East edge. Actually, the can was empty and trash was piled haphazardly around it—something I've seen far too often. Why not put it into the can? Of course, there was so much junk that it would fill the can to overflowing, but still...!

Laying on the table with my Skid-lid and Shimano sandals off, I shut my eyes and philosophized. If we Humans would expend just a fractional amount more effort, how much better an environment we'd leave to our posterity. Are we living just for the moment, that flicker of time that we exist on Earth, maximizing our comfort at the expense of all other living things? Can the nearly seven billion of us who call the third planet from the Sun home really take care of our home?

I don't know how long I slept, but was ready and eager to keep pedaling upon waking. The Sun was now about two palms high, another two hours before nightfall. Clouds peppered the sky, and a tailwind helped me. US290 soon intersected I-10, where I had two paved choices: East to San Antonio or West to El Paso. Peeling right on the ramp, I stopped shortly where the shoulder construction went from superior to oiled aggregate of earlier horrors. Fortunately, it was not newly laid and, though not nearly as smooth, it is broad, as all shoulders should be. *NO* paved rural roads, regardless of classification, should ever be built without them.

This was something of an extremely satisfying, momentous occasion for me, and stopped to tweet. Twenty-six days ago, I was on this same road, albeit 477miles/763kms East for my longest daily distance (106miles/ 197kms) from Fabens to Van Horn. That had been such a pleasure to pedal—that section of I-10 had been rebuilt of hardened concrete several years ago and is now very safe, very predictable, very fine. Our tax dollars well spent.

John Eyberg

Today is the seventh, my workshops start on the eighteenth, which gives me eleven days. Barring any mechanical problems—and by now, I couldn't imagine anything else going wrong—that's less than *fifty* miles/80kms per day. My confidence brimmed over—this would be an easy conclusion to my Trans-Texas Bicycle Odyssey.

Looking West, I saw wavering images of downtowns El Paso and Juarez with the ASARCO tower piercing the sky, framed by the Franklins and Sierra Juarez. No where else have I ever seen such a distinctive image. Oh, I've seen many skylines and features around the World (thank you, Navy, and ancestors for the inheritance), but often they are so similar as to be indistinguishable. Among the most memorable that have come under my gaze are often known only by a singular such characteristic: Gateway Arch, St. LouisMO; Space Needle, SeattleWA, Roman coliseum, Pula, Croatia (formerly Yugoslavia); Statue of Liberty/Empire State Building/Twin Towers (no longer in existence), New York CityNY; The Eye, LondonUK; CN tower, Toronto, Canada; Eiffel Tower, Paris, France; Peter and Paul Church, St. Petersburg, Russia; low-water bridge, Upper Buffalo River, PoncaAR; downtown trolley, Melbourne, Australia; Cape Spear, coastal battery/lighthouse/ Easternmost point in North America, St. John's, Newfoundland, Canada; L'Anse aux Meadows National Historic site, Canada; Great Wall, China; Sachsenhausen concentration camp incinerator stacks, Berlin, Germany; Banaue Rice Terraces, Philippines; Mitad del Mundo, Ecuador; Acropolis, Athens,Greece; Bridge of the Americas, Panama; SammySammy and his treehouse, Hornby Island, Canada; Katy Trail MOPAC trestle, BoonvilleMO; Gruenenberg Castle mosaic, Melchnau, Switzerland. Each and all have a specific memorable feature that has stayed with me far longer than the hub-bub of a busy downtown or outskirt. And so it is with the ASARCO smelter tower, an inverted funnel to disperse waste gas up into the atmosphere and away from the humans on the surface. The plant is no longer operational, but it is an unused reminder of the two features (the other is the very actively used railroad) which fundamentally made El Paso the dynamic city it is today.

My reverie was broken when the jake brake staccato slamming of a diesel engine in an 18-wheeler sounded, along with a cloud of black smoke spewing from the exhaust pipes and the pavement vibrating like an earthquake. Then, across the grassy median in the Eastbound lanes, I heard another sound, a long intermittent bus horn sounding and I pumped my hand into the sky in response. This had become a habit since numerous motorists and passengers were waving and tooting at me when they passed by. I felt sure the noise was for me, and if not, that's OK—I'll take it anyway.

Then my cell buzzed with a message, and after reading it, both my arms shot up, shaking in a wild frenzy. Amy, one of my colleagues, had texted me about seeing my very visible Doublevision, which meant there could only be one person in charge of it—me. So that was the noisy vehicle.

Amy was accompanying the small group (Mike Dee's Big Adventure), organized by ESC Region 19 Rick, on their way to Austin. Mike Dee is a hero to many people because in spite of his blindness by age 20, he overcame the inherit challenges, earning a college degree in communication and finally achieving Executive Producer status with radio station Power 102.

Reinvigorated, I resumed pedaling with gusto—and I started counting down the mile markers. I knew I'd not pedal into El Paso tomorrow, instead they became a gauge of how much closer was my goal. My exhilaration was tied to my energy, which was continually sapped by the heat. I barely made it to mile marker 475 before having to stop and re-evaluate my position. The fission inside me had dwindled, with a similar reduction in kinetic action and ability to push the pedals. The long, steady downhill stored in my memory banks of this road was interrupted with the reality of more uphill, and cooling my internal reactors with a massive flood of fresh water was necessary.

I sucked the water bottle dry, then recharged it with tepid water from one of my six water bladders, sucking the bottle dry again before refilling it once more. After a moment's rest, I continued, slowly pushing forward.

The temptation to stop in Segovia was strong; I could easily find a campsite in the truck stop area, as I had in Sanderson and Van Horn, and decent food would be available 24 hours, should I need or want it. But my real need and want was to get to Junction before darkness—which *had* to be just over the next hill.

Alas, it turned out to be more than a hill—creeping up it, the Sun faded fast and I stopped at the crest to turn on my lights. I looked in vain for the less-than-distinctive skyline of Junction; I couldn't see *any* sign of the Kimble County Seat. Given that disappointment, the lights of motor vehicles lumbering uphill thrilled me, a sure sign that I'd be moving quickly as gravity pulled me down.

Unfortunately, my rapid descent was eliminated by the shoulder. I had to weave a path between excessive debris and move no faster than my headlamp could show. In other words, I was creeping along, being careful not to run over some steel belted tire scrap or broken glass or anything that would give me a flat. I was eager for motor vehicles to come up behind me on I-10, where far stronger headlamps would illuminate this hazardous shoulder far enough ahead, enabling me to move faster.

But there were no such vehicles. While the Eastbound lanes were chock full, it was as if all Westbound traffic had exited the road at Segovia, where the operators were enjoying a good meal and perhaps a night's stay. I was alone on the road. In total darkness save for my lights and much to my horror, I heard the same beast that had terrified me when pedaling through the Van Horn mountains in darkness twenty five days ago. No way was I going to stop now, but wanted to get out of there quicker.

Then I had an idea.

I *could* use the right hand-traffic lane to both move faster and avoid the debris.

Then I shook my head; *NO, NO, NO,* that's absolutely crazy, far too dangerous. No motor vehicle would be able to slow down enough, much less stop, to avoid contact with my Doublevision and I'd definitely be killed. So I crept along, dodging an enormous amount of the flotsam and jetsam occupying the shoulder while hoping for the headlights of a motor vehicle. It was maddening; I kept going slower. And slower. And slower, while the batteries in my headlamp grew weaker. And weaker.

I was going to have to stop to put in fresh batteries.

I had but one possible solution.

I desperately steered left into the traffic lane. Immediately, my Doublevision rocketed forward, no longer restrained by my incessant braking. It was amazing. Amazingly dangerous—stupid, in retrospect—but infinitely *faster.*

While always keeping my eye out for Westbound motor vehicles, I also saw the glimmer of the city of Junction. Fantastic! Why didn't I do this earlier?

Then the headlights of a fast-moving motor vehicle exploded behind me, putting me squarely in its path as well as illuminating the surrounding road. I *had* to get back onto the shoulder. But I was going way too fast. I'd surely wipe out on some debris!

Then the headlamps gave a huge benefit, showing me the exit to a rest area. I road atop the solid white lane line, veering right, moving down the ramp. The motorcar sped by me, neither hesitating nor slowing down as if I didn't exist. And with my own diminishing lights, I *didn't* exist. Afraid to ruin my remaining brake, I lightly grasped the caliper in my left hand, coming ever so slowly to a stop. Turning on my other helmet light, I found the first picnic area, vacant, accessible, and my home for the night.

While sitting on the kneewall eating an MRE, I peered West. Gentle warmth overfilled my body and brain. Closing my eyes for a moment, I felt closer than ever to home...

I was sure I could see the star of El Paso, glowing from it's anchorage on the South face of the Franklins. It had been a beacon that guided myself, along with brother passengers Bruce and Nils when I had spontaneously motored us into Mexico at Caseta in daylight, then meandered our way back into the USA via Juarez in darkness during the early '90s. I could also see the aircraft warning lights of the various transmission antennas and microwave towers erected along the spine of that mountain, including the array in East El Paso. Then the downtown luminosity from skyscrapers reflected on the grand, lofty ASARCO towers.

What a vista!

Blinking, I saw a remarkably similar 2004 visage. Back then, while perched on the window ledge of the *Auberge de jeunesse Leo*

Grange, Clichy, France, I was bemoaning the fact that we (Katy, Erik, Ellen, and myself) were inside a room *cinq étages* above the ground and not elsewhere. I could see "elsewhere" while looking South—the lights mounted on *la tour Eiffel* were visible in the distance. It pained me to think that we weren't underneath those lights, or possibly amongst the lights, after having ascended the narrow stairwell, something Katy, Erik, and I had climbed several hours before in daylight. It was warm then, too, and drinking water had slopped out of one of our canteens, spilling all over me...

I came back to reality with a fluttering of my eyelids. My water bottle had flopped over and was leaking warm fluid onto the kneewall where I sat, thoroughly saturating my shorts. Only the clear lights of Junction were visible; how ridiculous that I could see either El Paso or the Eiffel Tower—both were much too far away.

Far worse, though, was my pedaling in the right-hand lane of I-10. Yes, it was faster and seemed the right thing to do at the time, but regardless of the exponential amount of experience I have cycling, it was foolish. Despite my own high rate of speed, that vehicle operator was overdriving it's headlights, descending upon me like an F-14 catapulting off a carrier deck, and lacking sufficient reaction time, would likely have been unable to swerve around me no matter how good my lights might be. Though I know a collision with the motorcar would kill me, the Doublevision was of enough mass that it wouldn't be a hit-and-run. However, the conclusion of the police report would read: "...the pedacyclist's failure to follow the rules of the road... despite having lights, Vehicle A was not being operated in legally designated space."

With adrenalin was still coursing through my body, that kind of thinking caused my heart rate to spike. I even trembled as a few drops of cold sweat trickled down my face and fell from my chin.

Checking my cyclecomputer, I saw that I had pedaled some 69 miles/110kms. At this rate, I'd be home within 7 days. As I tucked in for the night, the reassurance of knowing that home was not too far away, another thought gave me additional comfort: my purchase of two more bladders for my buffaloes in Houston had significantly increased my freshwater carrying capacity, a definite need for my impending transversal of the Chihuahuan Desert—no more repeats of the Valentine near-dessication! And after the harrowing arrival to the safety of this rest area, peaceful sleep easily overtook my body—once my pulse slowed.

OVERNIGHT TWENTY-SEVEN:
I-10/JUNCTION REST AREA

I like early morning pedaling, just before Sunrise, when the accumulated heat of previous day had dissipated overnight and a coolness pervades the atmosphere. Motor vehicles had become rare in both directions on I-10, although a few 18-wheelers could be seen grinding East or carefully swooshing West. The quiet was calming as I slowly gathered myself, thinking about breakfast at my favorite stop in Junction, the Sunshine Cafe and Bakery, when I began the day's cycling.

My route was easy; just a bit on the shoulder, downhill to the stop sign for FM2169. I noted the gas station and regretted for a second about not at least eating a little bit before leaving the superb rest area. The hunger-inducing scent of *chorizo*, bacon, eggs and hot cakes saturated the air, most likely emanating from the tiny suburban outpost or the Days Inn, both overlooking the Llano River.

Turning West, the road became a surprisingly good overlook of Junction, the Llano River, and it's lovely through-truss bridge over Lake Junction. Merging with loop road 481 and pedaling over the still water, I considered a quick plunge, but my hunger for food was greater, in addition to remembering Linn's warning about Weil Disease. I did make a few other stops, though, the first being at the historic maker on the Western approach of this fine bridge. The 1937 steel girder construction was typical of many, many such structures and doubtlessly became part of a government-funded (something which continues through today) effort to relieve effects of the Great Depression.

Pedaling along these quiet streets, I saw a combo Exxon Gas/ Subway and nearly stopped, but it was too early. Later, after satisfying my appetite, I'll return here to buy lunch and fill up my water buffaloes with ice before heading West. I did stop for the Deer Horn Tree, erected in 1968 by the Kimble Business and Professional Women's Club.

Admiring the structure, it struck me that this is the Junction's tower, which, other than size, is like the ASARCO tower in El Paso. Interestingly, it makes me think of Jackson's Hole, Wyoming, the only other place I'd ever seen such an impressive collection of antlers. It is something that I—and probably anybody else who sees this—will always remember, though my particular memory right now is for a delicious food stop.

Pedaling on, Junction was waking up as people were starting to move about, open up stores and begin another work day. I noticed that a Kimble county road crew was sliding on work gloves and starting to assemble their gear for the day.

I had to stop.

"I want to thank you guys for such fine roads," I said to the boss, giving him my personal card. "It was such an amazing change going from Gillespie County into Kimble on two-ninety yesterday."

Lance nodded his head in agreement.

"But, what happened to the shoulder on eye-ten real close to two-ninety?" I asked. "It was really trashed out, and so incredibly slow."

"Well, uh, Juanito,' he replied after looking at my card, "money tells us what we can an' can't do, an' there ain't enough of it to do a real good job, which includes cleanin' it up. We don't have the manpower, neither. Sorry about the shoulder."

"Seems as though that's true all over," I said. "I got on two-ninety at Hempstead, and it was really beautiful, until I got just West of Giddings, then it became real bad until Elgin, when it was good again, 'till Dripping Springs, when it became dodgy most of the rest of the way, until Kimble County. I was told the same thing you're telling me in McDade: money. However, your rest area just up the hill there is super-good. I had a real good night's sleep there!"

"We like it, too. Glad to hear you liked it an' our roads—we don't hear that very often. Thanks!"

Some of the other workers sidled up to us when I expounded on my Trans-Texas Bicycle Odyssey.

"You timin's real good, Juanito, with all these high temperatures," Lance said, heavy with sarcasm. "We have to knock off mid-day because of the heat. You be careful, now; it get's real bad from here West, OK?"

Nodding my head yes, I was supremely confident, answering, "I think getting here was the worst, and as long as I don't have a headwind, I'll do fine. Thanks for your concern, Lance."

Continuing West on Main Street, I passed a very busy Isaack's Restaurant, which had a prominent neon marquee that held the promise of air conditioning. I slowed down, considered it for a brief moment but pedaled on—my commitment was to the Sunshine Cafe and Bakery. Approaching it shortly, I thought it strange that it wasn't busy; in fact, no vehicles were in the parking lot except for mine. Was I too early? It looked deserted, and a sign posted on the window informed me that it was closed due to injury. As if I deserved some kind of special treatment, I peered through the windows to see if someone could serve me alone—after all, this is the best place to eat in Junction.

Sadly, I had to accept the inevitable and began to backtrack— something downright disagreeable to me, though not nearly as much as when I tried to cross the Brazos River on I-10 a week ago. Shrugging my shoulders then waving at the heavy equipment operators who were leveling the adjacent lot, I pedaled East on Main Street. Isaack's it is!

Just like the 59 Diner a few days ago, I took an entire slot for my Doublevision and could easily see it from where I sat inside. Not only was I able to have a powerful and by now a desperately needed brekkie, I was also permitted to plug in my Nokia to recharge.

"If you headed West, there's quite a dead zone between here and Sonora," the amiable waitress prophetically told me.

It had started warming up fast, and I appreciated the icy cold a/c. Better yet was the friendly service, low prices, and rave reviews posted on the wall. There were also hunter postcards available for purchase—you know I bought a few.

Thinking that this was real competition for the Sunshine Cafe, I started to leave when an SUV pulled up in front of me and the driver motioned for me to come over.

"Here, hon," she said, gingerly handing me a large cup of coffee so as to not twist her bandaged arm. "The workers told me you had stopped, and I don't want to lose a valuable customer like you! As you can see, I'm unable to work, so we had to close down for now. But I brought you a coffee."

Now, *that* is the kind of service which will certainly keep me returning!

Quite full of coffee (and the Hunter's Special), I was glad to have backtracked—I needed to get to the Subway anyway, and now had a postcard to mail to McRae Car Care Robert, a double-barreled devotee of this area. It was warming up real well, and I knew I had to get underway as quickly as possible. I also knew it was a good day's pedal West to my next overnight, Sonora, and needed to buy lunch to go from Subway.

Larry, who was in charge of the Exxon side, guffawed after hearing my goal when I asked for a foot-long toasted Sweet Onion Chicken Teriyaki sandwich with double avocado and spinach on 9-grain wheat, hold the lettuce and mayo.

"You're not gonna' make it on that 'cause the machine's broken an' we only got flatbread available."

Undeterred, I made the same order, except this time requesting neither the bread nor the toasting, adding, "I hope your ice machine is working better."

It was.

In fact, besides recharging the bladders, a freshwater lever beside the dispenser made it too easy for me to also make the bladders fat like an inflated balloon, filling all the spaces between the chunks of ice with that precious fluid. I smugly paid for the flatbread sandwiches, laughing with Larry that my lunch might not be the best, the icy water more than made up the difference.

He wished me well on my journey as I walked out to stuff four of the bladders into the two blue denim water buffaloes hanging on either side of my saddle-chair, and the other two into the Doublevision seat bag. There! Looking more like an octopus all the time, and I'll have more than enough water capacity for my final week of pedaling. I excitedly pushed off, quite satisfied to finally be getting underway. Next stop: Sonora.

Pushing my Doublevision along Main Street, I knew I hadn't started early enough—it was incredibly hot. Crossing the North Llano River, I saw it was dry, with the parched riverbed showing cracked Earth with a few brown weeds bent over like old men. Pedaling into the shadow of the I-10 bridges overhead, the temperature plunged into pleasantness, very much the same way as had when resting in culverts along US90 while Eastbound.

Seeing McDonald's on my right and knowing that I was going to be spending the rest of the day pedaling in this intense heat, there was no question about stopping. My mind had become fixated on a frozen Strawberry-Lemonade available only from the iconic double-arches. I wheeled into the broad plaza, a true tourist stop if I've ever seen one, with crowds drawn to fast-food, T-shirts, and, most importantly, the air conditioned spaces.

Lanita quickly saw to my specific order and I returned to my Doublevision, regardless of the inside comfort. I was still mindful that I needed to get a move on and it wasn't getting any cooler. In fact, the few minutes I was outside saddling up, the frozen drink had become more of a chilled sugary sweet syrup. I had to suck down half my water bottle after drinking it to keep that viscous liquid from gumming up my throat.

I re-entered I-10, taking the shoulder, purposely avoided the frontage road because of my uncertainty that it continued very far. There was no way I wanted to maybe have to backtrack. Also, that side road had a goodly amount more asphalt showing, which would doubtlessly be soft and slow me down. I saw the split billboard noting that the Caverns of Sonora were at exit 392, and the Days Inn, next to the Sutton County Steakhouse was only 55 miles/86kms to go.

Ascending the long hill ever-so-slowly, I finally came to a stop by a bridge in the limited shade of a scrawny tree. Looking over the side, below me was the North Llano River, the same which had been bone-dry in Junction but now had a surprising pool of water in it. That must be the reason why the tree had any kind of leaves at all.

Later, I found myself at exit 438 and a choice: continue West on I-10, or North on loop road 291 to Roosevelt? The promise of food and cold water in that site was powerful strong, but I simply didn't know, never having been there before. Its symbol on the map equaled Dryden; what if it was less? I couldn't risk spending any time in pursuit of something that may or may not exist.

I did take advantage of stopping though, and refilled my water bottle from one of the water buffaloes. A slight amount of water had leaked out, soaking the denim holster which, during the process of evaporation, was keeping the bladders inside it cool, though the ice was long gone, melted away in the heat. I was ready to push on.

Gulping a mouthful of cool water, I choked.

It was the foulest tasting water possible!

The smug feeling I had about getting free fresh water at the Exxon station back in Junction disappeared; what I had really done was fill up my bladders with *carbonated* water. I couldn't believe it! I have 38 miles/61kms of rolling terrain in intense mid-afternoon heat to go, and no fresh water to drink? This is a disaster, not unlike when I was camped between the fence and US90 just South of Valentine, except for one huge difference: all other vehicles were whipping by me, and none of them were Border Patrol.

I could return to Junction, backtracking and fighting a headwind all the way there, both of which were definitely not part of my agenda. Or I could continue on. I mean, it's only carbonated water, it's not like saltwater, which is completely intolerable. After all, haven't I been drinking Mountain Dew most afternoons, and isn't that basically caffeine, sugar, and carbonated water? This stuff might not taste so good, but it won't kill me. With new resolve, I resumed pedaling, albeit a good deal slower, hesitatingly sucking small swigs from my water bottle.

My Westward movement became infinitely more difficult. The great satisfaction I had felt last night while sitting on the kneewall was rapidly disintegrating with every swallow of the warm flat drink. Berating myself, why didn't I buy some bottled water instead of thinking myself clever for getting it free at the soda fountain? My mouth twisted in a half-smile like comical buffoon at the thought of being an real soda jerk.

Now I understood why Erik refused drinking the bottled water at the Il Patio restaurant in Moscow—it too was carbonated.

The memory of that trip pushed my lips into a proper smile, when, in 2004, we (Katy, Erik, Ellen & I) had traveled to Europe on part of an inheritance I had received. After Ellen had returned home from Amsterdam, the three of us had five more weeks to continue traveling, much of it by train.

We had just completed an uncomfortable 32-hour haul on Deutsch Bahn from Berlin to Moscow, the greatest challenges being Katy's injury, lack of food, and potable water. We were famished upon arrival at Belorusskaya Station, and finally sated ourselves at the *Il Patio* restaurant, which accepted my VISA credit card since I had not yet acquired any *rubles*. Unfortunately, the only bottled water available was carbonated, and it was quite intolerable to Erik then— just as I was finding it difficult to stomach now.

Within an hour, the intense afternoon heat immediately abated in the shade of an overpass, where I stopped for a much needed rest. Parking my Doublevision on the broad shoulder, I leaned against the blasted out cut, consuming the sandwich I had purchased earlier for this exact reason. Since it was not toasted, my usual way of portage, it became a horrid dual assault upon my body: the clammy bread followed by gagging water. I managed to get it all down, and my eyes were closing. It was time to sleep.

Removing my Skid-lid and Shimano sandals, I lay upon the sharp rocks. I looked at my Doublevision, the flags completely horizontal from the East tailwind, and considered going to it for my Z-rest. But it would be a lot of work: I'd have to put my sandals back on, trudge to the bike, unlash the mat, return, take the sandals off, lay back down...! Whoa, that was just too much effort and I was already practically asleep. So I compromised. I've laid on rough surfaces all over the World, and this would not be too different.

The Sun woke me later, having descended enough to replace the shade. I groggily re-assembled myself and began pedaling again, somewhat queasily, thinking about what another Crazy Cat super wrench, Frank, had told me about tailwinds. Since the wind was behind me, it couldn't evaporate my sweat and cool me off as effectively as a headwind. I know full well the importance of staying cool, even in the dire heat to which I was subjecting myself, having suffered heat stroke in ColumbiaMO while an undergrad almost three decades ago. That terrible water was not good tasting, but it sure was good to put on my scalp, which made me think about Skid-lid.

This exceptionally fine helmet was my first and most effective means of head protection. I felt very fortunate to have purchased it in 1980, after I fell and hit my head in the parking lot of a food co-op. At that moment, I knew luck was on my side—my skull had not cracked nor did I get a concussion. I also knew that luck might not accompany me in my next fall (and **everybody** falls!), so I immediately contacted Skid-lid in San Diego. Within a week, I was wearing this light, partial shell, soft-crush helmet that offered maximum ventilation.

All time best helmet ever for bicycling! (www.juanitohayburg.com)

Unfortunately, this helmet is constructed without a top center tab and was unable to pass the Snell Penetration Test, in which a sharp cylindrical object is dropped from above. Without any helmet material there, the pike naturally goes straight through; if a human head was there, the cranium would be pierced with death a likely result. This also became the deadly piercing for Skid-lid; being unable to be certified "passing"—along with glee from the vicious competition in the helmet market, the company went broke.

In the late '70s and early '80s, when Skid-lid dominated sales, other helmet manufacturers were constructing solid shell, hard-crush helmets—good for one time use only—that were often riding on the bike, not on the bicyclist's head because they were incredibly hot due to lack of ventilation. Once Skid-lid was out of the market, the other manufacturers immediately understood the Skid-lid wisdom and began incorporating vents in their helmets. The irony is that, nowadays, every helmet has extensive venting—something Skid-lid pioneered!

The bridge shade had been nice, but now I chased a different kind of shade, that which is provided by the few clouds overhead. I wanted anything but the Sunlight hitting me directly, piercing, if you will, just as lethal as pike dropped overhead.

My aggravation continued back out on the road because often, just as I was about to enter the cooling shadow of a cloud, it would recede before me slightly faster, teasing me, leaving me unhappily gasping, having pushed a wee bit harder to get into it. I had ill thoughts about how unfair, even cruel, that this atmosphere seemed to be antagonizing me—and making me a bit faint, though I was grateful for the tailwind.

Regardless, my slight dizziness was a warning sign I took seriously. Heat stroke is no laughing matter—it is very much a deadly matter and I needed to keep my brain engaged. I started to make iterations of two simple rhymes, adding and subtracting words:

"How now brown cow? Cow, so brown, how now? Now, now, brown the cow? Say, cow, are thou brown? Now how brown the cow? Cow? Brown? How? Now? Thou? Me? Thee?..."

and

"I would if I could but I can't so I shan't; I shan't because I can't although I would if I could..."

My first real test, though, was approaching mile marker 428: *"Ciento veinte nueve punto novecientos, ciento veinte nueve punto ochocientos, ciento veinte neueve punto setecientos, ciento veinte nueve punto quinientos..."*
Good. Keep on pedaling.

Approaching mile marker 427 was entirely different; I couldn't remember any Spanish. I knew I was in trouble, and began looking for a place to rest.

With I-10 going directly into the Sun, the glaring rays were intense and I could feel myself baking. There was not a shred of shade anywhere, not a tree, bush, outcrop, nothing. *Nada.*

Approaching mile marker 426, I couldn't even remember neither **English** nor the rhymes. I knew I was beyond trouble, I was a **very serious risk** for heat stroke, I **had** to quit pedaling and get into shade. Then I saw what had been my savior so often before, the little yellow rectangle, meaning a culvert ran beneath the road.

Hallelujah! Saved!

Parking my Doublevision on the shoulder, I wasn't totally wiped out—yet. I still had enough sense to grab a water buffalo, my camera, and cell phone, before meandering to the culvert. I was shocked to find that this was going to be a challenge. Standing on the round steel rib, it was high-dive distance to the gravel road below. I looked for an easier access, but the ridge was too steep. Maybe gravity could help me get into that prized space of coolness? But how would I get back up?

Gravity almost did take me down, but I flopped flat and stopped my plunge.

My Stylus Tough passed it's first real fall, as did my Nokia snicker-style cell, and my water buffalo survived, losing not a drop of that distasteful stuff. I guess it is better to have bad water than none. I cleared away brambles and gravel from that angled ledge, making myself a small resting place, sheltered by an overgrowth of branches which would be thick with leaves in wetter times. For now, though, I was grateful to have this skeleton of shade.

Wiping my forehead, I realized that I was in the most serious situation yet over the previous twenty-eight days: *NO SWEAT!*

I wasn't thirsty—my belly was bloated from drinking the carbonated water, so I immediately saturated my head and shirt. Then I rationalized: bicycling is the best thing for me and if I'm going to die, then this is the way I want to go. Struggling, I sat up and took my death pix.

Laying back down, random thoughts, like marbles scattered about a Chinese checkers board, entered my brain—snippets of the scroll of my life. I knew the end was near.

A former history teacher, I saw myself as a pioneer, with this isolated spot marking as far as I could go and would have become both my homestead and graveyard. I was fighting with Paul, my best friend from Kos Harris elementary school, when I fell from his picket fence. My best friends from high school, Bubber, Dincho, & KJ, were involved in typical adolescent stupidity. Paul and Anniego watching over me as my broken bones mended. Brother Nils and I biketouring Eastern Europe. Ellen, speaking with my father—I'm so glad they met before he died. She and I biketouring the lower loop of Yellowstone National Park. My mother, recently singled, sharing hostel quarters in Manizales, Colombia, when the big band next door deprived all of us of more sleep, but didn't stop Betty and me from hearing a talented Sunrise crooner in a bar there. Katy and Erik pedaling behind my Stumpjumper on an Adam's tandem trail-a-bike. After receiving an inheritance, we traveled as much as possible: around North America, going abroad to Europe and Northern Asia, reconnecting with longtime friends Pat, Chris (and his wife Christine + their children Lena & Julian); then, without Ellen, we went Down Under to make new friends (Tania, Gangles, Alon, Beat) and some adventurous stunts on South Island which caused me a half-day in clinic for a bungeed shoulder. I will *never* regret spending time or money that way. This, my Trans-Texas Bicycle Odyssey, is definitive confirmation that I'm *NOT* pre-offspring young anymore. I have aged. I have gained too much weight. I'm simply not the same though my brain refuses to accept the inevitable.

If possible to relive it, I might have corrected some mistakes, but wouldn't trade the adventures, the heartaches, the joys, for anything. I felt calm, peaceful, and closed my eyes, ready to pedal the final biketour.

With my Doublevision parked on the shoulder, my body would be easy to find. (www.juanitohayburg.com)

I bolted upright into a sitting position and vomited. What little I spewed was red, red as the frozen strawberry-lemonade I had eaten at McDonald's several hours ago. I sat there for a while, thinking.

OK, I didn't die. But I might have coughed up blood. And I'm pretty sure I finally made it to my boot camp weight of 180 pounds/82 kilograms.

I fished my cell phone out of it's case and pushed the presets for Ellen. I was leaving a message for her when she came on line. I whispered my status, but heard no response. Was I already on my final biketour? Then the phone vibrated, and we began communicating by text message.

"You must be in a dead zone. I could hear you, but you couldn't hear me."

"Yes, dead zone would be accurate.I may have to stop pedlg 4 awhile!"

"Are you ok?"

"OK,maybe.I,m going to rest a few hours in shade"

"Are you sure? Remember your heat stroke in Columbia?I packed you in ice."

"i'm not sweating"

"Do you need me to come and get you now?"

"yes,i think so.I am not able to cool my body enough. Gil or Mike could come. Let them use the truck"

"No, I'll rescue you. I'm coming now. Where are you exactly?"

"Thank you. I am between mm 425 & 426, Westbound. It will take you sevrl hours (8-9) and u'll have to refuel the truck as least once probably twice(VanHorn & Sonora),but it is ready to go.If I can move closr,I will, but I'm not moving 2 well rite now.I'll let u know.Thank u!"

My phone gave a triple beep, then went black. I closed my eyes, thankful that the battery lasted as long as it did. Laying there, a different kind of peaceful calm enveloped me. I felt better, but still much too weak to do more than pour (carbonated) water on my body.

It was still daylight when I heard, "You must be the emergency we were told about."

Opening my eyes, I saw a police officer looking at me as he continued, "Can you move? Do you need an ambulance?"

I was surprised by the energy that surged through my body, and I rolled over onto hands and knees to get up while answering in a weak voice, *"I sure am glad to see you! How did you know?"*

He extended his hand to help pull me up, telling me, "I'm Bill Webster, Sutton County Deputy Sheriff'; guess that was your wife who called and gave us your exact location. She said somethin' about you havin' heat stroke..."

"I was real concerned because I quit sweating, and even thought I might die right here, but after communicating with her, I started feeling better. And now you're here. Yes sir, I'm feeling right chipper!"

Standing up, I staggered, nearly fainting.

"Don't look like your quite as well as you think," he said. "You just rest down there more while I get my truck and take you to town."

"That's great!" I replied. "Maybe you could drop me off at the Sutton County Steakhouse? There's a motel attached to it."

"Sure, I know it well, eat there regular. I'll be back soon. You get some more rest," he told me, then asked, "People've died out here from dehydration and you're lookin' dry. Do you want a bottle of water?"

He saw his answer when my eyes grew wide at the thought of *fresh* water, and handed the clear plastic 500ml container.

It was ice cold; I cradled it in my hands, caressed my neck and forehead with it as the droplets of condensation felt like an air conditioner on high speed had been directed at me. Then I twisted the top open, cracking the seal and sucked that most precious of all liquids down into my body, feeling the very best water today passing through my mouth into my throat.

The impact was immediate, with rejuvenation not unlike when Border Patrol agents Lily and Jay had stopped to investigate me camped between 90 and the fence last month. They, like Deputy Sheriff Webster, had ensured my survival. I should not have been surprised at how quickly he, driving his double-cab, delivered a broken me and my Doublevision 25.2 miles/40kms to the doorstep of Devils River Days Inn, Sonora.

A similar experience occurred to me two years ago, when Ms. Barbara Brown delivered me and my broken Doublevision to Global Reach/Yarbrough/Montana in El Paso—a two-hour haul that would have taken me at least two days, or more, retrace.

At the other extreme, hypothermia had also been a challenge. Long ago, back in my Stumpjumper days before Ellen, I had camped in December with two Swiss women—interestingly, both were named Patrizia—at Pacific Rim National Park, Vancouver Island, Canada. After parting, I began my return cycle East on the Pacific Rim Highway in dastardly cold weather, freezing on descents and recovering slightly on ascents. When Mary Anne & Hubert Leber (Salt Spring Island) slowly motored by me in a Datsun pick-up truck, they were gesturing for me to quit pedaling and join them inside their hot motor vehicle—hand signals sufficed because rolling down the window would let out valuable heat! I can still remember cramming in the front bench seat with them, shivering uncontrollably, unable to speak due to my jaw chattering without stop. By the time we stopped in front of Roli's Homestyle Cooking restaurant, Port Alberni, my stuttering thanks were inadequate for their saving me from what could have been a certain death. I finished warming up after a several hour-stay inside that great eatery, where other concerned patrons bought me plenty of hot oyster chowder.

Whether freezing or baking, I know I'm alive to talk about it because the above named inviduals went out of their way to assist me. To say the least, I'm exceedingly grateful, and will always return the favor by going out of my way to help other stranded persons, *especially* if it is a weird looking bicyclist.

Sitting in the double-cab with Deputy Webster, I tried to slowly suck down two more of those chilled water bottles, and would have had a third if it wasn't time for me to offload at the motel. He refused any form of payment, declaring that he was just glad to not be filing a report on another person who succumbed to hyperthermia.

Holding our handshake a bit tighter and longer, I agreed, "Me too!"

We offloaded my Doublevision and gear, leaving it piled beside the office.

Going through the door, I met receptionist Adrianna, who quickly booked me into groundfloor room 217. "He got you here alive; we certainly aren't gonna' let you die on us. Now that you're our guest, go around the corner and get yourself right into the pool!" she commanded.

No argument from me, though I did ask for, and receive, another water bottle.

I performed my assigned task admirably, easily finding the gated pool. Changing clothes, taking off my glasses, doing *anything* other than getting massively wet was not important. I hesitated for a nanosecond before belly flopping into that aquatic reservoir, that pond of pure liquid, the sure elixir for my arid ailment, and completely submerged myself. I could feel my internal and external temperatures dramatically decrease, nearly passing out from the pleasure. Resurfacing, I gasped voluminous amounts of hot air, saw the shapes of other guests lounging about in the twilight, and closed my eyes, floating like a dried up branch, my arms and legs splayed out as if they were twigs for holding long disappeared leaves.

I started to climb the ladder when that Santa Ana-like wind hit me and I fell back into the water, exhausted. If I could only stay here all night...!

However, I was still thirsty and no way was I going to drink pool water. Going to the shallow end, I pulled myself onto the ledge and rolled away to a chair, where I could steady myself while standing up.

From there, I unsteadily limped toward room 217 although unable to see it. Another massive double-cab pick up hauling an equally massive trailer blocked the view. However, the front grill did provide me with a decent handrail, though I didn't really want to use it as such. I'd hate to alienate the operator.

Just my luck—I guess—he was standing by the door, and I felt that my touching his vehicle might not have been the best choice.

"So you're in this room?" he gruffly questioned me.

"Uh, yes," I meekly replied. "Checked in an hour or so ago..."

"This *my* room, I always stay here when comin' through!"

"So?"

"So I want you out of *my* room. There's a room on the second floor which you can have. Got the key for you right here."

"Not to be unpleasant or anything," I told him, "but I'm checked in here. 'fraid you're out of luck, friend."

Apparently he was no friend, because he glowered and sputtered mostly unintelligible less respectful remarks as I unlocked the door, went inside, closed the door, loudly putting the chain on and engaging the deadbolt. Then I turned the a/c on full blast before flopping down onto a bed. In a short while, I remembered to take my wallet out of my pocket, laying the soaked contents out on the bureau top beside the television. Can I use age for an excuse? Or maybe I *am* a bit baked in the brain?

There must be an ice machine around here. Seizing a bucket with it's plastic sleeve, I found the ice machine and filled both till brimming. I also saw that guy arguing with Adrianna, doubtlessly about having to be on the second floor instead of close to his rig. Back at the room, I made a cup of delicious ice water, sucking every bit of it down—twice!

I moved a chair to make a clear path for my rig to occupy, and began to transfer it, along with my other belongings from the office. I could see that the guy had not been able to persuade Adrianna to relocate me, and was tramping up stairs to the second floor. Fine by me—I still had to get completely into this room and was extremely glad to not have to ascend with my Doublevision or any gear.

Remembering my Nokia was in the camera bag, I retrieved it and plugged it in. Surprisingly, it rang. Confused about who could possibly be calling me, I answered.

"Good! You're off the road," I heard Ellen saying. "Reserve the room for another night because there's no way I want to try to drive eight hours there, then turn around and drive eight hours again. See you tomorrow."

Numbly I nodded, put it down, then used the house phone to call Adrianna, as instructed.

I went back to that wonderful wet pool for another refreshing dip, then returned to my room. As soon as I closed and locked the door, I stripped off all my clothing (shorts, shirt, socks, sandals) and took a long, cold tubbing. Stepping out of it, I had left far more than just a ring—the dirt, sand, and gravel had taken up residence in that large basin, and it looked just like a model floodplain, with heavier sediment lodged upriver from the drain, progressively finer elements making their way to the clogged outlet. Wearily, I cleaned the drain and stepped back in, this time showering, using soap and shampoo, eventually cleaning my wrinkled skin—a good sign of rehydration.

Thoroughly exhausted, I flopped back onto the bed. Strange, I wasn't hungry but couldn't get enough water inside me. Equally strange, I was neither tired nor could I sleep, even though I shut my eyes tight. Very strange indeed.

OVERNIGHT TWENTY-EIGHT:
DAYS INN SONORA, ROOM 217

I turned on the TV, found a Harry Potter movie to distract me. Maybe it was some kind of a marathon, because it was followed by another. During the third such showing, I jerked upright and flew into the bathroom, vomiting.

It was horrible! Nothing came out of me except belches, long and sustained. I continued to kneel over the toilet, the pain was excruciating with my stomach churning and constant dry heaves. I don't know how long this gut-wrenching session lasted, but by the time I returned to bed, the third Harry Potter had ended and was now well into the fourth movie.

My eyes closed and I finally fell asleep.

I woke to the sound of "Hedwig's Theme" and saw film credits rolling at the end of another Harry Potter move. At least my ears and eyes were still working, but the rest of my body was slow to move.

Except for my innards, which had left a stinking stain on the sheets. I needed help.

The help came when gravity assisted me to the floor, and I began the ordeal of pulling myself up to a bent-over stance, not quite ready to take on the world but at least back to the bathroom.

The weakness that pervaded my body would have made a snail look like a speed demon when I stepped outside. At least I had sense enough to re-clothe myself, including sandals, before going in search of food.

My first stop was the office, so that I could obtain a breakfast chit. Next was the restaurant, a logical choice considering the coupon in my trembling hands. It was crowded, but a solo guy at a table pushed a chair out for me to sit upon.

"Ya look like ya been through a wringer, pal," he said.

"Actually, I've just been pedaling from El Paso since the eleventh of June," I said. "My goal was Louisiana and seeing my children in Houston and Austin after my turn-around at the Sabine River, returning for three workshops, but a bit of heatstroke caught me yesterday out between mile makers four twenty five and six. Thank goodness I was able to contact my wife by cell—she is such a smart cookie—and she contacted the Sutton County authorities. Deputy Webster came out, got us—me and my bike—and delivered us here last night."

"Yeah, I remember seein' ya," he said. "Ya look a mite better now, an ya' got your coupon. A little food'll bring ya' back to present, though it's a bit warm right now. Not as warm as Lajitas, where I came up from, so be glad ya' didn't pedal there."

"I'll bet it's a degree or two warmer there," I agreed. "Last time I was there was for expensive gas in my fourRunner."

"It's still costly," he said, "but if you keep your wits about you, Lajitas is a great place to stay, even in the blistering Summer."

His order of hot cakes and eggs, and the waitress who brought them then looked at me, not overly critical, but her words and look accurately expressed that near-universal opinion which wives always seem to have when they rescue their husbands from some less-than-well-though-out activity.

"I heard you talkin' an' you do have a right smart wife. That's just how we have to be. An' that was no ordinary lawman that saved you—he's Bill Webster, formerly a long time sheriff who retired but currently helpin' out as deputy sheriff. He comes in here a lot."

"But now to you—our overnighters with the ticket get to order from this menu. What'll you have?"

It looked tasty enough—until the smell of my tablemate's order invaded my olfactory senses, causing a wave of nausea to pass through my body.

"Uhhhh, nothing for right now," I replied. "Thanks for reminding me that while I'm the only one pedaling, I'm not alone and really do depend on others. I want to acknowledge Sheriff Webster, retired or not. I should get him a gift certificate here, eh?"

Shortly, we completed our transaction with her solemn promise that next time he comes in for a meal—likely later this week— she'll personally deliver his food, and my thanks. Satisfied with this arrangement, I still had to somehow nourish my declining body.

I slowly shuffled on the sidewalk toward the Alco, just on the other side of I-10. Wandering the aisles inside, I found a wide variety of items useful for both a tourist or serious resident. The most important to me, of course, were gallon jugs of Glacier Clear Water at the bargain price of 99 cents apiece. Of course, I couldn't carry more than two; not only were the jugs bulky but the weight of nearly 17 pounds/8kgs, plus fruit snacks, was almost too much for me.

In fact, I only made it to the North edge of the parking lot, sitting on the sidewalk in a daze. This was becoming unbearable. I poured one of the water jugs onto my head, soaking me, my clothing and creating a hot puddle to lay in; even though shaded, the concrete mass beneath me still retained ample solar radiation.

That heat wasn't particularly conducive to my staying there, and neither was it good for the gelatinous candies. That was an easy problem to resolve—I ate them.

I didn't throw up.

Feeling a bit of pep, I picked myself up and shuffled North on US277, pausing briefly in the shade of the I-10 overpass. Looking over the guard rail, I had an epiphany about the Devils River—it is so named because only dry heat flowed through it. My next stop was the swim pool. Surely I must be getting better—I remembered to take my wallet out of my pocket.

Returning to my room, I cranked up the a/c again and sprawled onto the bed. Turning on the television (Those remotes are really quite wonderful.), I saw the Harry Potter marathon was repeating itself. It made no difference to me, because Ms. Sandwoman had visited and I was finally getting desperately needed sleep.

Mid-day, I had an unbelievable experience when a sliver of light woke me as the door cracked open. Then Ellen stepped in and, I swear upon a thousand gleaming Doublevision recumbents, a halo surrounded her head. She rushed to my side, touching my forehead, declaring, "Your still warm. Good thing we're staying tonight. Have you eaten yet?"

"No," I responded with a stronger voice, "haven't been able to keep anything down except for water and the gummy beans I bought a little while ago. How about you?"

"Subway in Fort Stockton," she replied. "I bought like you and still have half a sandwich for you."

"Thanks. Maybe I'll eat it later," I said, then added, "Thank you so much for coming like you did. I'm feeling loads better now, and maybe another night here is all I need before finishing my biketour."

She gave me the same incredulous look as the waitress did several hours before in the restaurant, then stated: "You're delirious. You nearly died out there and now you think I'm going to allow you to pedal again? No way. This is it. You're finished!"

Visions flashed through my mind's eye: people lining the streets cheering as I pedaled in front of the Rose Parade, PortlandOR, 1977; a drunken miner attempting to topple me by throwing his mop into my spokes when I pedaled at the head of a St. Pat's parade in RollaMO; escort led by Officers Guevarra & Serrano of the El Paso Police Department and Agent Davis of the Border Patrol, all bicycle units, while triumphantly pedaling into El Paso on bicycle friendly routes—particularly re-built Paisano Drive which also accommodates refurbished trolleys to the ASARCO ballpark—past the rejuvenated Hart's Mill/crossing/ markers, past the brilliantly repainted and tuck pointed ASARCO towers to a well-organized, extremely busy non-motorized POE/ Boundary Marker #1/museum/park/swim hole and trailhead for the international border (bike) trail. There, I met Roberto from Crazy Cat with numerous other cycling groups, and we raised our wheels in recognition of making our Hidden Gem of the World a hub for bicycle tourism.

My delirium showed that perhaps I still needed a bit more recuperation time?

In a low, resigned voice, I murmured to my number one savior, "ok, I'm finished"

ACTUAL ITINERARY (all dates are in 2011)

11JUN: Fabens, 38miles/62kms; front tire flatted, gear cable broke
12JUN: Van Horn, 106miles/170kms
13JUN: US90 berm (about 3miles/5kms) South of Valentine, 50miles/80kms
14JUN: Ft. Davis, 43miles/60kms
15JUN: US67/90 Paisano Pass rest area, 47miles/75kms; 5miles/8kms West of Alpine, no derailleur
16JUN: Marathon, 40miles/64kms
17JUN: Sanderson, 64miles/102kms; rear tire flatted
18JUN: US90 rest area, 32miles/48kms; 11miles/18kms East of Dryden
19JUN: Langtry, 30miles/48kms
20JUN: Comstock, 36miles/58kms
21JUN: Del Rio, 45miles/72kms
22JUN: US90 rest area, 43miles/69kms; 5miles/8kms East of Brackettville, rear Magura broken
23JUN: Sabinal, 64miles/102kms; two consecutive rear flats
24JUN: US90/Montgomery Road/Mr. W. Fireworks, 53miles/85kms
25JUN: Floresville, 58miles/93kms
26JUN: Lexington(Gonzales), 69miles/110kms
27JUN: US90A shoulder between swamp/guardrail, 74miles/118kms; foot lacerated
28JUN: son's apartment, Houston, 63miles/101kms
29JUN: respite, no pedal
30JUN: Academy Sports/Performance Bikes/Subway #2254, 7507 Westheimer:turnaround point,
       10miles/16kms
01JUL: by two crosses, route 359, 63miles/101kms; 10miles/16kms South of Hempstead
02JUL: Carmine, 64miles/103kms
03JUL: daughter's apartment, Austin, 79miles/126kms
04JUL: Hyde Park subdivision and back, 7miles/11kms
05JUL: *Casa de Pablo* (close to Perdernales Falls SP) 48miles/64kms
06JUL: Fredericksburg, 47miles/75kms; gear cable breaks again
07JUL: I-10 rest area, 68miles/109kms; 5miles/8kms East of Junction
08JUL: Trans-Texas Bicycle Odyssey terminated due to heat stroke symptoms, 43miles/69kms,
       between mile markers 425 & 426; texted wife, she contacted authorities; Sheriff Bill Webster
       (ret) delivered me/Doublevision to Sutton County Steakhouse/Days Inn-Devil's River, where I
       began recovery from brink of death

STATS

27 days: 11JUN-08JUL2011
total distance: 1374miles/2198kms
average daily distance: 51mpd/81kmpd
highest single day distance: 106miles/170kms
lowest single day distance: 0/0
one brief rain (Del Rio)
100+F/40+C days: 23
tailwinds: 10 days
headwinds: 14 days
Eastbound: 17 days
Westbound: 8 days

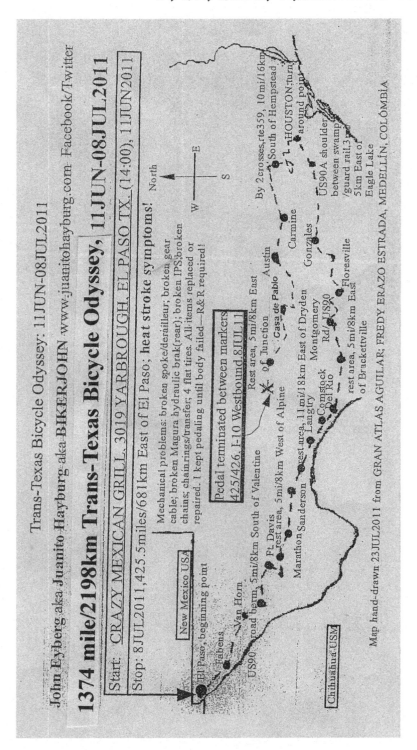

Trans-Texas Bicycle Odyssey: 11JUN-08JUL2011

John Eyberg aka Juanito Hayburg aka BIKERJOHN www.juanitohayburg.com Facebook/Twitter

1374 mile/2198km Trans-Texas Bicycle Odyssey, 11JUN-08JUL2011

Start: CRAZY MEXICAN GRILL, 3019 YARBROUGH, EL PASO TX. (14:00), 11JUN2011

Stop: 8JUL2011,425.5miles/681km East of El Paso; heat stroke symptoms!

Mechanical problems: broken spoke/derailleur; broken gear cable; broken Magura hydraulic brak(rear); broken IPS broken chains; chainrings/transfer; 4 flat tires. All items replaced or repaired. I kept pedaling until body failed—R&R required!

North

W E

S

Pedal terminated between markers 425/426. I-10 Westbound 8JUL11

New Mexico USA

El Paso, beginning point

Van Horn

US90, road berm, 5mi/8km South of Valentine

Fabens

Ft. Davis

rest area, 5mi/8km West of Alpine

Marathon Sanderson

rest area, 11mi/18km East of Dryden
Langtry

Comstock
Del Rio

Rest area, 5mi/8km East
of Junction

Casa de Pablo

Montgomery

Rd./ US90

rest area, 5mi/8km East
of Brackettville

Austin

Carmine

Gonzales

Floresville

By 2 crosses,rte359, 10mi/16km
South of Hempstead

HOUSTON;turn
around point

US90A shoulder
between swamp
/guard rail,3
5km East of
Eagle Lake

Chihuahua USM

Map hand-drawn 23JUL2011 from GRAN ATLAS AGUILAR; FREDY ERAZO ESTRADA, MEDELLÍN, COLÓMBIA